ACADEMIC FREEDOM
AND CHRISTIAN SCHOLARSHIP

ACADEMIC FREEDOM
and
CHRISTIAN SCHOLARSHIP

ANTHONY J. DIEKEMA

WILLIAM B. EERDMANS PUBLISHING COMPANY
GRAND RAPIDS, MICHIGAN / CAMBRIDGE, U.K.

Wm. B. Eerdmans Publishing Co.
255 Jefferson Ave. S.E., Grand Rapids, Michigan 49503 /
P.O. Box 163, Cambridge CB3 9PU U.K.

Printed in the United States of America

05 04 03 02 01 00   7 6 5 4 3 2 1

Library of Congress Cataloging-in-Publication Data

Diekema, Anthony J.
Academic freedom and Christian scholarship / Anthony J. Diekema.
p.   cm.
Includes bibliographical references (p.   ).
ISBN 0-8028-4756-0 (alk. paper)
1. Academic freedom — United States.
2. Church colleges — United States — Curricula.
3. Church and education — United States.   I. Title.

LC72.2.D54 2000
378.1′21 — dc21

00-032153

www.eerdmans.com

Dedicated to the
Board of Trustees
and
Faculty
of
Calvin College

Contents

CONTENTS

Foreword

One might think that twenty years in a college presidency would earn the occupant a goodly stretch of complete bed rest. When Anthony J. Diekema got off the hot seat at Calvin College, he took advantage of his unaccustomed leisure to write a book. Book-writing professors may marvel that a former college president would — or could — write a book, especially one that meets a real need. But in a day when holders of that office typically make themselves scarce on campus to chase dollars far and wide, President Diekema, while not neglecting fund-raising, actually presided over his college. The spirit in which he did so is represented in the title of one of his major internal documents, *Servant Partnerships*. It fits with his attitude of service that he would dedicate this book to Calvin's board and faculty, for he seemed to us less our boss than, well, our servant partner.

Since the author has turned to one of those dedicatees for this Foreword, I take this occasion for a few personal remarks. Readers should know that this Foreword is written by the faculty member who, by the president's own count, wrote him the greatest number of memos of criticism. Close readers will discover that within this book he has felt equally free to criticize me. Impetuous professor and imperturbable president could argue with each other because we were at one in seeking to fulfill the purposes of the kingdom of God. Our personal amity was much reinforced by regularly worshiping together in our small inner-city church. At work we were in deep accord about what the college was doing, and why, thus allowing us to debate the questions of how. Tony provided the atmosphere for us faculty members to speak our minds freely, even to him. So I will swallow my mild embarrassment at his crediting (or blaming?) me for provoking him to write this book and, in reciprocity, eagerly claim the honor of being his friend.

Although Tony would be the first to hope that, as the college moves from strength to strength, his tenure in office will not someday be looked back upon as Calvin's golden years, I wish to say what good years those were. Building faithfully on the sturdy foundation laid during the twenty-five years of his predecessor, President William Spoelhof, Tony led the college to the considerable degree of national eminence that it enjoys today. This he did by attending primarily not to bricks and mortar but to professors and programs — especially to professors. The Calvin faculty has historically played the central role in institutional decision-making. Tony's self-effacing manner and democratic spirit allowed him to promote faculty leadership and to welcome warmly those many colorful colleagues who during his tenure joined the already-forceful faculty. During the years 1976-1996 — to mention just one index of faculty development — the scholarly productivity of the Calvin faculty made a quantum leap forward. (Fittingly, the Diekema name is affixed not to a building but to a fund for faculty scholarship.) This accomplishment came under presidential leadership that carefully husbanded the college's commitment to the primacy of excellent classroom teaching and never flirted with the widespread imposition of a publish-or-perish regimen for judging faculty quality.

Now the president has joined his professors in the arena of book writing. Writers need distance from their normal daily distractions, and so professors often take refuge in quiet libraries, sometimes far away. For his study and writing, the president sought out fastnesses in Wales, Spain, and even remote New Zealand. His need for distance might be thought ever so slightly inordinate. Some might imagine that the man was tincturing his driven Calvinist conscience with a small dose of epicurean delight at lovely landscapes. There is a better explanation. The turn-of-the-century Dutch polymath, Abraham Kuyper, stands second only to John Calvin himself as an energizing engine of thought at Calvin College, and Tony was simply pursuing with relentless logic the literal implications of the key Kuyperian dictum that every square inch of this earth belongs to God and thus is ours to explore.

The distinctive mandate that characterizes Calvin College nurtures scholarship that engages the surrounding culture and then submits it to discerning Christian critique. Diekema fulfills both aspects of this mandate. His chosen subject of academic freedom is supremely important to the academy in general and to Christian colleges in particular. Diekema has done his share of heavy lifting and ransacked the scholarly tomes on his subject, and this effort enriches the theorizing conveyed in this study. But he also is a practitioner who has lived through some hurricane cases that required difficult judgment calls. The combination of theory and practice is what gives this book its unique place in the enormous scholarly literature on academic freedom. Those readers who in our hurried age are inclined to skim books should slow down whenever they come upon those campus episodes that tested the author's presidential mettle, for they will see in them, as careful readers will appreciate more fully, what most (though not all) of his faculty saw during the episodes described, that is, how a rooted man exercised judicious leadership in tense times. All will observe academic statesmanship by one who always took the long view.

Professors are particularly attuned to pointing out external threats to academic freedom, and Diekema does not slight these threats. They are a recurring motif in the story line of every church-related college, though they are also increasingly familiar to public institutions answerable to legislatures. But Diekema is particularly shrewd in delineating those internal threats that many a college president would rather not put on display, since they are hard on public relations. Here he boldly takes on both old and new threats to academic freedom. Diekema sharply challenges the failed modern nostrums and insupportable rigidities of the American Association of University Professors that persons at religiously affiliated institutions are uniquely positioned to espy. He is equally clear-eyed about the depredations of politically correct postmodernists who cannot write the word *truth* without putting quotation marks around it and who would enlist the university in the pursuit of power instead of the search for truth. Moreover, a man practiced at caution turns quite provocative when he challenges the concept of tenure and suggests decoupling it from the concept of academic freedom to which it has been long attached. The many secular scholars who worry nowadays that the North American academy has come to resemble a darkling plain on which ignorant armies clash by night will find in this volume much to hearten them, and if they are surprised that their ally is an unapologetic Christian, they may even rethink whether Jerusalem can have anything to do with Athens.

Nevertheless, those who stand to gain most from reading this book are those — faculty members, administrators, trustees, students, constituents — attached to a Christian college. At the top of the list are those belonging to one of the member institutions of the Council of Christian Colleges and Universities, among which Calvin College is acknowledged (usually appreciatively!) as a leading institution. Such readers will observe how many proposals and suggestions are aimed directly at them. Chief among these potential beneficiaries are administrators, who will be encouraged by the evidence that "courageous president" is not an oxymoron.

Were I limited to one word to summarize Diekema's achievement, I would choose *balance*. This study offers something to ruffle readers on both wings of the political spectrum. Here we find rights and responsibilities, freedom and duty. As a sociologist, Diekema expresses his indebtedness to Durkheim's balancing of individual and communal imperatives. As a Miltonist, I think of the Puritan poet's belief that the path of true liberty lies between servitude and license. By far, the greatest contribution to Diekema's balance comes from his enduring love for the Reformed tradition of the Christian faith. This tradition strives to cultivate the life of the mind and the life of the spirit at once, and as one. Forgetting neither that we bear God's image through creation nor that we are sinful beings in need of the salvation provided through Christ's sacrifice, Reformed people seek to be God's obedient agents of redemption in all precincts of human activity.

The insights that President Diekema has gained through his two decades at Calvin College he attaches to the wisdom accrued through long ages. The result is a wisdom of a sort rare in today's confusing welter of opinion, often so deficient in historical anchorage. And he offers it in this book as a labor of love — for God and for the academy. He merits a place among the company to whom the poet Wordsworth's line pertains: ". . . what we have loved/Others will love, and we will teach them how."

Edward E. Ericson, Jr.
Professor of English
Calvin College

Preface

This book is a personal, interpretive, and didactic treatise on academic freedom through the eyes of a practitioner. It is the odyssey of an adventure, with interpretations and prescriptive advice gleaned from events and experiences along the way. Although intrigued by the topic from early undergraduate days — when one of my favorite professors was almost perpetually scrutinized by the board of trustees over issues of his academic freedom — its significance became increasingly apparent to me over a forty-year career in higher education, especially during twenty years as the president of Calvin College. During those years, while called increasingly to defend the academic freedoms of both the faculty and the college, I generated an assortment of insights that I thought were worthy of more attention, and perhaps even a series of articles. I longed often for the time to do more reading and research, and then to write on the topic, but administrative responsibilities prevented it. Then, upon my retirement in 1996, the board of trustees of Calvin College granted me a six-month sabbatical leave to pursue a topic of my choice. The choice was easy, for by then I had come to see the often confused and misunderstood phenomenon of academic freedom as essential — indeed, top priority — to the entire enterprise of higher education. Just the opportunity to pursue it in depth would be a luxury; it would be both challenging and the fulfillment of a dream.

In September of 1995 Jeane, my wife, and I departed for Wales, in what became the beginning of a year of study and travel abroad in Wales, New Zealand, and Spain. I had already done a good bit of reading on the topic in the United States and thought I knew some of the foci I would find worthy of a series of articles. But more reading at the extensive libraries of the University of Wales at Aberystwyth and Swansea, and exploration through the computer-assisted facilities of Trinity College at Carmarthen, soon enlightened me to the extensive (and often confusing and redundant) literature on academic freedom. Synthesis and interpretation became imperative, and my plan to write a variety of tidy, focused articles became much more complicated. I forged ahead with the articles anyway, but became increasingly aware that it would be difficult to make them "hang together." Then, after learning of my concern and reading a few of the early manuscripts for the proposed articles, my good friend and colleague Professor Ed Ericson simply queried: "Why don't you write a book?" It sounded more like a solution than a question. Although more than I had bargained for, a book would help to hold the varied dimensions of the project together. Later, Ed's constant encouragement helped me "stay the course" toward a book.

So the project expanded, and so did the adventure as we headed off to New Zealand. I continued to read, and synthesize, and reflect, and interpret — and I started to write anew. As in Britain, we traveled, we hiked (including the Milford Track), we found new friends, we worshiped in a host of different churches and cathedrals, and we tried to immerse ourselves in the culture. I spent many days in the libraries of Canterbury University (Christchurch) and the University of Otago (Dunedin), the Sir Robert Stout Law Library (Dunedin), and the Higher Education Development Centre (Dunedin) — days delightfully unencumbered by tight schedules and endless meetings, telephones, fax machines, and electronic mail. These activities, taken together, began to give shape to the book that I'd never intended to write. After return to the United States and a short summer in Michigan, we departed for Spain and a similar adventure in the heart of historic Seville. But now the reading was mostly completed, and writing became the primary focus. Eventually, it resulted in this book.

As one might expect from a college president on a subject most often addressed by faculty, and among them usually by those who have been the "target" of actual academic freedom cases, this is neither a totally sympathetic nor a thoroughly intellectual volume. It is rather an historical reflection on the extensive literature, interpreted against the backdrop of personal experience and participant observation, in which didactics and the presentation of proposals often prevail over more ordinary exposition. It is meant to incite as much as it is meant to inform. It is partially autobiographical in that it is written by an unabashed defender of academic freedom who wishes only to prescribe some movement in an academy that has seemingly lost its way toward an ethos of freedom. Perhaps there is truth to the old adage that "fools rush in where angels fear to tread." But I believe there is reason for hope.

Acknowledgments

I am grateful to all those who aided and supported me in this project. The board of trustees of Calvin College deserves special thanks for awarding me the sabbatical leave that was, ultimately, the stimulus for this book. Writing it has been an experience more rewarding than the trustees will ever know. And it would never have happened without the leave and the year abroad. In Wales, the Reverend J. H. Richards used his family relationships to secure for us a delightful flat in the seaside village of Pendine; Graham and Mona Thomas, our host and hostess, provided good friendship and cultural socialization; and Sylvia Jones, Assistant to the Principal of Trinity College in Carmarthen, generously arranged for campus space and facilities for my work. In New Zealand, Graham Webb, Director of the Higher Education Development Centre at the University of Otago, provided a very comfortable office in the Centre and used his good offices and gracious staff to arrange for all needed help and facilities. Betty Osmand, our hostess in Dunedin, made available to us a most pleasant and quaint apartment overlooking the scenic Dunedin harbor and Otago peninsula. Generous to a fault, Betty, with her hospitality and unique cultural flair, was most helpful in our acculturation to the region. She will always have a place in our hearts. In Spain, Esther Paredes Lagoa, Director of the Trinity Christian College Semester in Spain Program and the Windsor School of English, along with her husband Aurelio, led us to a charming apartment in the heart of old Seville, which became our home, my office, and the point of departure for our travels around the country. And they graciously entertained us in their home and oriented us to life in the native haunts of old Seville. Carmen, a superb teacher in the Trinity program, generously conducted a series of tutorials for Jeane and me in which she unraveled immensely helpful fragments of language, history, and culture. Her skill, along with charm and patience, made our stay and work in Spain a rewarding and memorable experience.

There are many others to thank, and no adequate way to say just how much their help and encouragement have meant to me. But let me try. I am especially grateful to that cadre of faculty at Calvin College who over the years, and in various honorable ways, pushed the boundaries of the extended community's moral order and, thereby, honed both my skill and patience in defense of their and Calvin's academic freedom: Hessel (Bud) Bouma III, Jim Bratt, Sam Greydanus, Phil Holtrop, George Marsden, Clarence Menninga, George Monsma, Ken Pomykala, Henry Vander Goot, Christiana Van Houten, Howard Van Till, and Rich Wevers. A few others could be added for their sensitive management of the freedoms essential to the sound educational value of film, drama, music, and art. By their dogged dedication to the pursuit of truth and their commitment to the values of community and civility and cherished Christian worldviews, they helped to establish that Christian scholarship and the academic freedom to do it can prevail and, indeed, thrive. Although they would not have expected it, I stand happily in their debt.

I also express appreciation in particular to colleagues Ed Ericson, Gord Van Harn, and David Hoekema, who read and improved early drafts of the manuscript and gave me sustained encouragement. My son, David Diekema, sociology professor at Seattle Pacific University, who by his persistent and penetrating questions about the manuscript reminded me of my Durkheimian bias and sociological roots, deserves special thanks. In the process, he exposed more explicitly my operating worldview, one that is theologically Reformed in the Dutch Calvinist tradition and sociologically communal in the heritage of the Durkheimian school of sociology. They comport well. Christine Wright was especially helpful in the technical preparation of the many drafts through which this book has wended its way. I note, too, the support of Calvin's librarians and computer technicians, and the many on campus who provided working space and encouragement in the final stages of this project. Finally, I thank the staff at William B. Eerdmans for all their work on the production of this book.

One person lived through it all from the first day in Wales to the last day of editing. And she did so much more. That is my wife, Jeane, fellow traveler, CEO of the Diekema "clan," loyal partner and ready adventurer for forty-two years. Without her love and constant support, none of this could have happened.

All of these people have in a multitude of ways made this book a better one; none bears responsibility for its failings. Those shortcomings are the sole property of the author, who hereby claims them, each and every one.

I

Introduction

The dawning of Christianity's third millennium finds many Christian colleges and universities in a search for identity. These institutions, once again, face the challenges of a new generation of students. In addition, they face a new postmodernist influence in scholarship and a declining influence of religion and churches in society. All present new contexts and new issues. Society's forward march will not permit a stable state for anything; it will not tolerate the status quo. Christian higher education must constantly confront the task of examining what it is and how it is to accomplish its mission in an increasingly secular academy. It must find a place to stand. Even then, any redefinition runs the risk of losing something valuable on the one hand, or being judged irrelevant on the other.

The beginning of the twenty-first century has been the reason, although mostly symbolic, for much reexamination in our society and the world. It goes far beyond the hype of the Y2K issue, and that is good. Each new age presents it own questions and crises, and I do believe we are now living in a time when the challenges are especially substantive, intensive, and pervasive. As a society we are confronted with a dramatic shift in our cultural worldview, or more accurately, worldviews. Indeed, I believe we live in a period when both increasing pluralism and rampant individualism collide in the social cauldron of what some have come to call the "culture wars." Reexamination, reassessment, and redefinition are both necessary and inevitable.

Of course, the dawning of new eras is what makes history interesting and life exciting. Reflect for a moment on the movement from the Classical to the Enlightenment periods. Higher education and intellec-

1

tual development shifted from God-centeredness to man-centeredness, from faith in God to faith in Reason. The power of that change in the way the scholarly task is defined has been significant. It had a dramatic and perhaps irreversible impact on all of higher education, and continues to present Christian higher education with challenges on every hand. But evidence now points to the dawning of a similar epoch of radical transformation — a new era — and another intense shifting of paradigms and worldviews.

It is no secret to those involved in scholarship that Enlightenment answers have become post-Enlightenment questions. The fundamental presupposition of autonomous reason's self-sufficiency has been found to be seriously flawed. Much of what has been built upon that presupposition has been rejected or is fast failing. Indeed, a new worldview, or set of worldviews, is taking shape that tends to relocate reason within a much more expansive range of human gifts and talents. A very pervasive rediscovery of values, spirituality, ethics, emotions, intuition, and human communal concerns seems to be shaping the new worldviews emerging in our society and all over the world. There seems to be a shift away from the Enlightenment culture to another whose parameters are still to be determined.

The emergence of a new era with new worldviews is an especially challenging and exciting time for Christian higher education. Worldviews are well known to us, and we embrace the concept as vital to our task and calling. They give us much of our identity and we take them seriously. We also know their risks and threats. A deliberate move toward radical relativism in the secular academy (postmodernism)[1] is one such

1. While postmodernism is not a specific focus of attention in this book, it is alluded to in a variety of contexts because it is a major intellectual movement in the secular academy today. We shall need to contend with it as we pursue better ways to defend and protect academic freedom in the twenty-first century. Postmodernism has been variously described in a rapidly developing body of literature on the topic. Key characteristics include rejection of traditional science and its methods; rejection of general theory and any attempt to discover it; rejection of the possibility of truth independent of a particular standpoint while embracing a relativity of perspectives, none of which holds a privileged position; and endorsing the abandonment of any universal standard of truth or excellence. It is systematically anti-systematic, and all voices and ideas and perspectives are equally valued. Truth, among postmodernists, is whatever you can get away with saying in whatever specific context you find yourself. Power lies in the context (the prevailing mentality) and, thus, power becomes

risk in this era, but it need not immobilize us. And while the exact shapes of the new worldviews that are emerging in our culture are not yet transparent, we can begin to detect their tendencies and directions. Most importantly, amidst the heat and debris of the culture wars, I believe we have an opportunity to understand and influence this "world in the making" in ways that will have lasting value. Our Christian colleges and universities exist to foster and enrich the interchange that must take place under these conditions, and they can enhance the continuing dialogue between faith and all of human knowing. It is a time when our Christian scholars can deepen the understanding of Christian faith within the different fields and disciplines of human inquiry. It is a new and open window of opportunity to challenge each field of intellectual endeavor with the Christian claims and worldviews about God and people, and the meaning of life.

Christian colleges and universities will have new and special opportunities in the academy during this period of cultural transformation. But it should be understood that it is in precisely such periods that the church and Christian community also feel the stresses of change and challenge to strongly held views and beliefs. It will be important for Christian colleges and universities to help guide the community of faith through this difficult period by providing perspective and insight, while at the same time seizing every opportunity to influence the academy and intellectual communities toward a fuller understanding of Christian worldviews. We must establish learning environments that can maximize the advantage of these opportunities for Christian scholarship.

Inevitably, there will be some conflict between these quite different roles. Handling these and other roles will require a freedom of inquiry and intellectual exploration for each of our scholars and institutions. The temptation to put restrictions on both faculties and colleges will be especially present in the church and Christian communities; on the other hand, the threat of being judged irrelevant in the secular academy will always be with us. To be Christian and scholar, or Christian and college, will generate charges that go beyond that of oxymoron. These times of change tend to be chaotic periods for everyone, but espe-

---

truth. Obviously, then, this movement influences our concern for the future of academic freedom. Indeed, if there is no truth but only power, the need for academic freedom ceases to exist.

cially for those called to make sense of it all. The latter falls squarely, at least from the perspective of faith and truth and learning, on the Christian academy. It will require solid trust and considerable freedom.

So Christian colleges and universities must be free to do what they are called to do — to search for truth and advance our knowledge and understanding — with all of the rights and privileges of academic freedom for themselves and their Christian scholars. And it will be important for all of us to know more precisely what this comes to in our day to day life in the academy and in the Christian community. So we need to explore that topic again, and together, in the hope and confidence that we can "stay the course" toward our pursuit of truth. This book is intended to facilitate the process.

Academic freedom is "suspect" in our society and especially in the Christian community. But I contend it need not be so. Academic freedom is not the right to "do or say anything you please" (Marty, 1997).[2] Academic freedom is always limited. In every college or university — whether public, private, or religiously affiliated — the rights of academic freedom are never unlimited or absolute. Every college and university has an identity and mission to which it must be faithful. All faculty members have a responsibility to the methods of their discipline, the nature of their academy, and the worldview they embrace. Academic freedom is always a contextualized freedom, and a responsible freedom. It is anchored in community and ethos. And it is important that we communicate this to each other and the society at large. We must do it better.

For anyone who has been caught up in the nasty knots of academic freedom cases, it is clear that the practical problems one faces are usually the result of theoretical and conceptual problems. There is, one soon discovers, no clear and widely accepted definition of academic

---

2. These parenthetical references are designed primarily for the serious student or scholar of academic freedom and the related topics in this book. Primarily, then, they simply cite other sources found in the bibliography, which address the topic at hand. I hope they will also assist in the differentiated use of the selected reading list. They do not necessarily imply support for a point being made in the text, but they frequently do so. But contrary views are sometimes also referenced. Usually they refer to a more extensive address of a specific issue only briefly cited in the text. However, where they follow the use of quotation marks in the text, they are the source of that quotation.

freedom and even less consensus on the way in which claims of violation may be assessed and adjudicated. It sometimes is hard to distinguish between the heroes and the villains. And there is little practical advice in the literature. On the other hand, the literature abounds with differing definitions and conceptual debates. It is thus important to deal with some of the conceptual issues, to develop a sound working definition of the concept of academic freedom, to assess the threats it faces, to acknowledge the significance of worldview in its implementation, to explore the policy implications for its protection and promotion in Christian colleges, and then, hopefully, to provide some practical advice to those who will be called upon to do it. These same people will need to be prepared from time to time to adjudicate and resolve actual cases on their campuses.

It will come as no surprise to those who have experienced some actual academic freedom cases, or have taken time to seriously review some of the literature on the topic, to find that this book does not provide answers to all the questions it raises. You will have expected that. Indeed, if it reveals a certain disarray in the academy on this topic, that, too, you will have anticipated. But you will know also that academic freedom is a highly prized ideal of very wide embrace and application in the academy. Furthermore, I am persuaded that it is absolutely essential for the advancement of Christian scholarship and the fulfillment of our institutional missions. For that reason it is important that we continue to struggle with both the conceptual and the practical dimensions of it, while all along acknowledging that we shall need to pay the price of some flexibility in the way it is implemented on the campuses. Indeed, it may be in that very flexibility that we discover some of the practical advice which leads first to better policy development, and then to more fairness and justice to both those accused and offended, and to more stability in the processes of adjudication for the campus community.

The Search for Definition

What really is academic freedom? The concept has been used in different contexts with different meanings and for different purposes. So defining it is not a simple matter; if it were, there probably would not be so many misconceptions of it and the principles underlying it. One writer has observed that "everyone seems to agree that academic freedom should be defended, but there is little agreement or clarity about what it is. Unless we know what it is and can justify it, we will neither defend it convincingly nor exercise it responsibly" (Bligh, 1982). Justifying and defending it has led to many variations in definition; some have merit for brevity while others try to be as comprehensive as possible. Barnett (1990) suggests one of the most tidy versions, with academic freedom meaning "that academic pursuits, carried out in academic settings, by academic persons, should be ultimately directed by those academic persons." One report suggested that we see academic freedom "not as job protection for life but as the freedom within the law for academic staff to question and to test received wisdom and to put forward new and controversial or unpopular opinions without placing individuals in jeopardy of losing their jobs" (British Education Reform Bill proposal, 1987). Another writer, trying to be more comprehensive, suggests that "academic freedom refers to the freedom of individual academics to study, teach, research and publish without being subject to or causing undue interference. Academic freedom is granted in the belief that it enhances the pursuit and application of worthwhile knowledge, and as such is supported by society through the funding of academics and their institutions. Academic freedom embodies an acceptance by academics of the need to encourage openness and flexibility in academic work and of their accountability to each other and to society in general" (Tight, 1988).

Such attempts are helpful, but there are hundreds of them. In fact, no dominant or common view of academic freedom emerges readily from my review of the torturous literature. This suggests little progress since almost two decades ago when Kaplan and Schrecker summarized a very comprehensive review of the literature on academic freedom as follows: "there is little consensus regarding the meaning of academic freedom although there is agreement that it is something worth protecting. The concept has been invoked in support of many contrary causes and positions. It, for example, was used to justify student activism and to repress it, to defend radical faculty and to defend their suppression, to support inquiry into admissions or promotions or tenure decisions and to deny such inquiry. It is at best a slippery notion, but clearly a notion worthy of analysis" (Kaplan and Schrecker, 1983). Perhaps, given the nature of academics and academic life — an endeavor which does not normally rate agreement very highly — this should not be at all surprising, even though the condition of academic freedom is central to that life.

It should not either be a surprise then that academic freedom — the fundamental right in the academy to pursue truth — is facing grave threats on many college and university campuses today. One reason among many for this is the popular notion that academic freedom means essentially that anything goes, that professors and scholars have the right to say and do what they please, a sort of unbridled license to violate any semblance of ethical or moral order. In common parlance, academic freedom has become something of a dirty word. Academics often seem unaware that academic freedom is in danger of being brushed aside by a public that has little understanding of what is at stake. In an age where the call for accountability is growing in many sectors of our society, it is obvious that such a popular conception of academic freedom demands a more explicit response; that is, a much more accurate articulation of the concept and a sound rationale for its essential place in the functioning of the academy. The fact remains, however, that there is no official or uncontested definition of academic freedom.

It is important to see the concept of academic freedom as functional only in the academy. True academic freedom carries no legal or constitutional sanction. It is not some objective "freedom" to be be-

7

stowed by law or some governmental entity. Rather, it is communal in character; it arises from the ethos of the academy, from the assembly of scholars on any given campus. It is a freedom restricted to the academic enterprise, and it is an implied right granted by the moral order of the academy. It arises from the essence, the very "soul," of the academy. It concerns the personal integrity and professional commitment of professors in colleges and universities everywhere. It concerns the collective and personal integrity within the academy which resists any threat or intimidation to the pursuit of truth from any source. It concerns the courage and conviction of academics to believe in themselves and in the values their institutions were founded to disseminate.

Although academic freedom is a concept closely related to the rights of freedom of speech and freedom of the press, I believe it must be carefully distinguished from them. Freedom of speech and freedom of the press are rights that are constitutionally granted and legally protected. Academic freedom, to the contrary, is a right granted only to teachers and scholars in the academy and by the academy. It is protected by long-standing custom and convention within the academy, not by statutes.[1] Nothing in our laws guarantees the enduring right of a teacher to speak the truth as she perceives it, or to pursue the truth according to the insight and light that is given her (Kirk, 1980). Only in extraordinary circumstances could she appeal to the general constitutional provisions for freedom of speech and of the press found in the Bill of Rights (Gordon, 1994; McConnell, 1993; Worgul, 1993; etc.). But then she would not be appealing to academic freedom, but rather to the statutory freedom which is guaranteed to all persons in our society. So, for purposes of a sound working definition, academic freedom exists only in the academy, and there only by custom and convention and

---

1. Some readers may question why I have not included students among those to whom the rights of academic freedom in the academy are extended. Simply stated, it is because students, at this stage in their intellectual development, are neither qualified nor equipped to handle the rights and responsibilities of academic freedom as here defined. They are, at best, scholars and teachers in training. They are transients in the academy, not yet full citizens. They are, of course, extended the rights of freedom of speech and expression. Furthermore, on those campuses where academic freedom is alive and well, students are usually extended the practical advantages and expectations of academic freedom in the classroom and in campus debates and dialogue.

ethos. It is a sort of "natural right" within the academy, a right without which the teaching and scholarly tasks (the pursuit of truth) are severely impaired.

History suggests that academic freedom is a "right" that is more of an aspiration than fact. And it never belongs to academics without a challenge. It must always be claimed by them as a community of scholars, sometimes with considerable difficulty and personal discomfort, and always with extraordinary moral courage when the claim is legitimate. It is an important aspect of the freedom of thought, the freedom of opinion, and the freedom of expression and speech; but it stands in a different order of "rights" or freedoms. So the distinction of academic freedom from freedom of speech is important in definition. In a real sense, just as freedom of speech is foundational to a democratic society, so academic freedom is foundational to the academic enterprise. And just as there are constant threats to freedom of speech in a democratic society, there are continuing threats to academic freedom in the academy. Some of the most prominent of those threats are reviewed here.

Based upon a comprehensive review of the literature, I conclude that most commentators, and I suspect most scholars, could accept a definition that describes academic freedom as a fundamental principle of the academy designed to protect professors from those forces which tend to prevent them from meeting all their obligations in the pursuit of truth. For it is still a basic premise in the academy (some postmodernists not withstanding) that the obligations of the professor are first and foremost to truth. Betrayal of that obligation to any force in the immediate environment, whether it be internal or external to the academy, renders the professor unfaithful to his or her calling and thus unworthy to belong in the company of scholars. Academic freedom is the right and obligation to constantly pursue truth, and to teach and publish it along the way toward the goal of finding ultimate truth. Thus, academic freedom is a specific kind of freedom, peculiar to a defined task and peculiarly valuable to the carrying out of that task. It is an idea, a principle, that is real in the academy; it takes on a life of its own only in the confines of the scholarly community.

I am also persuaded, however, that the task of shaping an adequate definition of academic freedom remains with us, and that it is further complicated by issues that are receiving more attention in actual academic freedom cases today. These include issues centered in the worldview vs. objectivity debates, the academic freedom vs. freedom of speech distinctions, the means vs. end discussions, the individual vs. corporate (institutional) academic freedom controversies, and, at least for Christian colleges and professors, the integral relationship between the biblical notion of Christian freedom and that of academic freedom. Furthermore, the historic relationship between academic freedom and tenure needs an up-to-date review and assessment. Each of these issues, among related matters concerning the need for a sound and consistent definition of academic freedom, are addressed later in this book. Some may require more extensive analysis by a variety of methods which are logical extensions of their treatment here. Finally, after these considerations, a comprehensive working definition of academic freedom is proposed. (See pages 84-86.)

III

Threats to Academic Freedom

A college is a very special kind of place. It is a place organized to create and transmit knowledge — tasks that are exceedingly difficult and important. It is a place where freedom takes on extraordinary meaning, where people come together precisely for the purpose of thinking, speaking, inquiring, and criticizing freely. It is a communal place. It is a place whose stock in trade is diversity of ideas, whose tradition enshrines dissent. It is a place unfriendly to fetters. It is a place whose very existence depends upon the careful preservation and promotion of academic freedom. It should come as no surprise then that academic freedom is one of the most cherished virtues of the academy. I believe it is precisely because academic freedom is so vital to the health and welfare of a college that threats to its survival seem ever present.

Threats to the preservation and promotion of academic freedom come from both within and outside the academy. They exist for all colleges and universities — public, private, and religiously affiliated. Sometimes these threats come in obvious "waves of zealotry." McCarthyism in the late 1940s and student activism in the 1960s are prominent examples (Hamilton, 1995). But most often they come in subtle form and fashion. They come as "wolves dressed in sheep's clothing." They sneak up on us. They all require vigilance on the part of both faculty and institutions. Some that have been observed and cited in bold strokes include the phenomena of political correctness (particularly as it is manifested nowadays in some of the single-issue topics like multiculturalism, pluralism, diversity, and feminism); prior restraint; censorship; and ideological imperialism. During my years in the academy, especially those years in the presidency, I have experienced and observed many of them firsthand. Something will be said about each.

Ideological Imperialism and Dogmatism

One of the greatest and most consistent threats to academic freedom over the years has been the phenomenon often referred to as ideological imperialism. We live in an age of ideology, an age of infatuation with political and religious abstractions, ideas, and social movements. We seek quick and simple solutions to complex and complicated problems and issues. Ideologies that purport to resolve our problems abound in our society and present a continuing threat to the free and deliberate pursuit of truth. Ideologies, no matter how rudimentary, tend to be totalitarian, dominant, and intolerant of other views. A mind ensnared by such an ideology quickly becomes a closed mind. On the other hand, the academy promotes a free and inquiring intellect in both its faculty and students. Whenever faculty are threatened by the possible submission of their worldviews and their pursuit of truth to the scrutiny of ideologies — of whatever stripe or stamp — they have ceased to enjoy any real academic freedom to accomplish their tasks and callings. The threat of such ideologies — often reduced to simple dogmatism — whether by powerful boards, constituents, unions, churches, peers, religious fanatics, or sects (and a host of others), is ever present in the preservation of academic freedom.

Such ideological enthusiasts (Hamilton calls them "zealots"), whether from the Right or the Left or a multitude of other ideological persuasions, will continue to assault what they judge to be heretical thought and speech. My personal experience certainly persuades me, but sound historical perspective also tells us this is inevitable (Hamilton, 1995). So it is especially important that faculty foster and defend competent voices of dissent against such assaults, however unpopular at the time, because it is upon such dissent that the ultimate advancement of our knowledge depends. It is not enough for faculty to defend only those voices with which they share political, religious, and social ideas. They must stand for openness and for the right of all honestly held opinions to be heard.

Viewed broadly, the one greatest threat to academic freedom arising from ideological imperialism is blatant dogmatism. Dogmatism seeks to banish all ambiguity or tentativeness by appealing to a kind of ultimate, static, and simplistic truth. The pursuit of truth is rendered unnecessary. And dogmatism insists that its truths are immune to criticism or change (Scott, 1995). There is, indeed, a natural conflict between the pursuit of truth and the dogmatism that accompanies most ideology. The academy thrives on raising and addressing difficult questions, searching diligently for the answers, and then sharing the findings that may lead to new insights and possibly some ultimate answers. But in my experience, more often than not, the process of searching for the answers is extended and laborious, and final answers are elusive at best. Such is the nature of the pursuit of truth, and dogmatism cannot tolerate such a deliberate process.

Tentative answers and living with some ambiguity are essential elements in the academic enterprise. On the other hand, the dogmatism that accompanies most ideologies seeks to banish that very tentativeness or ambiguity. Dogmatism denies the need that scholars have to pursue truth by a logic of inquiry, wherever it might lead. Contrary to dogmatism, and quite ironically, a critical function of the scholar and teacher is to advance our knowledge by calling into question some of the widely held and accepted beliefs of the various ideologies that pervade our society. So it is not surprising to observe that often ideology and academic freedom are at opposite poles.

Ideological imperialism often arises from within the academy itself. Professors, too, and perhaps too often, fall victim to ideological imperialism. Dogmatism does exist in segments of the academy, and it often falls along disciplinary lines. In too many cases it is observed that a professor is more concerned about protecting his or her own authority and belief system than about the search for truth. In the most extreme cases, such academics actually strive to bend their colleagues and students (and even institutions) toward their own will or belief. Appealing to their freedom to propagandize, to indoctrinate, and to persuade by the power of their authority as senior members of the academy, they may seek to compel colleagues, students, and the college as a whole to submit to their ideology (e.g., Hamilton, 1995; Silber, 1973). Postmodernism has moved some even further in this direction. Academic freedom was never intended to protect the academic who engages in such blatantly coercive activities.

13

This is obviously an extraordinary abuse of the true meaning of academic freedom, but it often feeds the popular view that academic freedom is simply a smokescreen for doing and saying whatever one pleases. To abuse the concept of academic freedom in this way is nothing short of converting the very liberty that academic freedom grants into the license it is committed to avoiding. Fortunately, such blatant intemperance has afflicted only a small minority of professors and scholars, but some current postmodernist mentality tends to promote it, and such cases increasingly find their way to the "courts" of academic freedom. Strategically, then, academic freedom must endorse an ideal of scholarly activity that is blind to power and authority in order to see how the abuse of authority in particular cases may constitute violations of academic freedom. Ironically, often such abuse from within the academy (e.g., tenured vs. untenured, etc.) is committed in the name of academic freedom.

There are also well-meaning efforts to protect and advance academic freedom that unfortunately can feed the "anything goes" mindset of many of our publics. Even respected educational leaders run the risk of overstating, I believe, the supreme position of academic freedom when they tend to ignore the existence of moral order and ethos in the academy and in the larger society. At least, by not acknowledging a moral order as a control factor in the academy, they tend to give academic freedom the status of end rather than means (e.g., Schmidt, 1992). This is easily misinterpreted and oversimplified beyond the academy as the license for professors to "do and say anything they want." To the contrary, it has been broadly recognized in the academy and established in the courts that academic freedom at any university — whether public, private, or religiously affiliated — is never unlimited or absolute. Every university has an identity and mission to which it must adhere. Freedom is always a contextualized freedom and a responsible freedom (Worgul, 1993; Marty, 1997). It exists in community. This latter message must be much more visible in our public discourse, as well as our internal discussions, about academic freedom. We must try to convey a more accurate view among our many publics beyond the academy.

The academy itself, through the vigilance and courage of its members, must protect against the imperialism of ideology. The college campus community requires freedom from any oppressive ideology, freedom from obsessive political and religious radicalism, freedom from any power that binds the intellect. Indeed, it requires the freedom for serving our society by teaching, studying, and thinking. Hamilton argues strongly that "the duty to foster and defend the academic freedom of colleagues is a critical cornerstone on which the rights of professional academic freedom rest" (Hamilton, 1995). I fear this will not come easily in the midst of postmodernism. Indeed, postmodernism seems pragmatically paradoxical in this regard; its emphasis on power militates toward ideological imperialism rather than freedom. Resistance toward it requires a high level of courage. And, sadly, courage has not been a necessary virtue in the academy. It remains puzzling to me how so often a small number of what Hamilton calls "zealots" can successfully coerce and intimidate others in an academic setting. The strong inclination to accommodate and acquiesce to "aggressors" has been pervasive in the academy for a long time. But that must change. Rigorous and communal self-regulation by the members of the academy itself will do much to preserve and promote the very special and natural right of academic freedom for our society. Academic freedom from my perspective is then a highly moral practice anchored in the ethos of the academy. It thrives in an ethos of freedom. It is a freedom aimed not only at the protection of individuals and institutions but at the collective well-being of the entire academy for better service to our society. It arises out of, and then serves, the community.

Political Correctness and Intolerance of Religion

Perhaps the threat most closely related to that of ideological imperialism in the academy is the phenomenon we have come to label "political correctness." Much can and has been said about this throughout our society, but it should be noted here that political correctness has a particular relevance to the academic community. Political correctness, simply stated, refers to a dominant view or political position in a faculty or academic community that makes it difficult for individuals to take contrary views or positions without negative implications or, at least, without some discomfort in the social milieu of the community. Political correctness, usually in subtle and unspoken ways, can put considerable restraint on faculty members who do not "fit the mold" of current think-

15

ing on the campus. In common parlance nowadays, it refers primarily to the single-issue causes of multiculturalism, feminism, and diversity (and so on) that tend to engage and excite most campuses. And let there be no mistake about it, academic freedom is needed at least as much to protect individual academics from other academics as from politicians, clergy, the press, and members of the public. Indeed, I believe a majority of current cases where academic freedom is threatened are of this nature (e.g., Hamilton, 1995). Political correctness can place severe limitations on a faculty member's academic freedom.

The most consistent and recurring illustrations of this phenomenon tend to come from Christian scholars on secular campuses. They often describe in various ways the anti-religious bias that pervades the academy in general and the specific ways in which it comes to fruition in the discouragement of religious perspectives and worldviews in the scholarly work of Christians. In my own experience as president of a religiously affiliated college, I recall some examples: the junior faculty member who found it impossible to secure a mentor to guide his doctoral dissertation topic that included a Christian worldview; the recent graduate who was confronted by her graduate school mentor and advised to find a "better set of presuppositions" (better than Christian ones) or a different graduate school; the candidate for a faculty position who argued that he needed to "relearn" how to articulate his Christian worldview because it had been entirely unacceptable during his years in pursuit of the doctorate. There are others of a similar nature. The pervasive character of this bias, with its manifestations in the life of the community, makes it very politically correct to keep religious views outside of one's scholarly and teaching activities. In such an environment it is politically correct for Christian scholars to focus on research and projects that avoid worldview issues and to keep their religious views and commitments outside their teaching and analytical tasks. And some postmodernists, to be sure, have promoted an even more blatant and aggressive bias against religious worldviews. This is vividly portrayed in an interchange between Stanley Fish and Richard John Neuhaus (in *First Things*, February 1996 issue). Fish, in essence, suggests that those holding Christian worldviews either orchestrate a "hostile takeover" of the academy or get out.

Political correctness in the academy today has an even greater and more direct influence on the freedom of speech than it does on academic freedom. The influence on academic freedom is more indirect. In fact, in recent years the concept of free speech seems to carry more ideological baggage than is ever acknowledged. Even Fish emphasizes it (Fish, 1994). But even before the concept of political correctness was a part of our vocabulary, Roger Heyns (Chancellor of the University of California at Berkeley in the 1960s) portrayed the Free Speech Movement at Berkeley as essentially a battle of different ideologies using the free speech argument to advance their cause. All extolled the virtues of free speech. But their enthusiasm for free speech was limited to their own views, not for opposing ones. Heyns was persuaded that they meant well, but he marveled at the "blindness" in such argumentation by otherwise bright and logical people. He marveled even more at the seemingly impossible task of bringing these opposing ideologies to recognize and acknowledge such blindness. They were blinded by the higher morality of their own ideology.

This was clearly the case for a variety of free speech issues on the Calvin College campus during my presidency there. Two brief examples may be helpful. In the spring of 1993, David Noebel — a conservative, Right-wing evangelical who then directed the Summit Ministries in Manitou Springs, Colorado — was invited to speak to the student Republican club on the topic of how to use the political system to defeat inappropriate state legislation. The speech was open to the public. About a week prior to his speech, it was learned that Noebel would be using a video entitled "The Gay Agenda" as an illustration of a tactic used in the process of defeating gay rights legislation in Colorado. A student went to the local gay and lesbian activist organization (in Grand Rapids, Michigan) and told them, "We have to shut this down." From that point the local activist group took what was happening at Calvin and turned it into a media event in order to push its agenda. The group's members brought considerable pressure to bear, demanding censorship of the video and the speech. The college refused. One of their leaders said to me in my office, "We see a window of opportunity here and we intend to use it." From that point on the issue quickly degenerated far from its original educational purpose and became a vigorous homosexuality debate prior to the appearance of Noebel. It was "used" by the local gay and lesbian activist group and "hyped" by the media. Unfortunately, as it turned out, Noebel displayed a rather blatant homophobic attitude and was less than courteous and civil in

17

presenting his material. That only added to the already high emotions centered on the speech. The large audience, on the other hand, was controlled and civil, asking somewhat provocative, yet sound questions after the speech.

Several days after Noebel's presentation, it became apparent that he and some constituents of his Summit Ministries organization were aggressively attacking the college, especially alleging the existence of a dominant liberal, Left-wing faculty and administration. Interestingly, the local Grand Rapids gay and lesbian activist organization was simultaneously alleging the existence of a conservative, Right-wing, and homophobic faculty and administration! The college was unsuccessful in persuading either side of its "blindness" toward the opposing ideology. Each was blinded by the higher morality of its own position.

Shortly after the event, and not unrelated to it, the college learned from various constituents that the Young America's Foundation — a conservative, Right-wing organization headquartered in Herndon, Virginia, whose purpose is to raise funding to support conservative speakers on college campuses — had sent a "Confidential Report" to a wide variety of its supporters across the United States alleging that the Leftist faculty at Calvin was preventing conservative speakers from appearing on the campus. The mailing included a "petition" to be sent to the "board of regents" along with a request for the recipients to sign the petition and send money to the Young America's Foundation. The president of the foundation, Ronald E. Robinson, was informed in detailed letters, telephone calls, and even a written appeal from a conservative faculty member acquaintance that his allegations were, in fact, blatantly false. Because of the organization's interest in speakers on campus, the college sent lists of speakers who had appeared on the campus, demonstrating that speakers came from many different persuasions: Right, Left, and almost everything in between. The college soon learned from Robinson that neither he nor his organization were interested in the truth as revealed in our "chapter and verse" responses; rather, they were interested in the fund-raising value of their allegations against the college. Indeed, the college learned that the organization sent out at least three subsequent mailings to even broader audiences, without any revisions or acknowledgment of the facts from the college. Neither were they interested in sending the "petition" to the college board of trustees. Careful analysis of the materials and methods used in this instance was very enlightening about the unethical practices and tactics some organizations use to raise funds and advance their cause. Truth and facts seemed irrelevant. It is unfortunate, indeed, that a wide variety of organizations in our country today — from both the Right and the Left, and a variety of single-issue groups — seem to have forgotten what truthfulness is all about, especially when they find that they can raise considerable amounts of money on the basis of deceit, innuendo, distortion, fear-mongering, and paranoia. For groups of this ilk, any concern for unethical actions and questionable tactics is blinded by the higher morality of their cherished ideology.

Today ideology is having a greater influence on who is invited to speak on campus, what the format will be, and who may respond, and it often ultimately determines who will object to the speaker's appearance. Even the "hate speech" that now tends to afflict major universities is a symptom of the use of free speech as a political correctness tool by both the progressive and neo-conservative elements of the campus communities. It is a double-edged sword. In this regard, political correctness is the practice of making judgments from the vantage point of challengeable convictions; that is, it is not a deviant behavior but rather a behavior that everyone necessarily practices to some degree. Thus, debates between opposing parties can rarely be characterized as debates between political correctness and something else; rather, they are often debates between competing versions of political correctness. For example, conservative ideologies will quite predictably clash with liberal ideologies wherever they are found together. Taken in this sense, of course, most free speech hassles on the campus are the legitimate substance of the academy. Indeed, where such hassles are not occurring there may be reason to question the health and vitality of the place. But there is more to the phenomenon.

Recently, Frederick Schauer, a noted First Amendment scholar, said what most people fear to say (due to political correctness implications) when he suggested that standard free speech arguments have all the earmarks of an ideology because it is assumed in our society that counter-arguments are dangerous and must be rejected by all right-thinking persons. Schauer observes that there is "little free inquiry about free inquiry and little free speech about free speech" in the current climate of political correctness (Schauer, 1992). It is a paradox, he says, that the current political-correctness orthodoxy of tolerance is intolerant of those "who have less protective rather than more protective views about freedom of speech" (1992)! Therein lies the irony of political correctness: it often refers to the views that are correct only from the perspective of those who espouse them, not necessarily the empirically dominant views. Almost anyone can use the concept to disparage the argument of someone else. Postmodernists especially emphasize this point (Wilson, 1996). It is true that the concept is sometimes used simply as a political and rhetorical tactic in argumentation, but it becomes destructive to academic freedom when it inhibits freedom of expression and free inquiry in the academy because of the fears suggested by Schauer.

Generally, it is the ideas and changes emanating from the academy, which various publics don't like, that are often categorized as political correctness in the broader community. Today this label might resonate with some perceived dominant repressive thought in colleges about feminism or multiculturalism or socialism. And, particularly in religiously affiliated colleges, the emotionalized "secular humanism" label is a favorite. There is often misunderstanding by those outside the academy on these issues, which leads to suspicions of a political agenda designed to undermine traditional and Christian values (Whitehead, 1995). These suspicions are generically no different than those historically associated by the Right with communism and the Left with McCarthyism.

During my tenure in the presidency during the 1980s and 1990s the polemics surrounding "political correctness" were long and loud on a variety of issues. Several examples of such political correctness labeling from both the Right and the Left come immediately to mind. One stands out as particularly illustrative. Attempts to cancel a scheduled appearance in 1995 by Charles Murray, author of *The Bell Curve* — the controversial national bestseller that identifies the differences in intellectual capacity among people and discusses their social implications — included emotionalized political correctness jargon from the Left indicting the Rightist correctness of the Calvin community for allowing such a travesty to occur. The "travesty" alludes to the controversy that the book had raised about the differences in intelligence along ethnic lines, especially race. It was argued that this event would cause irreparable damage to the college's efforts toward increasing ethnic diversity. Although the book is not about race, the one chapter dealing with ethnic differences had been the focus of national media attention and, consequently, much controversy in the public square. The call from the Left was to cancel, to censor. Supporters of Murray's right to present his research findings openly, on the other hand, argued in terms of academic freedom and free speech, and they often expressed dismay at the Leftist correctness mentality, which wished to silence free expression for the sake of a wrong-headed multiculturalism. Their position was based upon Murray's solid academic credentials and nationally recognized stature as a social scientist, along with the excellent reputation of his co-author, the late Richard Herrnstein, a highly regarded psychologist and senior professor at Harvard University. The call from the Right was to allow free expression and promote academic freedom. Ultimately, the college stood firm in its conviction that censoring responsible perspectives and research is antithetical to a Christian liberal arts education. The event occurred, was not focused on race or ethnicity, was well attended and well received, and I believe affirmed the college's philosophy that the campus community must engage issues worthy of thoughtful and critical assessment.

Similarly, although distinguished from Murray in that they are members of the faculty and enjoy the rights of academic freedom, the numerous attempts to silence Howard Van Till (author of *The Fourth Day*) and Hessel Bouma (editor of *Christian Faith, Health, and Medical Practice*) by the religious Rightists were dominated by allegations about the Leftist correctness of the college and the pervasive "secular humanism" that that political correctness represented. By the same token, the strong supporters of academic freedom for both Van Till and Bouma often did not refrain from labeling their critics as representing a political correctness of religious conservatism and pro-life fanaticism. Over and over again, the concept of political correctness was used to disparage the arguments of the opposing views. This phenomenon became as predictable as the robins of spring in Michigan. And it inevitably carried with it a potential threat to academic freedom and free expression on the campus. Each case required careful and deliberate assessment. These controversies often did little credit to any tradition of civil debate and dialogue within the church and Christian community. Both from the Right and the Left, contrary views were usually labeled as a political correctness fostered by the college. A more pervasive ethos of freedom is needed, especially beyond the campus.

Political correctness in its broader definition, of course, is not a new phenomenon in the American academy. Academic institutions have always been quite capable of being oppressive to their individual members in this way. The oppression carries a new label, but it has been present from the beginning of the academic enterprise in our country. Indeed, it was perhaps the early church-affiliated colleges of our nation (Harvard, Yale, etc.) that gave rise to the phenomenon. Most of these early colleges insisted that their faculty be denominationally correct — that is, that they be members of the church that supported and subsidized the institution. Important here, of course, is the fact that these "correctnesses" were not made explicit in mission statements, faculty recruitment policies, and the like. Thus, in subtle and unwritten ways, they became firm expectations or exclusions — a type of institutionalized imperialism reflecting the culture and orthodoxy of the place. Similarly, a variety of other unspoken criteria such as race, nationality, and ideology have been the substance of politically correct decision making in American higher education from the very beginning. In fact, it has been stated that the American Association of University Professors (AAUP) was founded in 1915 to defend academic freedom and to protect the rights of Leftists and agnostics to secure and retain faculty positions (Lipset, 1992).

From an historical perspective, it is interesting to note how what once may have been religious dogmatism in the academy has become a pervasive intolerance of all things religious. Hoekema (1995) contends that in most classes, if they are taught in creative and challenging ways, questions will arise that bear on fundamental issues of personal convictions and views of the world. Professors ought not shirk or be silent on these matters, he says, but rather should address them honestly and openly. Indeed, faculty members who cannot, or will not, respond to religious and worldview questions in the classroom are not truly qualified to be professors, for they are depriving students of areas of inquiry that are important for their nurture and understanding. Hoekema makes a sound case for the legitimacy of worldview considerations and religious questions, along with political ones, in the classroom.

Perhaps it is the presence of religious dogmatism in the early history of the AAUP that has made it reluctant to address the need for revision and updating of its academic freedom definition and statements, especially in regard to the relevance of worldview to the definition and

22

implementation of academic freedom in the academy. More likely, however, is the fact that the AAUP long ago turned its primary focus to matters of tenure and job security and has become a sort of labor union focused on faculty benefits, collective bargaining, and contract negotiations. In either case, it now seems to me that intolerance of religion has become quite politically correct in the membership of the organization and in its leadership. Indeed, throughout its history, the AAUP has demonstrated by its actions a much greater concern for any limitations on academic freedom at religiously affiliated colleges than for widespread limitations on religious expression at secular institutions.

Although the political Left seems to have dominated most college faculties in the past, the political Right in their supporting constituencies continues to have some presence. This is particularly true in religiously affiliated colleges, although by no means limited to them. The past decade has witnessed many limitations imposed by certain religious denominations, the more notorious cases representing only the "tip of the iceberg" of such cases around the country. I can name at least three such cases that gained considerable national attention, partially due to major AAUP investigations of each case. They include the Catholic University of America, where the distinguished liberal theologian Charles Curran was barred from teaching Catholic theology out of concern for orthodoxy by the Church authorities in Rome; the Southwestern Baptist Theological Seminary, where the Radical Right of the Southern Baptist Convention gained control of the governing board and drove out a moderate president and dean because of stricter views of biblical inerrancy; and the Concordia Theological Seminary, where officials of the Lutheran Church Missouri Synod dismissed a professor for teaching "false doctrine" related to the status of women. These cases, and many others, simply demonstrate a continuing presence of the Right in the academy and their ability to "clamp down" on faculty members and administrators seen as coming from the permissive Left. They also demonstrate the naivete of the AAUP in its statement back in the 1970s that most religiously affiliated colleges and universities no longer needed or desired to place a limitation on academic freedom on religious grounds.

Opinion polls and attitude surveys have observed a predominant orientation toward the political Left among college and university faculties over the years. While there has been some variation from time to time, the academy has always been significantly more to the Left than

23

the population as a whole (Lipset, 1992). It should come as no surprise, then, that at a time when our society has moved rather deliberately to the Right, conservative and even moderate speakers, faculty, and books have become politically incorrect. Conservative speakers of almost impeccable academic credentials (including former professors such as Jeane Kirkpatrick, Charles Murray, William Bennett, and even Daniel Moynihan) have been forced to cancel lectures, or have them appropriately "sanitized" by contrary views on the same platform, because of actual or threatened protest demonstrations. Hamilton (1995) attributes an entire "wave of zealotry" currently observed in the academy to the fundamentalist academic Left, and he identifies it as the most pervasive threat to academic freedom today.

It is on the strength of such evidence, for example, that political correctness as a real phenomenon threatens the protection and promotion of academic freedom. It is in precisely these cases where college administrators, and especially presidents, must do what often faculties will fail to do — that is, defend to the ultimate the right of academic freedom as it comes to fruition in freedom of speech and open dialogue on whatever keen issues seem especially relevant at the moment. All of us in the academy ought to question whether we have come to the point where some of the "hot potatoes" of political correctness have become so explosive that deliberate thoughtfulness and fair play get thrown out the window. There has been, regrettably, a failure of nerve on the part of too many administrators in recent days where these issues have surfaced, especially when the controversy is associated with ethnic, racial, and gender matters. Being on the "wrong" side of these issues in some settings can cost professors their jobs, their tenure, their benefits, and their good names. Courageous key administrators — deans, vice presidents, provosts, and presidents — are today the primary force of any significance that can bear upon the present situation. Faculties will not (Hamilton, 1995). Recently, some promise for the future may be found in potential supportive roles of groups like the National Alumni Forum and the National Association of Scholars.

As I've already said, political correctness nowadays is most often referred to and found in selected single-issue concerns such as multiculturalism, feminism, pluralism, scientism, humanism, and the like. All have merit and should certainly be addressed in the academic community. But when a given solution or methodology for addressing these matters takes on a prominence or life of its own in the community, often to the detriment or exclusion of other concerns, it becomes politically correct to embrace that solution and the methodology for attaining it. This leads to the squelching of contrary approaches and contrary views, thus limiting the debates and discussions that these issues deserve, especially in an academic community committed to the search for truth. Interestingly, in all too many such cases, the only real values are found in the single issue (the -ism), while the criteria of truthfulness so essential to academic freedom are judged to be illusory and deceptive. Thus the value of academic freedom is denied while these single-issue values are given special prominence and status.

We must learn from the past in responding to both present and future threats of this sort. The academy must never become captive to the agenda of special interests, no matter how deeply they are felt or how passionately they are presented. I have yet to see a sound example of how such single and special-interest preoccupations have promoted the pursuit of knowledge. Most have proven harmful. Interestingly, people driven by single interests (and self-interest) tend to choose similar tactics and social strategies; they often act alike in a given situation. From McCarthyism in the 1950s to the Free Speech Movement of the 1960s to the "zealotry" of the Radical Left in the 1980s and 1990s, the threats and the results are strikingly similar. Single interests necessarily and inevitably prod people into conformity. Truth, on the other hand, by its very nature diversifies human thought and discovery. Truth, along with justice, is rarely found on only one side of complex issues. In political correctness circumstances, then, truth is relativized beyond the reach of academic freedom. In such cases the college or university may be failing to serve as the "intellectual experiment station" intended, but rather as a home of orthodoxy, reaction, and conventionality (Thomson, 1993). The canons of the campus may vary, but when the canons of single-issue causes and political correctness reign, academic freedom is threatened. It is the obligation of the academy to be forever vigilant among its own for just such single-mindedness and lack of tolerance.

The logical extension of such dynamics in the academy can often lead to the kind of ideological imperialism cited earlier. At least it will feel that way to faculty with contrary views. Some illustrations in "real life" are often cited by faculty members who see these phenomena as infringements on their academic freedom (R. Scott, 1995; London, 1995;

Hamilton, 1995; etc.). Others are documented in more general writings about the harassment of professors who express views that are not politically correct (Bernstein, 1994; Cheney, 1995; D'Souza, 1991; etc.). It matters little whether the commentators are from the Left or the Right. Because the issues (gender, race, class, etc.) have merit and are so important, and because they will have a considerable impact on the long-term welfare of our society, it is easy for a faculty member to be misunderstood and "labeled" when contrary approaches are suggested. These good and deserving issues, then, often come as "wolves dressed in sheep's clothing" where academic freedom is threatened and at risk.

Some of these modern day single-issue threats lead to a reactionary nostalgia among some academics, which, in turn, becomes a threat of its own. Such nostalgia need not have any direct relationship to the reality of the past, but it does create a view of academic freedom that is more destructive than helpful in the current climate. It builds on a wrong-headed arrogance about a fine notion — that is, that academics are a very special group with special privileges conferred by society. Perhaps because they have lost sight of the obligations and responsibilities that accompany that status and privilege, their faulty nostalgia immobilizes them. They do nothing to protect academic freedom against these threats; they ignore the threats of postmodernism and the rising tribe of antinomians; they "grouse" about change and idealize the past. They create an unreal world for themselves. The academy, for them, is a cloister of peace and contentment for the scholar, a place where no one need be "managed" or even appraised, a place where they simply should be curious and unattended. They produce little or no scholarship. Their teaching is mediocre at best, and often woefully out-of-date. They resist evaluation and assessment. They vegetate. They marginalize themselves; they become less than full citizens in the academy. They become "deadwood," bad examples. Each campus has a few, some more than others.

Such nostalgia is totally incompatible with the new mixture of technology and competition in our society and in higher education. Nostalgia does nothing to aid in the protection of academic freedom in a changing academy. Rather, such nostalgia represents a regressive mentality at a time when the academy must be focusing on new and progressive approaches to scholarship and the delivery of education. Such changes will undoubtedly have implications for academic freedom. Indeed, we need to be focusing today on how the academy may be expanded, as new groves of academe spring up outside the college and university in corporations, research entities, privately sponsored "think tanks," and governmental agencies. These new entities also need the assurance of academic freedom. Indeed, some may have greater commitment to an ideology than to the search for truth, thus rendering academic freedom of little merit. These need to be uncovered for what they are and be confronted by the academy. These changes, along with the threats inherent in postmodernism, need not threaten the existence of academic freedom so long as the academy carefully assesses what such changes mean for the unbridled pursuit of truth and then commits itself to finding new ways to assure its protection and promotion. Such new ways must be communal in character and should always militate toward an ethos of freedom.

Prior Restraint and Censorship

Censorship of opposing views is one of the strongest drives in human nature. Throughout history we have learned of one group or another that has been labeled too dangerous to be heard. We have heard of books and literature too dangerous to be read or placed in libraries. Indeed, the drive to interfere with the wrong thoughts of others can come from any direction: from the Right or the Left, patriots or traitors, capitalists or socialists, feminists and multiculturalists, and a variety of others. Often, of course, the urge to interfere with the wrong thoughts of others arises out of good and honorable motives. Usually it is an honest effort to enhance a virtue that, in the process, is exaggerated until it becomes a vice. The censors usually extol the virtues of free speech while carving out their exceptions in the name of a higher morality or a nobler cause.[1] They mean well.

Prior restraint and censorship are ever-present threats to academic

---

1. While this phenomenon can be observed on any college campus and throughout our society, nowhere was it more blatant over an extended period of time than during the 1964 Free Speech Movement at Berkeley. Roger Heyns's observations (see p. 17 above) about that movement are particularly illustrative. My own experiences and observations on the campuses of Michigan State University, the University of Illinois, and Calvin College resonate precisely with those of Heyns.

freedom. Sometimes these threats come from well-intentioned, but usually misguided, efforts to give a higher place to the value of harmony in the campus community than to freedom of expression and debate. Both come as "wolves in sheep's clothing" because they can seem so perfectly harmless in the existential situation and so much easier to accomplish than the alternatives. But inherent in such efforts is often the fundamental assumption that the purpose of education is to induce correct opinion rather than to search for wisdom and to liberate the mind. In this regard, these threats are no different than those that come with political correctness.

Obviously the values of civility, mutual respect, and harmony are rightly prized in the college community. But they must be fostered in the process of doing what the college is called to do — to search for wisdom and truth wherever the search may lead — rather than preventing it by prior restraint or censorship. In my personal experience and by my observation of similar incidents on other campuses over the years, I believe that a college should rarely, if ever, bow to the threats that normally accompany calls for censorship or prior restraint — disruption, violence, withholding of financial support, political punishment, and the like. All in their essence fly in the face of the essential purpose of the academy and militate against an ethos of freedom on the campus.

Prudence always requires that academic officers and presidents take such threats seriously when they arise. Careful review of the issues is essential, and deliberate efforts to clarify any possible misunderstandings are imperative. Prudence will then often demand strong stands, where justified by the facts and an understanding of the prevailing ideologies in the conflict, and forceful articulation of the role of the academy in the face of such ominous threats. I experienced directly a variety of such threats during my tenure as a college president. Because in almost every case of attempted censorship or prior restraint there are faculty involved, two absolutely essential principles are at risk. Both complicate the controversies that result. One is the principle of strict confidentiality on personnel matters required by law and moral code (often in the face of unrestrained and unrelenting slander and defamation of a faculty member's character). The other is the principle of due process as necessary for justice to be accomplished and the law to be satisfied. The latter requires time and great care (often in the face of continuing call for a "rush to judgment"). Despite the threats, and the

28

enormous pressures for immediate resolution, academic administrators and presidents must "stay the course" of academic freedom and integrity. And they must lead their boards along the same course. Institutional integrity cannot be compromised, for a college's survival without it is purposeless. The higher education landscape is littered with colleges that do not enjoy such foundational integrity and clear purpose, institutions that collectively represent a wasteland of good intentions foiled by demagoguery, authoritarianism, and undue personal influence. I am convinced that none should join them.

Exceedingly instructive in these matters of prudence was the controversy that resulted over *The Fourth Day* (Van Till, 1986) on the Calvin campus and throughout the college's supporting and church constituency. While too complex to provide all of the details of that controversy here (which could be a book-length case study by itself), some of its dynamics are classic ingredients of many academic freedom cases now and in the past. They illustrate well the need for prudence.

Soon after its publication in March 1986, *The Fourth Day* began to receive two almost diametrically opposed reactions. Some reviewers and correspondents gave the book high praise for sorting out a number of confusing issues concerning the relationship of Christian faith and natural science and for offering a means of clarifying the muddied waters of the contemporary creation-evolution debate. From others the book received harsh criticism including allegations of denying the authority of the Bible, rejecting clear biblical teachings, accepting a host of heresies that flow from taking natural science too seriously, and blatant violation of church creeds and doctrinal positions. From these latter critics came calls for censorship of Van Till and his writings and for his removal from the classroom and his college professorship.

Although representing a minority view, the negative critics were loud and lasting. The charges against Van Till and *The Fourth Day* expanded rapidly from among the church constituency, and they were increasingly reckless and unrelenting. Voices demanding judgment were multiplying rapidly, even from those who admittedly had not read the book or heard Van Till speak on the issues involved. Established "due process" college procedures were set in motion and, because some of the allegations focused on ecclesiastical and creedal matters, a special five-member study committee of the board of trustees was established to assess the legitimacy of those issues. The internal proceedings resulted in the college's defense of Van Till's academic freedom while awaiting the results of the study committee. The study committee proceeded with deliberate care, without undue haste or a "rush to judgment," and submitted a report of findings to the board of trustees after a full year of study (Witvliet, 1991).

The study committee report became the baseline from which calls for Van Till's censorship and dismissal were rejected and his academic freedom assured. Addressing the full spectrum of concerns expressed by the critics, the report offered words of both caution and encouragement on the issues while standing solidly in defense of Van Till's freedom to explore them. It judged that Van Till's interpretations did not violate church doctrinal and creedal standards. It included words of appreciation for Van Till's scholarly explorations and judged that they held the potential of being fruitful contributions to a complex, longstanding, and emotion-laden discussion on the creation-evolution issue. It also noted that the college and its faculty are called to provide leadership in the enterprise of Christian higher education, including a "calling" to speak vigorously and knowledgeably to the entire community so that an effective Christian witness is presented to a scientifically well-informed world. It recognized the need for academic freedom within the context of a hearty commitment to the Christian faith and encouraged the faculty to conduct its scholarship with intellectual integrity. It represented a foursquare endorsement of the college's mission and purpose in providing solid Christian scholarship with the intellectual integrity that can stand as a beacon in a world too often darkened by anti-intellectual obscurantism. It was a courageous and straightforward report, and it provided a solid place to stand.

Van Till's response to the report was admirable and equally encouraging. It included the following comment: "I shall continue to study the Bible with full respect for what it teaches concerning history and I shall endeavor to express my views on both theological and scientific matters as clearly and as fully as possible. Without any reservations, I shall continue to seek a deeper understanding of both God's written Word and God's created world, and in that search I welcome the light that each may shed on an understanding of the other. To close one's mind to the results of either faithful biblical scholarship or competent scientific investigation would be intellectually dishonest — an approach that I vigorously reject. As an expression of a firm faith, a

Christian scholar must be willing to follow good evidence wherever it leads."

Not surprisingly, while providing that solid place to stand, the report did not satisfy the serious critics. Their assaults on Van Till and the college increased in both volatility and frequency. All of the usual tactics of the "zealots" were implemented: emotionalized language, deception, innuendo, defamation of character, guilt by association, threats of withdrawal of financial support, rumor-mongering, blatantly false charges, fear-mongering, full-page newspaper ads of ad hominem slander and libelous accusations, and much more. Some churches initiated formal actions within the ecclesiastical system and brought formal charges to the board of trustees. Pressures to censor and remove, now expanded to include others (including selected faculty and the president of the college), mounted in several constituencies and intensified at the level of the board of trustees. Some of these tactics will be discussed later, but suffice it to say for our purposes here that the report's foundational posture in defense of academic freedom was maintained throughout the controversy and that it also had enthusiastic support, although less vocal, among the various constituencies of the college. But the controversy was far from over.

Because many of the allegations against Van Till and the college in the advanced stages of the controversy included charges of various "heresies," the ecclesiastical (denominational) system also conducted its own investigations of the Van Till writings and related issues. While supporting these independent inquiries and insisting that they be conducted confidentially with careful deliberation, the college and board of trustees became increasingly weary and distracted by the extended controversy. Concurrently, and solidly supported by his academic freedom to do so, Van Till willingly and eagerly took many opportunities to present his views to gatherings of friends and foes alike. He traveled extensively throughout the United States and Canada, which also over time became wearying and distracting from his ongoing tasks of teaching and research. While prudence prevailed, by almost any standard the process was taking too long.

Soon both prudence and process were threatened when I observed a "crack" developing in the solid support of the board of trustees for the early study report and the academic freedom it defended. One trustee was beginning to buckle under the pressure and leaked confidential information from board proceedings, including some personal information about Van Till, to some key critics of the college. This threatened at least two vital principles essential to the fair adjudication of academic freedom cases: confidentiality and due process. Immediate corrective action was needed. It was imperative, I judged, for me to send a strongly worded confidential memorandum to the executive committee of the board of trustees calling for reprimand of the errant trustee; admonition of the critics who knowingly distributed confidential information inappropriately acquired; expression of regret for the breach and reassurance of confidentiality and due process for Van Till; and a public response to the incident including the resolve to assure due process and confidentiality in all remaining proceedings and to resist all external influences on final adjudication (Diekema, 1990). Obviously this was not a desirable turn of events, nor was it a pleasant task for me to orchestrate with the board of trustees, but it did serve to get the case back "on track," and it did result, finally, in a fair and just conclusion. From start to finish, complete and final adjudication within both the college and the ecclesiastical system (Synod, 1991) took almost six years (1986-1991), too long, but prudence prevailed over a "rush to judgment." Most importantly, the case ended with academic freedom and institutional integrity solidly intact. Despite the negatives that come with long processes of adjudication, I am persuaded that a fair and just outcome falling on the side of academic freedom promotes an ethos of freedom on the campus for many years into the future.

Finally, given the nature of this particular case and its direct focus on the relationship between Christian faith and natural science, I was especially gratified to observe that Professor Van Till was named a recipient of the coveted Calvin Alumni Association's 1999 "Faith and Learning Award." It represents a wonderfully reassuring vote of confidence for Van Till, from thousands of his former students, and a public affirmation of academic freedom for the college.

What is important in these cases is the mission of the college and the fundamental purposes of the enterprise. That mission and purpose — the aim of teaching and learning in any college worthy of its name — is to enlighten the search for knowledge with sparks of creativity and imagination, and to liberate the mind from habitual thinking so often dulled by custom and convention. That is never accomplished by censorship or prior restraint. Ideas are alive, and they need the invigoration of fresh thought and unencumbered perspective. Ideas that are not challenged soon become straitjackets. Presuppositions and first principles must always be scrutinized. On many great questions of life, truth is a matter of reconciling competing views, of weighing neighboring values, and of keeping the mind free and open to new light even as we redefine and hold to our convictions and enhance our worldviews. This is vital to the promotion and enhancement of the academy for faculty and students alike; but even more importantly, it is the only way by which the academy can fulfill its obligations to its primary constituencies and the society at large.

College and university faculties are particularly exposed to the lust to censor in the name of higher moralities or principles. It is in the nature of their work to challenge beliefs and to subject them to inquiry, analysis, and revision. And it is only natural that when one's own cherished beliefs are concerned, a large number of us strongly resist the central premise of a liberal intellectual system that all knowledge claims are revisable. Change is often painful, but when cherished beliefs are at stake the mental pain is even more severe. So even faculty committed to this intellectual system can have second thoughts about that commitment when their own cherished beliefs are scrutinized or challenged by others. This is inherent in the life of the academy and its members. The example of Galileo seems forever relevant.

The "Chilling Effect" and Self-Censorship

Nothing is more destructive to the maintenance of morale in a faculty than the "chilling effect" that comes with the use of college authority to restrain or censor. Indeed, I believe the most devastating threats to academic freedom come not from outside or from blatant tyranny, but rather from well-meaning persons who have little or no understanding of the long-range negative effect of their actions to inhibit the essential freedoms of the academy. Well-meant but misguided concerns for the fact that the academy's freedom can or may offend some group or individual can have lethal effects on the long-term health of a college or university. When offensiveness is used as grounds for suppression, it opens the road to widespread censorship and restraint because almost everything of consequence in the life of the mind will be offensive to someone (Schmidt, 1992). But most important is not the punishment suffered by the professor whose freedoms are restrained; rather, it is the much greater problem caused by the response of many others in the academy who will avoid a similar fate by steering clear of controversial and unpopular views or topics (Ericson, 1991; Tight, 1988; Shils, 1993). The latter is the essence of the "chilling effect" — that is, the real long-term negative results in the academy of those vague powers to punish any speech or publication, which in turn render the academy ineffective in the performance of its role in society.

Self-censorship is often a result of the "chilling effect." As one writer puts it: "It is not the iron fist of repression but the velvet glove of seduction that is the real problem." Faculty simply do not always say what they believe, or what they know to be true, because they don't want to deal with what may be the resulting hassle — peer alienation, negative student opinions, or the ire of a constituent community. Self-censorship is often a matter of personal convenience for faculty. They simply assess the potential costs before speaking out, not because of fear of specific consequences, but because of a more general assessment of a "nuisance effect." They count the costs in time, in social and peer relationships, and in career opportunities. Past experiences, observation of what has happened to others, and an assessment of the political correctness atmosphere of the community all play a part in the subtle self-censorship that takes place with and among faculty each day. And while there may be some positive effects to judicious self-censorship, it ultimately has a negative effect similar to the chilling effect on the academy and academic freedom (Glazer, 1996).

The chilling effect must be avoided at all costs precisely because the cost is so outrageously high. Examples of such effects abound in the literature, spanning the landscape from the extremes of McCarthyism in the 1950s and student activism in the 1960s to the acknowledged complexities of the Curran case at the Catholic University of America in the 1980s (Schrecker, 1986; Shils, 1993; McCormick et al., 1990; and many others noted in the reading list). And while the chilling effect nowadays often comes from the abuses of what Hamilton (1995) identifies as the "permissive academic Left," there are an abundance of recent cases in religiously affiliated colleges where the guardians on the walls for the Religious Right have clamped down on faculty and administrators in ways that have violated both academic and personal freedoms. A board of trustees terminated the appointment of a female professor for displaying a small "Support Gay Rights" button on her briefcase. A male poet's tenured appointment was withdrawn by the administration when sexually explicit language was discovered in a past piece of his published works. A young male faculty member's services were summarily terminated by the president after he was seen having coffee with a female student. A female professor was denied tenure after an article written by her appeared in a student publication and included criticism of church leaders for not extending the priesthood to women. Other examples abound. Abuses of academic freedom continue to occur across the entire spectrum of American higher education — public, private, and religiously affiliated (Kurland, 1996; Hamilton, 1995; Walhout, 1999). Each contributes to the lasting and substantial damage caused by the chilling effect.

It is especially troublesome when several of these threats intersect in existential situations on the campus. That is when academic freedom is most vulnerable to the spirit of the moment. Unfortunately, many campuses today experience the intersection of selected single-issue interests (feminism, racism, diversity, gay rights, etc.), a political correctness related to each, and a chilling effect precipitated by an increasing number of students and faculty who assert that vague notions of interpersonal harmony are more important to the academy than freedom of thought and expression. But such an assertion is clearly incompatible with the independence and creativity of the academic mission and enterprise. Ironically, it is often this intersection of the competing values found in single-issue interests that promotes a more open and diverse intellectual environment; but in the radical enthusiasm for presenting them as single issues they actually function to limit discussion and inhibit honest disagreement on the campus. A college campus, if it is doing what it ought to be doing, is by its very nature a bit controversial and disorderly. The paramount end of the academy is the search for truth, not some wrong-headed notion of harmony, even though an honest sense of community is also a cherished value on the campus. Admittedly, it is hard to adhere to fundamental principles in an environment that clouds their value by good causes supported by well-meaning people. But where the fundamental ethics of academic freedom are not well established, or where an ethos of freedom is nonexistent, both faculty and administration bend quickly to whatever political winds are blowing the strongest.

Such adherence to principle and ethic always requires the long view, the vision of what the future must be, rather than the bending to intense pressures of immediacy so characteristic of our frenetic times. Because the academy is so often divided on such current issues, strong and visionary administrative leadership is essential to the protection and promotion of academic freedom. Ironically, and unfortunately, it is exactly such an environment of division and doubt that all too often has produced a style of academic leadership that is averse to risk, skittish about defending academic values, and inclined to negotiate about almost anything. History has clearly demonstrated that most administrators too often urge compromise, and often capitulation, to the aroused ire of a student or a parent, a colleague or a constituent. Rarely have they opted to confront accusers, demand solid evidence, and undertake a full investigation. Quick resolution of the immediate "problem" is the dominant short-term goal.

Although sometimes difficult to document by empirical study, it is clear that the current threats to academic freedom have had a negative and chilling effect in the academy. They have limited the range of discussion and debate that occurs in college classrooms. Professors and students are fearful of presenting views that are "far out" or "politically incorrect" on issues such as diversity, race relations, gender differences, sexuality, abortion, and the like. On these and related issues, discussion has narrowed, and the issues are more limited and constrained.

Other effects have been the diminishment of lightheartedness and the increasing absence of humor. Jokes, both in and out of the classroom, have all but disappeared for fear that they might offend someone. The atmosphere of interpersonal relations among faculty colleagues has changed by the disappearance of much of the congenial teasing and disagreements about ideas and political issues that formerly enlivened the faculty meeting and coffee room. Behavior has become much more formal, stilted, and lacking in zest and spontaneity. The simple joys have gone. Silence is more and more often deemed "golden." Also, for faculty, the increasing fear of lawsuits — from students, parents, colleagues, and constituents — has promoted silence and noninvolvement. Increasingly, "getting involved" seems only to hurt one's career. Unfortunately, these realities have guided the chilling effect that has altered faculty behavior on many campuses. Students, too, have been affected — often, I fear, in a loss of vibrancy and quality in the education they experience.

Governmental and Institutional Influence

Other matters can be cited as occasional threats to academic freedom. At least nowadays, however, they seem less frequent in the arena of higher education than in some former times. There have been occasions when general societal or state values have constrained the way in which colleges and universities conduct their business, even at the level of curriculum and courses. The coming into being of overzealous state boards of higher education (and other so-called coordinating agencies) in a variety of states several decades ago occasioned such threats. Today, perhaps, it may be the indirect influence of the federal government that imposes a subtle but significant threat. While often brought to bear by administrators and other academics, these influences tend to come through efforts to comply with governmentally required, or "encouraged," ways of doing business. Whether in the arena of "diversity" interests, or project funding, or student financial aid, or affirmative action, such influences can have significant effects on colleges and universities. For example, the federal government's concern for diversity, and many institutional initiatives to "celebrate diversity," have concluded in an unintended demand for conformity. Ironically, almost every college and university now finds itself conforming to diversity demands. And while these matters have generally been addressed on the level of institutional academic freedom — that is, institutional autonomy — they eventually often have implications for individual faculty freedoms (Hamilton, 1995).

Certain rules or sanctions imposed by the institution in response to such threats can reduce essential freedoms for the enhancement of the quality of education and research delivered. Even requirements, for example, that every member of the faculty should teach so many hours per week or publish so many research papers per year lead to inflexibilities that represent lack of freedom. Not all of these would be recognized as threats to academic freedom, nor qualify to fit that rubric, but they suggest the need for constant vigilance on the part of the academy and its various members. Sound institutional academic freedom policies must be honed and embraced. Freedom from undue interference and freedom to teach, write, publish, and profess truth as it is found represent extraordinarily critical functions of the academic enterprise. They must be defended and promoted on all fronts. Furthermore, the academy and its individual members must always be seeking new and effective ways to be fully accountable both internally and externally for this trust. Especially to the public at large, we must explain the results of such freedoms and their contributions to the "public welfare" and the "greater good" of society. We must demonstrate in lay language wherever possible the payoff for an indispensable public trust.

Toward Vigilance Against the Threats

It appears clear that academic freedom is usually threatened most by attempts to enforce conformity. Indeed, every move toward demanding conformity involves some sort of claim to certainty that should be challenged or scrutinized. It is often these varying claims of certainty or "correctness" that the academy is called to pursue and assess in its search for truth. As we have seen, such threats are often found under the current guise of political correctness — that is, those moves toward insistence on conformity in multiculturalism (diversity), feminism, and the like. Religion and sectarianism are lesser players on the academic freedom stage today. Indeed, while religious sectarianism may once have been the principal threat to academic freedom, it may now be the case that one of the greatest threats to real freedom in the academy is the intolerance of religion. The barring of religion, in fact, is often so severe and complete that students are deprived of a vital source of cultural understanding and the bases of our societal values. Hoekema (1995) makes a strong case, by comparing political views with religious views, for the open expression of religious views in classrooms throughout the academy.

The solution to such threats to academic freedom is not to be found in governments and external agencies; rather, I believe it is to be found in the renewal of the academy itself. Unfortunately, faculty tend not to be the greatest defenders of academic freedom, except their own. In fact, the history of academic freedom cases is persuasive in demonstrating that faculty do not come to the defense of their colleagues on behalf of academic freedom, but only in those cases when their own or a shared ideology is at risk (Hamilton, 1995). In fact, the literature suggests that most academics do not give much thought to academic freedom. That certainly comports well with my personal observations. For many faculty it has not been an issue at all, and thus they are usually indifferent when sanctions are visited upon a colleague in some other discipline. Indeed, there are many academics who disapprove of those who "rock the boat," who cause commotion, who instigate external criticism of the college and attract the disfavor of prominent persons outside the college. They are often unsympathetic with colleagues who become the focus in academic freedom cases, regardless of the merits of the specific case. There are varied reasons for this, but all suggest that academic freedom is always at risk due to both indifference and contrary opinion in the academy. Indeed, if academics wish to assure the intellectual high ground of academic freedom in the future, I believe they will have to wake up to its importance, work for it, and struggle each year to hold it. They must understand the nature of community and then set forth to establish and nurture a vigilant community and, ultimately, an ethos of freedom within it.

So a sound sense of the nature of community is foundational to academic freedom. I learned long ago, primarily through the study of the theoretical works of the distinguished French sociologist Emile Durkheim during graduate school days, that one needs always to view and understand any community in the context of the culture and ethos that it develops and then defends by an evolving moral order. In one of his classic works, *The Division of Labor in Society* (1893; translated in 1933), Durkheim sets forth the essential character of communities of various sorts, and the fundamental principles by which they function. For our purposes here it is important to acknowledge, with Durkheim, the vital role of the character — shared ideas, beliefs, sentiments, interests, and so on — of any community in the development of a moral order by which it ultimately nurtures and regulates the behavior of its members. All communities establish moral orders with boundaries beyond which they do not allow their members to go without some reaction and repercussion. It is within these moral order boundaries that we observe a community's *raison d'etre*. Indeed, it is these moral order boundaries that give communities their unique qualities and characteristics. A fundamental idea that Durkheim develops in this work is that as a community becomes more complex and differentiated (pluralistic) the moral order that holds it together necessarily becomes weaker and changes in character.

Later, in another of his classic works, entitled *The Rules of Sociologi-*

cal Method (1895; translated in 1982), Durkheim addresses the resulting phenomena of normality and deviance in a community, and he contends that deviance is normal. He argues that some deviance from the existing moral order will occur in any community where moral order exists and is taken seriously. Challenging the moral order is both a necessary and a risky activity, for it is in pushing against the boundaries of the moral order that we find both creative genius and detrimental noncompliance, both social progress and social regress (Erikson, 1966; Moynihan, 1993). All communities, then, face the tensions and challenges that accompany the maximizing of progress over regress. Where such tensions do not exist, a community is either dying or in a chaotic state of radical change where moral order is nonexistent. We find in Durkheim a dynamic moral vision anchored in a deep respect for both the dignity of the individual and the social solidarity derived from the moral order of a community. Tension, then, is both inherent and good in a healthy community. Indeed, Durkheim essentially states that a community that loses its moral order, or its will to protect it, has already died or is doomed to extinction. In a meaningful Durkheimian sense, then, any community must always be patrolling the boundaries of its moral order. Otherwise it evolves into something it wasn't before, or ultimately falls apart and dies.

Academic communities are no different. A "community of scholars," wherever it is assembled, takes on the same vital character, and the principles by which it functions, as all other communities. It is the shared mission and purpose of the faculties and the institutions that host them — combined with their guiding beliefs and ideas and worldviews and values — that constitute the academic "community" that must patrol and protect and enhance its moral order. Questioning the moral order of any community is dangerous, but in the academic community it is part of the role definition of the faculty to do exactly that on behalf of the society we serve. So it must be done honestly and openly within an ethos that reflects the sanctity of both moral order and academic freedom, and of the inherent tensions between them. It is within such a shared mission and role definition for academic communities that Durkheim, in his work entitled *Moral Education* (1961), argues that the most important role of educational institutions is the development of good, moral citizens. From my early graduate school days, along with foundational Christian presuppositions arising from the theology of the

Reformation as transmitted through a Dutch Reformed heritage, Durkheim's paradigm regarding the nature of community and moral order has had a pervasive influence on my thinking about academic freedom and an ultimate "ideal type" academy.

It is helpful, I believe, for all of us in the academy to view academic freedom as an essential component of the moral order we are willing to embrace and patrol. The Durkheimian message is clear in this regard: you cannot live in a community and enjoy all of the benefits that go with being a member of it and, at the same time, not be willing to actively support its moral order or patrol its boundaries with integrity and courage (Durkheim, 1973). You cannot be part of the academy and willy-nilly attack its moral boundaries with impunity. In short, you "cannot have your cake and eat it too." Rather, if the boundaries of the moral order are to be pushed or altered, such challenges should be anchored in thoughtful and deliberate discussion and civil debate based upon the scholarly pursuit of truth. A healthy tension is always present, of course, but where academic freedom is — along with other components — at the core of the moral order, deviance from it will be carefully monitored while vigorously protected. Such deviance is intended to maximize progress while deterring regress. For this to be done sensitively, yet rigorously, the academy must constantly nurture an ethos of freedom.

Perhaps if academic freedom were not so important it would not be threatened, or we wouldn't perceive the threats in the same way. But its importance is drawn from its critical role in the constant search for and proclamation of truth. If teachers and scholars are to fulfill their obligations to society, then academic freedom must reign. Some have suggested that there should be an academic loyalty oath — that is, as doctors have a superior obligation to the Hippocratic Oath, so college and university professors have a superior obligation to truth that might be embodied in a kind of Socratic oath — imposing on them as their only duty to the community not to please it but to teach it and provide it with truth (Kohr, 1993). I have come to embrace this as a good idea needing further development; for faculty need to be reminded more often of their high calling, and they must know that truth is often contrary to a community's momentary interests and beliefs. Truth can be dangerous, often causes painful pause, and always requires thoughtful reflection in a community. Sensitivity is essential, for the mix of high

41

calling and pain can often stimulate controversy — with loud, immediate, and partisan reaction.

Methods for guiding the community through these rough waters with positive results must constantly be sought. And because the culture of a college community is largely defined by the faculty — and where that culture honors academic freedom — I believe a collegial body should be appointed or elected that is willing to publicly defend its members against the "zealots" and against internal self-interests. Call it something like a council for the promotion of academic freedom. Such a group should be composed of some of the most thoughtful and deliberate members of the campus community, the majority being members of the faculty and others selected from academic administrators and students. It must be characterized by a profound political disinterestedness, subject to neither political correctness nor the personal self-interests of faculty. Its sole focus must be academic freedom; its responsibility must be to see that no one — professors and zealots alike — transgresses the limits on which academic freedom depends in the campus community. Although not directly responsible for the adjudication of specific cases, it must take more than a passing interest in academic freedom cases on its own campus and those that receive national attention. Analysis of these cases can be helpful in identifying the nature of the threats and in keeping the entire campus vigilant. It may be called upon for advice from time to time, both by those responsible for policy development and by those responsible for adjudication of specific cases. It must have the respect of the entire community, including the president and board of trustees. It should militate always toward an ethos of freedom on the campus. Its overarching role should be to promote a healthy vigilance against the threats to academic freedom.

Such an official body could do much to moderate the attacks on thought and speech, and academic freedom would likely prevail. It should have top priority stature on the campus. Unfortunately, and regrettably, this has not been the predominant pattern in the past (Schrecker, 1986; Hamilton, 1995; Trachtenberg, 1997; etc.). My experience as a college president persuades me that the pattern must change from one of silent acquiescence with such attacks by critics to one of active and public defense of academic freedom. I believe the best way to accomplish this is by the development and nurture of an ethos of freedom on each campus, and then through careful and deliberate establishment of policy governing academic freedom. Such policy development is addressed later in this book, for the academy must "stay the course" toward academic freedom.

One final observation is worthy of note. Often when discrepancy between truth and social correctness occurred in the past, the community persecuted its teachers. Some of the extremes are well known. It poisoned Socrates. It crucified Christ. It imprisoned Galileo. But add to that the hundreds of outstanding scholars and teachers who, because of truths they discovered and professed, or because of persons or institutions they offended in the process, have been denied university appointments, or tenure, or access to avenues of publication (Schrecker, 1986; Lattimore, 1951; Kohr, 1993; Huer, 1991). Unfortunately, many such cases are quickly forgotten because the victims often leave the scene and their unpopular ideas are squelched. Indeed, it is precisely so that the community shall not again be able to indict its greatest members on the grounds of social disloyalty (even subversion) that the phenomenon of academic freedom was created. In this historical context, then, academic freedom must always entail the freedom of disloyalty whenever political loyalty comes in conflict with the only master that teachers recognize in their capacity as scholars — truth as it is found in their scholarship and the worldviews they bring to it. It is inevitable, then, that academic freedom will always be under threat and will need all of the protections the academy and society can muster. Eternal vigilance is essential.

IV

Academic Freedom
in the Context of Worldview

Using the Durkheimian paradigm for community, the moral order of any true "community of scholars" includes, among other elements, the essential components of academic freedom and worldview. Both are imperative for the pursuit of truth and the ordering of discovered truth into a unity of knowledge. Thus, both must be components in the shared mission and purpose of scholars and the institutions that host them.

A worldview is a way of thinking about life and the world in its broadest dimensions. It incorporates the core beliefs and values that derive from such thinking, and it provides a working perceptual framework for understanding and giving meaning to such thought. By its very nature — thinking — it strives for unity in all knowledge and for an ultimate truth. It pervades all of one's thought and is foundational to all scholarly and intellectual activity. There are many and varied worldviews in the academy. Some are known, defined, and clearly articulated; others are nebulous and confused. Some exist but are not known or acknowledged. All begin somewhere, with presuppositions and first principles. All influence intellectual activity and behavior. Ideally, each should be defined and articulated by those who hold them. For they are essential to a sound understanding of academic freedom.

Academic freedom in the Christian context, then, is anchored in a worldview. Christian worldviews are essential points of departure for academic freedom in Christian colleges and the broader Christian academy. This section of the book attempts to chart direction toward giving

44

full legitimacy to a Christian worldview in the larger academy, as it focuses some of the critical issues for establishing academic freedom soundly in the Christian academy. It also embraces the concept of academic freedom as a logical extension of the biblical concept of Christian freedom.

Worldview and Enlightenment Objectivity

When one reviews the current literature on academic freedom, it is quickly apparent that the pervasive underlying principle governing the pursuit of truth is a methodology of objectivity. This tacit assumption of objectivity seemingly derives from the work of scholars in the hard sciences, those fields where the confirming methodology is one of replication. By replication one's findings (truth) can be proven beyond a doubt. In such cases, the protection of the scholar's academic freedom seems to be readily accomplished even when the results of the work challenge widely accepted beliefs. Perhaps the work of Galileo is the archetypical example. There was no refuting his discovered law of gravity because it could be replicated easily and repeatedly both by physicists and laypeople. But this kind of objectivity governs the methodology of only a few disciplines, and indeed, even in these disciplines there are areas of the scholar's work that can be challenged. For example, even in the case of Galileo, some of his most grim critics (who wished to limit his academic freedom) came from within the walls of his discipline and the academy. Even in the "hard" sciences, objectivity can be betrayed by subjective bias and personal belief. And in all of the sciences, one's view of the world — one's worldview — plays a significant role in the pursuit of truth.

Arthur Koestler, in his book on the trial of Galileo entitled *The Sleepwalkers* (1964), observes that "professionals with a vested interest in tradition and in the monopoly of learning" always tend to block the development of new concepts. "Innovation is a twofold threat to academic mediocrities," he writes. "It endangers their oracular authority, and it evokes a deeper fear that their whole laboriously constructed intellectual edifice might collapse." So the Aristotelian scholars in the seventeenth-century universities dealt intolerantly with Galileo. Ironically, even the academic discipline (those colleagues considered to

45

be professional experts on the issues), which serves to protect the academic freedom of individuals within it, can operate in ways that deny some of them that very freedom. Those who have been involved in academic freedom cases firsthand will often agree. Indeed, speaking to the negative aspects of the historic relationship between academic freedom and tenure, John Silber (1973) writes, "Infringement by tenured professors of the rights of non-tenured faculty to develop their intellectual interests according to their own professional judgment . . . represents by far the most serious and most frequent violation of academic freedom in our colleges and universities." In any event, this kind of "unassailable" objectivity as the modus operandi for scholarship was an early concern for those with a broader interest in the universal protection of faculty and the academy.

The first president of the AAUP, John Dewey, in an early essay on academic freedom, pointed with concern to the lower scientific status of "the social and psychological disciplines and to some phases of linguistic and historical study . . . those most intimately associated with religious history and literature." Scholars in these fields, he said, needed "the utmost freedom of investigation" because they dealt more closely than technical scientists with "the problems of life," and were thus more likely to come up against "deep-rooted prejudice and intense emotional reaction." Although today the technical scientists are similarly vulnerable, the history of academic freedom cases since Dewey's time has certainly proved these words prophetic.

Increasingly today, even the task of finding "professional experts" for assistance in the adjudication of academic freedom cases is complicated by the nature of modern knowledge. The American academy has entered the age of the interdisciplinary team rather than the master of the discipline; indeed, in one academic discipline after another discrete boundaries crumble. Chemical engineers and biologists must pool their wisdom to become biotechnologists; international economists are lost without political scientists; the old boundaries between electrical and mechanical engineering become increasingly meaningless as both depend on design, computing systems, and business sense. Knowledge and inquiry go increasingly beyond the traditional categories, requiring new approaches that appear much more flexible than the old models. All have an influence on how we implement and adjudicate academic freedom in the academy.

So Dewey was right in raising the red flag concerning objectivity as a far too limiting methodology for a large segment of the academy. Many other commentators since Dewey have raised similar concerns, but little has found its way into official pronouncements and policy statements regarding academic freedom. Furthermore, in the meantime much has been written about the impossibility of doing scholarship that is "value free" and of pursuing truth from an entirely "neutral" perspective or view of the world (e.g., Tight, Barnett, Hawkesworth, Shils, Marsden, Ericson, Monsma). Much of this has been broadly accepted in the academy, but again, little has made its way into policy definitions or statements about academic freedom. Cognition, or knowing, is now more commonly viewed as a human practice in which truth is seen as subjective, mediated, and contextual. Worldview makes a difference. Because all intellectual activity begins somewhere, with presuppositions and first principles, it is more honest and liberating to acknowledge and articulate one's worldview than to pretend it doesn't exist. Consequently, a sound working definition of academic freedom must acknowledge the inevitability and legitimacy of worldview in the scholarly enterprise. It must affirm worldview's legitimate place, along with that of objectivity, in the methodologies operative in academic freedom cases and policy statements.

But change can be strange. It is certainly a more common assumption today than in the 1950s when I was a graduate student that education is empty and of limited value unless it has a moral component. Radical empiricism, at least in the social sciences, reigned back then. The belief today is increasingly that a traditional liberal education — an education that does not attempt to further particular values — is inadequate. This belief has almost become commonplace, especially in the academy itself. In recent years, open expression of values and ideologies (some even call it indoctrination) has almost become an academic responsibility as more and more faculty maintain that an unbiased, objective, ideology-free pursuit of knowledge is a transparent myth. A large proportion of the professoriate today sees truth as relative and believes that professors have a civic and moral responsibility to reveal truth to students as they see it. Objectivity for many is no longer either valued or sought. It is commonly believed today that scholarship cannot be disinterested.

There is more than a passing irony in this. Higher education, both

47

in Europe and in the United States, had its beginnings under the sponsorship of the church and religious associations in which both theology and philosophy were predominant disciplines. It is an often noted and undeniable fact that many of the leading universities of the world, both past and present, have flourished under church sponsorship and religious direction. It would be sheer stupidity to deny the high quality of scholarship that emanates from some of the major Catholic and other religiously affiliated colleges and universities around the world. Even to suggest that these institutions cannot provide an environment in which sound academic freedom thrives is evidence of a narrow parochialism that is, in its own way, sectarian. Surely, those who wish to reject a religious sectarianism — as, indeed, they must — should not embrace a secular sectarianism in its place — as they usually do! While it once may have been true that religious dogmatism was the principal threat to academic freedom, it may now be the case that the academy's intolerance of religion is the greatest threat to that freedom.

I find it odd that, in spite of increasing consensus in the academic community that one cannot construct a purely objective, neutral, bias-free, and rational perspective, the AAUP and other scholarly associations have not challenged the continuing assumption in academic freedom definitions and cases of the sole legitimacy of objectivity and pure rationality. The current consensus is that all thought is contextual and therefore value-laden. All presuppositions of such contextualized thought may be challenged. The absolute inevitability of worldview considerations in everything we think and do and say seems now to be quite universally accepted. Everyone seems to acknowledge that all scholarship takes place in the context of specific presuppositions, a definable social milieu, and an array of religious beliefs and commitments of the scholar. Yet there remains in the academy the predominant objectivity-rationalistic model with its presuppositions and assumptions (Thomson and Finkin, 1993).

Perhaps it isn't strange at all. But it is essential to pursue the fallacy of this model for the sake of Christian scholarship and its potential place in the marketplace of ideas. The predominant secular academy, I am sure, is more comfortable with the rationalistic approach and has managed to define academic freedom in such a way that is congruent with the presuppositions of a totally rationalistic and objective model. It simply comes to a faith in reason. Thus, the argument that faith in reason, at base, is no different than faith in God must be aggressively pursued. Some postmodernists notwithstanding, there is little doubt that faith in reason has an assumed legitimacy in today's academy. But what is reason for the rationalist may not be a reason for me as a Christian; indeed, it may embrace assumptions that are incompatible with the principles that ground my perception and judgment as a Christian — from a Christian worldview. Reasons (taken from any perspective or worldview) do not confirm or anchor your faith; they are extensions of your faith and are reasons for you because of what you already believe at a level so fundamental and foundational that it is often hidden from self-conscious scrutiny. Generically, then, there is as much legitimacy in a worldview based upon Christian presuppositions (beliefs) as in a worldview based upon the presuppositions (beliefs) of rationalism.

Part of the armament often used by the rationalists is the concept of the "open mind," allegedly a mind that is open to new and different approaches. But the open mind as sometimes assumed in the radical rationalist arguments runs dangerously close to being an empty mind. Presumably for the rationalist, an open mind would be not unduly committed to its present contents; it would be so structured (or perhaps unstructured) that it lacked a framework in relation to which the world of action and speech would be intelligible. It would be a mind so open that it was anchored by no assumptions, no convictions of the kind that order and stabilize perception; it would be a mind without shape and substance, thus a mind without the capacity for keeping anything in it. A consciousness not shored up by a set of beliefs whose negation it could not think through would be an empty mind, or no mind at all. So even an open mind must, it seems to me, include some belief system that can be changed by argumentation in order to be part of the debate. An open mind is not the exclusive property of the rationalists, as they would like us to believe so that they have an elevated status in the discussion.

It follows then that there is nothing totally "free" of worldview. The notion of reason is presented in the academy as if its meaning is obvious to anyone no matter what his or her religious background, political affiliation, educational experience, ethnic tradition, gender, ad infinitum. But it is really, in fact, simply one among other notions that have different meanings in relation to different assumptions and background conditions. This must be openly and honestly acknowledged in academic freedom definitions and discussions. In addition to the common assumptions about objective evidence and logic, worldview must also be acknowledged in the adjudication of academic freedom cases. The academy must actively promote the reality of presuppositions that constantly intrude into our worlds of ideas and thoughts — presuppositions that, until we recognize them for what they are, have not been a part of our previous experience. Thus, an academic freedom case cannot be fairly and honestly adjudicated without consideration of worldview because opposing arguments usually rest upon radically opposed presuppositions about what is desirable, possible, and even real.

The existence of worldview, no matter how limited or unclear, in the work of all faculty provides the impetus to make worldview a part of the definition and review of academic freedom cases. Once it is part of the definition, it seems that appropriate guidelines for its assessment in specific cases can be suggested. Indeed, the reality of worldview in all matters pertaining to academic freedom may well provide the nexus for bringing individual and institutional considerations together in a more compatible fashion. It may well make institutional mission and scholarly calling more prominent in the consideration of cases. It may lead to greater concern for compatibility of institutional and faculty commitments at the critical points of initial employment, reappointment, and the granting of tenure throughout higher education. In any event, a sound working definition of academic freedom must give attention to both the reality of worldview and its continuing evaluation.

Differing worldviews must be acknowledged, then. Real academic freedom is dependent upon their careful articulation and consideration. This is essential if we are to avoid the chaos that would accompany the relativism inherent in simple acceptance of any worldview being equivalent in value to any other. Acknowledging worldview differences does not lead to radical relativism; rather, it demands that each worldview be fully defined and defended. It requires debate among worldviews, arguing point and counter point, thrashing it out, and presenting bodies of evidence to one another. Presuppositions and first principles thus would be scrutinized and open to challenge. All worldviews would abide by the minimal rules (standards of evidence and logical argument) necessary for a pluralistic scholarly debate. It would involve the search for truth on a level playing field — without external, unchallengeable authority. Not presided over by a position from outside or one set of preferred presuppositions, it would be a continuing and vigorous debate in the academy's public square where truth would need to arise out of the debate itself, if at all. Indeed, it is an idealized debate in which everyone's "cards are on the table" and the stakes are known to all. It would be fair.

Given where the academy is today on the matter of worldview and academic freedom, a level playing field as described briefly here is all the Christian scholar should ask for. A playing field where worldview is in clear focus would be an idealized search for truth — especially for the Christian scholar and those others who have carefully worked out perspectives and assumptions. Students and faculty alike could engage the issues with a mental and intellectual rigor that always holds out the possibility of changing minds.

Indeed, I believe the focus of the Christian community of scholars (perhaps enjoined by others with defined worldviews) for the next decade must be toward exposure of the logical fallacy inherent in the predominance of the present faith in reason over all other worldviews. The agenda should include the downfall of that "political" predominance and the clear articulation of arguments for exactly what it is — political — and what it is not — a superior system of thought that stands above other worldviews. This would be a giant step forward for the Christian scholar and a challenge that would bring the best and brightest to a new appreciation of the academy.

Many secular scholars would be "at risk" under the conditions of such a level playing field. In spite of the fact that presuppositions and assumptions are increasingly acknowledged, most contemporary scholars tend to think of their knowledge as fairly unbiased in character and rational in acquisition. Indeed, for some, their confidence is so great that they rarely question their present state of mind, or from whence it came. Many professors carry on with their academic routines blissfully ignorant of their biases. Nothing will be more difficult for such academics than to explain clearly the worldview that guides their search for truth, especially when they have no idea about what they already know to be true. But a level playing field will require that they both know it and be able to articulate it. They will need to know from whence they come intellectually, what their basic presuppositions are, and how to articulate them clearly. They will need to know themselves; a professor who cannot debate worldview issues is hardly qualified to enter the discussion. For that matter, how can a professor who cannot respond to worldview-type questions in the classroom truly challenge students to think through alternative views and perspectives? How can such a professor truly teach? The introduction of worldview considerations to the discussion has the potential of improving the intellectual climate for all of higher education.

When one acknowledges the legitimacy of worldview as integral to academic freedom definitions and cases, this acknowledgment also allows for the inclusion of ethical and moral issues. The inclusion of these considerations does not negate the importance of the ideal objectivity; rather, it simply acknowledges their existence as real objects in the search for truth. All scholars should seek the ideal of objectivity in the subject of their expertise; that is, they must allow that subject to be what it intrinsically is. Regardless of worldview and personal inclination toward biases, the scholar may not distort or ignore the commonly known information that must be fundamental for the pursuit of truth in a discipline. The scholar must not permit preconceptions or biases to guide the scholarly endeavor, but rather must acknowledge their existence and in some cases assess their influence in the pursuit of truth. That influence, appropriately assessed and evaluated, may then become a legitimate part of the findings. Thus, there is a very legitimate place for consideration of moral order and ethical practice in academic freedom matters (J. W. Scott, 1995; De George, 1997). Issues of right and wrong, for example, may be appropriately addressed.

Moral order and ethical concerns mean that evaluation must be a process continually at work in the pursuit of truth. The scholar must evaluate the findings in the context of processes that are operating in the pursuit of truth. The scholar may, indeed must, have an opinion about what has been found and how it impacts the academy and larger society. This includes the moral order of that society and the ethical practices that guide it. Opinions, then — appropriately acknowledged and assessed — may become part of the substance of academic freedom judgments. So while we must see academic freedom as a universal principle in the academy, we must also acknowledge that its content is rarely clear-cut. Specific cases are usually complex and contestable; they include differences of interpretation and debate about these findings.

It seems clear, then, that academic freedom can never be boiled down to an essence. Rather, it lives in the ethical and moral space of a "community of scholars" — between the ideal of an objective and autonomous pursuit of understanding and the specific historical, institutional, and political realities that condition that pursuit. It must recognize that value-laden theoretical presuppositions organize and structure research and give meaning to objectively observed events. It must acknowledge that identifying relevant data and significant problems for investigation, as well as selecting strategies for problem solving, requires the abandonment of the myths of totally neutral knowledge and value-free inquiry. It does not require abandonment of conceptions of truth and objectivity. It simply acknowledges that all judgments and knowledge operate within the limits of fallible human cognition. Consequently, the most useful working definition of academic freedom will see these factors as important, not only for the protection of individual scholars, but also for the advancement of our collective well-being as a society seeking truth and justice (J. W. Scott, 1995; Hawkesworth, 1988). These factors are integral components of academic freedom. (See pp. 84-86.)

Academic Freedom and Christian Worldview

I contend that a sound working definition of academic freedom must allow for the legitimacy of worldview. This seems clear on the basis of widely held notions in the academy that there is no such thing as totally objective perspectives on reality. Over the last thirty years a keen awareness of the limits of Enlightenment reflection has developed in the academy. The belief that one can construct a purely objective, bias-free, and rational perspective on any subject of discourse has come to be seen as a dream forged in myth. Such an awareness does not reduce the value of objectivity and scientific method in the conduct of research and scholarship, but it acknowledges that everyone has a worldview, a way of thinking about life and its meaning, even though it may not be consciously held or intellectually understood. Our worldview guides our behaviors, often unknowingly and imperceptibly, and it shapes our values. Ironically, such widespread acknowledgment has helped to bring considerable consensus to the premise that all thought is contextual. It has helped to clear the way for insisting on worldview development in the academy.

Postmodernism, to the contrary, has jeopardized such effort by challenging entirely the search for truth. But this is only a temporary obstacle that actually should eventually militate toward the legitimacy of worldview. I believe postmodernists will soon come to discover that the cost of championing the idea that there are no truths is very high. The contention of its most radical proponents that we can know nothing will soon mobilize the academy against such a position. The "hard sciences," for the most part, rejected it long ago (Wilson, 1998). Most other scholars also realize that without some acknowledgment of truth and the legitimacy of pursuing it, there can be no standards of evaluation or methods for science and research. To the extent that postmodernists close the door to the continuing pursuit of truth, I believe they will be found wanting and, eventually, dead wrong. For if there are only equally valued opinions, there can be no moral order in the academy. And in Durkheimian terms (Durkheim, 1933, 1982), moral order is essential, and it will certainly win out because without it communities and societies cease to exist. In short, order will win because it is what makes the human spirit and the real world work. Without standards for evaluation, postmodernists will eventually find it impossible to establish first principles and presuppositions to be assessed in the academy's public square. And without some order and acceptable methods, even the radical pragmatists and individualists among us will find that "it doesn't work." Without some acknowledgment of truth and the methods for pursuing it, a "community of scholars" is nonexistent. Mutual support for anything is impossible; chaos is rampant. I contend that postmodernism will ultimately be rendered DOA — dead on arrival — by rigorous assessment in the academy's public square. Maybe, and ironically, postmodernism's lasting contribution will simply be in opening doors to the legitimization of worldview in the academy. That, indeed, is worth the increased vigilance required to subdue this hostile force of postmodern power.

All scholarship, then, is conditioned by a worldview of some sort. Few today would deny the fact that all scholars come to their subject and task with presuppositions. At least, they have some working paradigm for viewing and structuring the world around them. The old fact-value distinction of legal positivism has been discredited both within and beyond the academy. This does not mean that there is no truth, but only that the true, like the real, is always encountered from and defined by a particular perspective. Holmes (1983) says it concisely: "Intellectual honesty consists in admitting that neutrality is not possible. It consists in confessing and scrutinizing one's point of view and the difference it makes, and in explaining how other points of view would have to disagree." To suspend belief in order to understand is now seen as an impossible task. In fact, as we noted earlier, most of the academy today would agree, at least conceptually, that worldview helps in providing order to accumulated knowledge. It serves to enhance our ability to see and then understand more clearly the truth of the world. Thus it is important to pursue the relationship between worldview and freedom, and for our present purposes, the relationship between Christian worldview and academic freedom in the academy.

Obviously, a Christian worldview must derive from the character and person of the Creator God. But this need not mean that there will ever be a single monolithic Christian worldview, even though that might be our ultimate objective. Such an idealized worldview, I believe, can exist only in the mind of God. Indeed, I would argue that a final absolutized Christian worldview is not possible in our fallen state. Rather, we should pursue the identification of those common elements which must be a part of all Christian worldviews. What is essential for a worldview to be called Christian? There are honest and legitimate differences among Christians about the specifics of a Christian worldview, and those differences can enhance the discussions among us as we pursue the identification of those elements which must be foundational.

Walsh and Middleton (1984) present a comprehensive discussion of Christian worldview based upon the biblical concepts of creation, fall, and redemption. They state with clarity, and illuminate with biblical illustrations, the nature of a Christian worldview and how it should be evaluated. In the process, they suggest the need for paradigm development that includes the continuing assessment of worldviews by their consistency with reality, their internal coherence, and their openness to learning from other worldviews and visions of life. They suggest helpful elements of a Christian paradigm and suggest that a Christian worldview must also come under the continuing and careful scrutiny of such a paradigm. The paradigm acknowledges the importance of pluralism both within and beyond the Christian worldview, and it guards against the cultural dominance of any one worldview which, given a totalitarian character, would become an imperialistic ideology. It cautions that any vision of life, including a Christian one, is always limited and subject to improvement. Finally, Walsh and Middleton serve us well by demonstrating how our worldviews affect scholarship and study.

In their defining and assessing of worldviews, Walsh and Middleton also provide invaluable guidance in shaping Christian worldviews and understanding differences among them. Most faculties already acknowledge differences among themselves on matters of Christian worldview, often attributing them to differences of cultural background, religious and denominational traditions, theological reflections, training in the disciplines, historical perspectives, and the like. However, such tolerance often is not found in their supporting constituencies. But these differences need not, and should not, lead to charges and countercharges of heresy and subjectivism of one sort or another.

So we should not first focus on differences. It will be unproductive. We need simply to acknowledge that no single viewpoint or system can ever exhaust the truth of reality. Each partial insight, no matter how adequate to its specific purpose, ultimately remains partial and requires correction. Moreover, we must remember that human insights are always human interpretations. There is simply no alternative to knowing truth than to know it in the prejudiced condition of concrete cultural life. Pluralism as experienced in most communities today certainly makes religious and theological pluralism a necessity in the Christian community. As Christians we need always to be fine-tuning our worldviews by testing them against reality as observed and with an increasing understanding of God's revelation. Christian worldviews, like all worldviews, must be open to correction and refinement. It is not heresy to admit that theological pluralism (like worldview differences) is grounded in the fact of legitimate cultural diversity expressed in plural meaning systems. Neither is it a sign of intellectual relativism. It is simply acknowledging that theological and worldview pluralism emerges from a plurality of living experiences that are always culturally mediated (Worgul, 1993; Walsh and Middleton, 1984). Neither is this ascribing to a relativistic vision of truth. On the contrary, truth exists and possesses a unifying force. But truth is mediated by culture. This is not relativism, but rather a simple recognition of the human condition.

The more productive alternative is to take these differences into account as we pursue what is foundational. We should first pursue the essence of a Christian worldview while leaving the secondary differences for further discussion and analysis. As I have often heard among

Christian scholars, we need "on fundamentals, unity; on all else, diversity." Given some consensus on the essentials, I believe the Christian scholar, regardless of discipline, can accept and come to terms with the secondary differences while holding to the foundations. A Christian worldview can be shaped in different ways as long as it has all of the basic elements which make it Christian — as long as it has at the foundation all of the essential characteristics.

Stephen Monsma has moved toward the development of a helpful paradigm in his article entitled "Christian Worldview in Academia" (1994). Monsma rightly argues that the key distinguishing mark of Christian scholarship is its being rooted in a distinctively Christian worldview. Furthermore, he suggests that the distinguishing mark of a truly Christian college or university is a Christian worldview that permeates the curriculum as a whole.

Christian colleges need to give increasing attention to worldview matters. They need to give constant attention to institutional mission and its extensive articulation. And then by logical extension that mission must permeate everything we do, giving internal consistency to teaching, scholarship, student life, administration, community relations . . . everything. We need to daily strive toward that end. I am persuaded that a truly Christian college is distinguished by a mission statement that articulates a Christian worldview and implements it throughout the curriculum, and by a faculty whose scholarship is anchored in that same worldview.

Pope John Paul (1990) provides definition to Catholic universities by mandating the following four "essential characteristics" as a part of mission. Every Catholic university "must have:

1. a Christian inspiration not only of individuals but of the university community as such;
2. a continuing reflection in the light of the Catholic faith upon the growing treasury of human knowledge, to which it seeks to contribute by its own research;
3. fidelity to the Christian message as it comes to us through the Church; and
4. an institutional commitment to the service of the people of God and of the human family in their pilgrimage to the transcendent goal which gives meaning to life."

These essential characteristics will assure, says Pope John Paul, "a Christian presence in the university world confronting the great problems of society and culture." Such characteristics are entirely compatible with any efforts to integrate worldview and scholarship in the academy. Indeed, the pope becomes very explicit about such integration when he describes research at a Catholic university as necessarily including "(a) the search for an integration of knowledge, (b) a dialogue between faith and reason, (c) an ethical concern, and (d) a theological perspective."

These, too, are essential for any Protestant college. Each needs to be articulated pragmatically and implemented on specific campuses. In regard to academic freedom, the pope states that the Catholic university "possesses that institutional autonomy necessary to perform its functions effectively and guarantees its members academic freedom, so long as the rights of the individual person and of the community are preserved within the confines of the truth and the common good." This, too, articulates the assumed integration of worldview and academic freedom within an ethos of freedom.

A Christian college is distinguished by its pursuit of a pervasive Christian excellence in all of its activities, but guided by a well-articulated worldview within an expanded statement of institutional mission. (An illustration of one such mission statement may be found in the appendix.) Indeed, this pursuit sees research and scholarship as informing teaching, sees the classroom as a stimulating arena for the interchange of ideas, and sees the college as a whole engaged in a communal search for knowledge which, in turn, is brought to bear redemptively upon this world. It is in such a context that Christian worldview has proven to be an invigorating and unifying stimulus to a creative Christian curriculum and to first-rate Christian scholarship. In addition to informed and rigorous critique of secular worldviews, such an environment leads to the establishing, reaffirming, and legitimizing of the cardinal premises of a "Christian mind" in contradistinction to those of "secular minds." Such an environment, in turn, stimulates the continuing and further development of the Christian worldview.

Given the critical nature of Christian worldview, then, what are some of the essential elements of it? What are the non-negotiables? The pope has suggested some for the Catholic university which can serve well at all Christian colleges. Being even more specific, especially for the individual scholar, Monsma (1994) is helpful with his list of five fundamental aspects of a Christian worldview. They are:

1. the belief in a sovereign God who created and actively upholds the universe;
2. the belief in the existence of a moral order in the world, a moral order revealed by God to humankind in various ways, but most clearly in the Bible;
3. the belief in human beings as image-bearers of God;
4. the belief that human beings were created good and perfect but in their inner natures are now corrupted; and
5. the belief that the God-man, Jesus Christ, has come to break the power of sin and to empower persons to live lives in conformity with the moral order.

Monsma concedes that a Christian worldview based on these fundamental core beliefs provides a perspective, a starting point, but that by itself it gives very few answers. He argues, though, that it is in the searching for the answers that a Christian worldview frees the Christian scholar to explore, and debate, and consider endless possibilities. That is the framework for the exciting task of the Christian scholar who is freed to follow wherever a Christian worldview and the facts may lead. It requires an ethos of freedom in the college.

Finally, Monsma also asserts that these five aspects of a Christian worldview "have been accepted by the Christian church for two thousand years — from the Apostle Paul, to the early church fathers such as Polycarp and Augustine, to St. Francis of Assisi and St. Thomas Aquinas in the Middle Ages, to the Protestant Reformers such as Luther and Calvin, to Ignatius Loyola of the Counter Reformation, to John Wesley, Jonathan Edwards, and Catherine Booth of more recent times, and today to both Pope John Paul and Billy Graham." Thus, Monsma argues that these beliefs constitute the common currency of a Christian worldview across the ages and across the manifold varieties of the Christian faith.

Given these observations about worldview and their role in scholarship, what are the foundational variables in a Christian worldview paradigm? Relying heavily on the observations of Walsh and Middleton (1984), Monsma (1994) and Pope John Paul (1990), the following list includes those aspects of a Christian worldview which should guide all Christian thought:

1. belief in a sovereign, Creator God,
   who actively upholds the world and entire universe;
2. belief in human beings as fallen, image-bearers of God,
   who were created good and perfect,
   who, now, in their inner natures are corrupted by sin (through the work of Satan, the devil);
3. belief in a moral order in the world,
   revealed by God in Scripture and the creation,
   which gives humans the power to establish ethical codes and communities;
4. belief in the Bible as the revealed Word of God,
   inspired and authoritative,
   subject to interpretation and fuller understanding by humans;
5. belief in Jesus Christ as the God-man,
   who breaks the power of sin in humans,
   who empowers humans to live by the moral order;
6. belief in human beings as servants of Jesus Christ,
   who live to serve God and humankind;
7. belief in the revelation of God through the active pursuit of truth in human knowledge and understanding,
   by the study of the Scriptures and creation,
   which gives humans the power of reason to integrate knowledge;
8. belief in the Holy Spirit of God in the world,
   who gives inspiration to individuals and human communities.

These elements of a Christian worldview should be the subject of debate and deliberation in the Christian academy, the church, and the Christian community. Perhaps there are some to be added. Perhaps some should be deleted. Perhaps each needs more explanation. To be sure, each can profitably be scrutinized from different theological perspectives and traditions, and some could be phrased differently as a result. So where they have not received adequate attention, let the lively and focused worldview debates begin, both within and beyond the Christian college. I doubt that one single Christian worldview will emerge from this, but I am confident that a series of coherent Christian worldviews will bring together varied theologies and philosophies which comport reasonably well at their cores. It will be a sound beginning. Certainly as it relates to the Christian academy, I am persuaded that our first goal must be to accommodate a healthy pluralism in Christian worldviews as we continue the search for truth. Increasing attentiveness to the reality and value of pluralism in the systems of Christian meaning will, I believe, eventually serve to enhance also the freedom of the broader academy in its search for wholeness and the unity of all knowledge.

During the years of my presidency at Calvin College, I observed with considerable interest the early beginnings and development of what has become the now thriving Society of Christian Philosophers. With the leadership of key faculty — the likes of Alvin Plantinga, Nicholas Wolterstorff, Kenneth Konyndyk, and colleagues from other institutions — and modest grants from a local philanthropist, the society was launched in 1978 as a small but independent subgroup of the American Philosophical Association. It soon initiated a newsletter and then a fledgling publication. The results were quick and clear. Membership and interest grew from throughout the association, and within a decade the society was one of the largest and most lively such subgroups. Its publication, *Faith and Philosophy*, now has an extensive circulation and includes contributions from a diverse array of scholars. About this remarkable development, Marsden (1997) says "they have changed the outlook of this fundamental discipline. . . . It is ironic, in the light of popular academic prejudices against religiously based thought, that it is in the field of philosophy, especially the philosophy of religion and epistemology, that Christian thinkers have made the greatest impact." Clearly, openly Christian worldviews rather than secular ones have guided this effort, and they have embraced the Christian pluralism which has made it possible. Furthermore, it is fair to say that — along with similar developments in other disciplines like the Conference on Christianity and Literature, the American Scientific Affiliation, and the Conference on Faith and History — the society has served as a model for, and provided much encouragement to, Christians in other disciplines as they also struggle for a "level playing field" in the larger academy.

Monsma's thoughtful address of what are the essential components of a Christian worldview can help us, I believe, in defining the relationship between worldview and academic freedom. Furthermore, it may help us to bridge the gap between the many secondary differentiating characteristics of the Christian faith and the essential nature of a common worldview for the nurture of academic freedom in the academy. It can help us put aside some of the doctrinal and traditional differences among the Christian community in favor of the essentials that lie at the heart of what makes Christianity truly Christian. Academic freedom which includes a legitimate and common worldview paradigm can help to advance a quality of Christian scholarship which avoids the traps of sectarianism on the one hand and accommodationalism on the other. We should work toward that end, and toward the practical implications of such a posture for academic freedom in the academy.

We know, of course, that such claims and pronouncements will be greeted with derision by some postmodernists. Essentials? Truth? Whose authority? What standards? Whose moral order? Whose values? Isn't the very vocabulary with which we discuss the importance of worldview sound evidence that the pursuit of truth leads back through an endless chain of convention and custom to nowhere? These are the sorts of harassing questions we shall hear in the background as we do our worldview work. But it may be exactly that worldview work which calls postmodernism to task. Where does it stand? What does it contribute to the cause of scholarship? What gives it legitimacy in the academy? What "trees does it plant"? It is a worthy project. Worldview may just be the "stranger" that is so badly needed in the academy today.

The full integration of worldview into definitions of academic freedom will do much to resolve some of the practical pitfalls of academic freedom cases today. Worldview provides a legitimacy to what may now be a primary misunderstanding in most academic freedom cases, that is, a common understanding of the prevailing worldview and an ability to articulate it clearly and precisely. The very integrity that accompanies a clearly articulated worldview will demand a positive, supportive, expansive vision of academic freedom. The integrity of the academy, and of any educational institution, resides in a process of free and open postulation, inquiry, interpretation, and conclusion. Worldview is essential to that process. For Christian institutions, a sound working definition of academic freedom will need to respect the canons of individual academic freedom, the autonomy of institutional worldviews, and a theological orthodoxy within a doctrinally pluralistic system of meaning. A challenging task, indeed, but worth a try.

While the task of scholars at any college is to keep alive, develop, and pass along the root ideas of a culture (and its worldviews), and while the task of the scholars at a Christian college is to engage those ideas, to examine them, and to challenge or affirm them as consequential for the Christian faith, the committed Christian scholar also feels the obligation to engage alternative points of view in order to learn from them, to be challenged by them, and to bring a Christian witness to bear upon them. It is the pursuit of such essential tasks in the Christian academy which demands the full protection of academic freedom.

Having established the legitimacy of worldview in the pursuit of truth, the place and significance of academic freedom becomes more clear. The task of the scholar now is not to deny perspective and context and worldview in thought; rather, it is to become more inclusively and keenly aware of what actually informs one's thoughts. Scholars must become more self-consciously aware of who they are and from whence they come to the task of scholarship. Scholars must be able to articulate clearly and concisely the perspective or worldview that guides them.

The implications of this for academic freedom are significant for both theoretical and practical reasons. The most obvious will be the practical. The scholar no longer needs to struggle with the mythical separation of the knower (scholar) and the known (reality). Rather, a significant part of the scholarly task now becomes the meaningful connection between one's operative worldview and the reality of the data under study. For the Christian scholar, at the least, the attempt to connect one's religious faith (worldview) to other realms of learning is highly meaningful activity. It is now important to acknowledge in academic freedom cases, for example, that there is always some faith position present, even if it is a faith in reason alone. That is now an essential ingredient in all academic freedom cases, rather than some often vague assumption of neutrality or objectivity.

Academic freedom no longer means value-free, unbiased objectivity in learning and reflection, but rather demands the free and open debate and dialogue between various perspectives of learning, and between the various personal and social contexts in which knowing takes place. Academic freedom now assures an open and level playing field in the academy's public square. Christian scholars now need not apologize for their Christianity any more than secular scholars do for their perspectives. Rather, it is now incumbent upon all, including secular scholars, Buddhists, Muslims, and even the radical relativists of postmodernism, to explain and articulate the worldviews that guide their work. Most importantly, secularism is now simply one alternative belief structure for the analysis and interpretation of reality. It is not the only one. Marsden (1994 and 1997), among others, has made the case both comprehensively and emphatically: there is no value-free inquiry anywhere, including the academy.

Consequently, just as other voices now need to be brought to bear in scholarly discourse, so too must the Christian voice be a participant in the conversation (Marsden, 1994 and 1997). Furthermore, I believe the Christian voice will make no intellectual sacrifice whatsoever in the process, but rather will demonstrate a marked advantage over most others in acknowledging its basis of existence and the essential relationship of that existence to Christian thought. The Christian scholar, along with others, not only belongs in the conversations of the public square, she will enhance its quality.

This new era for academic freedom, flowing logically out of careful scholarship into the limits of the Enlightenment and the rationalist paradigm for thought, need not diminish the significant contributions of the Enlightenment to Western culture and scholarship as we have come to experience them. The role of reason in formulating the paradigms for sound analysis and understanding remains as an important enhancement to our scholarship and the advancement of knowledge in our society. Objectivity remains a cherished goal in all scholarship, but not the only one. Reason remains a highly valued human gift (now among an array of such gifts) for continuing use by all scholars. More importantly, the granting of legitimacy to the contextuality of thought (worldview and perspective) now provides for the possible enhancement of our knowledge and understanding through the sharing of principles of understanding across contextual lines. This will only serve to strengthen the role of academic freedom by permitting the legitimate introduction of other perspectives, including the religious.

The integration of worldview into academic freedom concerns has another positive payoff in the academy. It will force much of the extreme polarization of opinion about differing worldviews to the surface for open discussion and debate. What has functioned covertly for a long time now becomes the focus of overt analysis and assessment. Entrenched positions, often characterized by intense moralism, are open to scrutiny in an environment which may alleviate the polarized atmosphere of the culture wars as we have come to experience them. Ideologies come under careful scrutiny. Even the nihilism and radical relativism guiding some postmodernists today now must come under the microscope and run the risk of being found wanting in the academy. Power and coercion models of all sorts will come under rigorous review. I believe the intense moralism of the "culture wars" will be unmasked and seen for what it is: an expression of anger fueled by the need for power, an analysis by emotion devoid of bearings in sound scholarship. Thus, it easily turns into an intense "my way or the highway" mentality. For as moralism gains the day, so does political correctness and its own dogmatism, which seriously undermines academic freedom. Open discussion and challenge of worldviews can avoid such inclination toward dogmatism and, thus, keep free and nurture the logic of inquiry needed by all scholars in the pursuit of truth wherever it might lead. Worldview will be seen as an academic asset, not a constraint. Academic freedom will be enhanced rather than diminished (Hardy, 1995).

Finally, there is also the benefit which accrues to the cross-cultural appreciation of varied worldviews, and, one hopes, the development of some international consensus about the definition and implementation of academic freedom. Especially in countries where dogmatic ideologies or religious fundamentalism prevail, the open and mutual appreciation of worldviews across language and cultural barriers will enhance understanding and tolerance. In some such countries today, there are entire generations who have been taught that one of society's worst enemies is freedom of thought. It is literally unpatriotic to think. Scholars are not allowed to follow the trail of truth.

While it may be hard to imagine for one socialized in a free society, some of the most totalitarian regimes have even demonstrated their ability to provide youth with ready-made ideals and beliefs. Think of Nazi Germany and Facist Italy in the 1930s and 1940s. Think of Cuba and North Korea. And more recently, think of the fanatic mobilization of Islamic youth against Salman Rushdie — the Indian-born, secular Muslim now living an "underground" existence in London since writing *The Satanic Verses* a decade ago — as a clear signal of how forces can be rallied against the freedom of expression. Yet the Rushdie case can bring our attention to the two sides of the issue of academic freedom, put best perhaps by the Director-General of UNESCO when he said, "It is every person's duty to respect other people's religions; it is also every person's duty to respect other people's freedom of expression." It is no secret that many Third World leaders are suspicious of and antagonistic towards anything that suggests academic freedom. Academics, journalists, writers, and publishers in these countries suppress and withhold information daily under such compulsion. The "chilling effect" is real to the extreme. Self-censorship abounds. It is time that those whose interests in education and academic freedom transcend the bounds of nationalism now mobilize to ensure that universities everywhere are free and academic freedom is guaranteed. While certainly not the total solution, an enhanced appreciation of and respect for differing worldviews can be an essential step in that direction.

There may also be another contribution made by the integration of worldview into our definitions and procedures of academic freedom. It may add strength to the argument that ultimately truth will be found. It will help, I believe, to reestablish that there is merit in the pursuit of truth. In today's world of relativistic thinking and valuing, we face the risk of losing all sense of the merit in truth seeking. Postmodernism is on the rise. An aggressive and intimidating sector of the academic community that views truth as simply an illusion that cannot be attained is gaining in strength (Hamilton, 1995; Veith, 1994; Shils, 1993). To the contrary, then, the notion of academic freedom rests on the view that the truth can be achieved, and that it surely can never be attained by coercion or by fear that external powers will inflict sanctions for any view which is contrary to their own.

These two worlds can live together only if worldview becomes an acknowledged part of academic freedom. Then, and only then, will both the ideological relativists and imperialists be forced to articulate worldviews that can be assessed and critiqued for what they are. Only then will the academy be able to preserve and promote academic freedom for what it was intended by the early founders of the AAUP, that is, the uninhibited pursuit of definable and observable truth. If, on the other hand, it is established that there are no criteria of validity or truthfulness, because any statement can be as true as any other statement, then it will be useless to attempt to assess the achievements of scholars and scientists. Indeed, if the antinomians among us are successful in abolishing the moral order and ethos of the academy, then there will be little for academic freedom to protect in the academy (Shils, 1993). So worldview, and the clear acknowledgment of the existence and legitimacy of moral order in society, just may be the ingredient of academic freedom that preserves it for the future. At least it deserves a discerning look.

Academic freedom, as understood in most secular institutions, is predicated on the view that knowledge is advanced only through the unfettered exercise of individual human reason. The authority of the rational methods derived by human reason is still supreme (McConnell, 1993; Marsden, 1997). But we have noted that this is far too limiting in the post-Enlightenment era of the academy. While some would argue for increasing political openness in intellectual inquiry, most would object to a specific religious worldview as incompatible with true intellectual and academic freedom. Hoekema (1995) points to the absurdity of such objections by citing classroom texts that describe the Pilgrims without mentioning their Christian faith or discuss Martin Luther King, Jr., without noting that he was a minister. Such blatant omissions in the facts of history and culture are mere symbols of the pervasive intolerance of religion in the academy even today. In response to the question "Why?," Hoekema cites three possible reasons: (1) fear of violating constitutional limits, (2) fear of professional disfavor, and (3) fear of inappropriate student reaction. He then presents brief arguments against each. In all of this, the lesson to be learned is simply that exclusion of religion does not preserve, but rather undermines, genuine academic freedom in the entire academy. Furthermore, academia has observed over and over again that nonreligious worldviews can be just as sectarian and dogmatic as religious ones.

Finally, it must be said that the grand, extraordinary fallacy of the AAUP's current position on academic freedom is its unwillingness to take worldviews into account and make them a legitimate part of the search for truth and, thus, of the equation for academic freedom. In spite of the fact that relating one's faith to the rest of one's knowledge has a distinguished intellectual heritage (Newman, 1931) — or perhaps because of it — most academics today regard it as inappropriate and unprofessional. Without a doubt, the AAUP position violates an increasing consensus in the academy; that is, the simple fact that all scholars come to their task and subject with presuppositions for viewing and structuring the world around them. By its actions, or inactions, it persists in the objectivity fallacy and embraces an unquestioned faith in

67

reason. Thus, it betrays — in the face of almost universal acknowledg-ment to the contrary in the academy — the fact that there remains a pervasive faith in reason (in the Enlightenment influence) and a deep down fear of religion or, perhaps more accurately, religious dogmatism. And while one can understand some of this in historical perspective, the academy cannot forever condone it or stand idly by as this grand fallacy continues (Marsden, 1997).

This outdated and unsupportable ideal, anchored in the Enlight-enment model of disinterested reason, continues to guide AAUP posi-tions and policies regarding academic freedom. The irony which accom-panies this, of course, is the fact that academic freedom — born of the need to protect a diversity of thought — now functions to force all scholars and colleges to conform all thought around a faith based solely in reason and the myth of objectivity. We've come full circle. Academic freedom — born of a spirit of freedom in the academy — now militates toward a likemindedness that will assure mediocrity of the worst sort. Particularly by its threat of censure, the AAUP has for years pressured individual colleges and universities to conform to this fallacy.

The next step toward resolution of such fallacies in the academy is the acknowledgment of worldview. This need not deny or denigrate the importance of reason and objectivity for the methodologies used in scholarship. But we should promote, by acknowledgment of worldview differences, a great diversity of perspective and presupposition at the in-stitutional level. Colleges and universities would vary considerably in the worldviews they embrace or tolerate; their moral orders and intel-lectual traditions would draw boundaries at different places, thus devel-oping true and mutually beneficial "communities of scholars." From such a wonderful mosaic of diversity could then arise a "level playing field" in the lively debate and discussion of the entire academy and the "public square." For anyone coming to play on such a level playing field there would be the clear expectation of rigorous evaluation. Those un-able to withstand such attention would eventually leave the field. While McConnell (1993) still argues soundly for exception to present AAUP guidelines, we should take it a step further to the integration of world-view into those guidelines. That would promote the mission of every in-stitution in that all would need to know and articulate (or develop) who they are (worldview) and from whence they come (presuppositions). All institutions and scholars would need to confront anew the fact that

68

the search for truth is always guided by preconceived notions about the nature of the field under investigation, by the most appropriate methods for ascertaining the truth in such a field, by the criteria for appraising theories, explanations, and interpretations, to mention a few. We would together confront the fact that these preconceived notions serve as "prior constraints" on the freedom of inquiry — for the positive purpose of ordering truth, and so that we can make sense of it and build on it. We would come to acknowledge together that most such preconceived notions arise out of a variety of specific scholarly communities (including the academic disciplines) according to an established tradition of inquiry and, for the most part, are taken on faith.

Interestingly, in a vigorous rejection of McConnell's (1993) rationale for continuing exception to religious colleges and universities, Thomson and Finkin (1993) present some argumentation that leads in the direction of worldview consideration for other than only religious institutions. While I'm inclined to think they would be horrified at the suggestion, they do present some useful rationale. They are obviously distressed by McConnell's assertion that the AAUP's "insistence on a single model of truth-seeking is inconsistent with the antidogmatic principles on which the case for academic freedom rests." In conceding that there is an internal inconsistency in the AAUP's demand that all institutions of higher education adopt its own (AAUP's) model of truth-seeking, they allege that McConnell is trying to replace the "secular model of academic freedom" with a "religious model of academic freedom" and proceed to argue against such a move. In their enthusiasm for rejecting the religious model — in a sort of win or lose showdown — they miss entirely the point of possible multiple models of truth-seeking which would have equal access to "the marketplace of ideas" and a "level playing field" for other perspectives (worldviews). The AAUP could provide strategic leadership in correcting this obvious inconsistency now; it would do well to establish a sound and principled stand for the twenty-first century, one which integrates the concept of worldview into all of its policies and procedures governing academic freedom.

Thomson and Finkin also concede that McConnell is right in saying that the choice of one model over another is really a matter of faith (that is, faith in reason or the scientific method vs. faith in God or a supreme being). But they then shift the argument to one of coercion; that is, faculty may not be "coerced" to live under a religious model of academic freedom. Here they betray a conspicuous lack of understanding of the amount of coercion that is present under either model; for there is considerable evidence of both in the literature. More likely, however, they assume it exists in religiously affiliated colleges and not in secular institutions. Be that as it may, the invitation for the consideration of worldview for all institutions comes by way of a question which they mean to answer affirmatively; that is, after affirming that religiously distinctive institutions do make important contributions to intellectual life, they query "could the same not be said of institutions distinguished by their commitment to a particular body of political or social or economic doctrine?" Yes, indeed, and much more! And that is exactly where worldview consideration and articulation could play a very useful role for all institutions. Perhaps Christian colleges and universities can lead the way.

The shifting of argument to a moral one, that of "coercion," deserves brief comment. We hear it far too often. It certainly arises out of a kind of warfare mentality — the need to see religion as the enemy. But it betrays a lack of knowledge about most Christian scholars and Christian colleges and universities. It overlooks the fact that most Christian scholars locate in Christian colleges embracing Christian worldviews because they share that worldview. They are there because it facilitates their scholarship and search for truth. It has no resemblance to "coercion" as Thomson and Finkin describe it. The scholars are there because they want to be there, they are enhanced by the compatible worldview that they themselves endorse. The worldview may be a limitation to some, but for these faculty it is a limitation they will for themselves and which they find to be an asset rather than a liability in their work. What seems to be ignored by these writers, and many others in the secular academy, is that a Christian worldview does not represent a coercive constraint on those who agree with it in the first place. Indeed, no one has to teach at a Christian college. Nor does anyone have to teach at any other college or university where any variety of such so-called constraints may exist.

All potential limitations, if self-imposed, do not represent a loss of freedom, but rather an exercise in freedom (Marsden, 1994). For example, those who share the Christian worldview of the Christian college are freed from the political correctness of pervasive opposing ideologies and free of the constraints inherent in the religious intolerance of the secular academy. This message is simple and clear, but many in the secular academy seemingly don't recognize their own intolerance; nor are they ready to acknowledge the orthodoxies from which they come.

Academic Freedom: Means or End?

Unfortunately, for many of our significant publics and some faculty, academic freedom is no longer viewed in the traditional sense of searching for truth through intensive study and careful reflection in the academy. It is now often perceived as part of the more general right of freedom of expression and speech. Many fear that academic freedom has become nothing more than the expression of any sentiment, any impulse, or any desire — and this has led to an "anything goes" mentality in many about the academy.

This suggests that a useful working definition of academic freedom also must see the essential nature of academic freedom as a means and not an end. The literature is full of criticism of the AAUP for not making this clear in its guiding statements on academic freedom (Nuechterlein, Logan, Ericson, Monsma, ad infinitum). Specifically attacked are the AAUP statements of 1940 and 1970 which, in their rigorous defense of the phenomenon called academic freedom, tend to give it a life of its own. It becomes an end, even an idol (Nuechterlein, 1993). Because the AAUP is the organization most often looked to for guidance in this area, and because it takes on the role of protector against violations of academic freedom through its investigative procedures and pronouncements, such criticism is to be expected and may be entirely legitimate. There does seem to be widespread agreement (although for perhaps quite different reasons) that the current AAUP official statements are inadequate in the context of current discussions (including postmodernism) within the academy.

Much of the confusion regarding whether academic freedom is an end in itself or a means to other ends is related to its confusion with freedom of speech or freedom of the press. The latter concepts constitute rights that are constitutionally granted and legally protected. Academic freedom, to the contrary, is a right granted only to teachers and scholars in the academy and by the academy. It is a freedom restricted to the academic enterprise, and it is an implied right granted by the moral order of the academy. It is anchored in the ethos of the academic community. It carries no legal or constitutional sanction. It is protected by long-standing custom and convention within the academy, not by statutes. It has come to be respected, however, by the courts and judicial system of the larger society (Van Alstyne, 1993).

Academic freedom, then, is clearly a means to other ends; namely, the pursuit, discovery, and promotion of truth within the context of the academy and for the benefit of society. Thus, academic freedom is a means that is limited by both its context and by the ends it seeks. The academy, in turn, is limited by mission statements and worldviews. Within them, however, the academy's pervasive ethos is one of freedom; freedom for institutions to seek and promote truth, freedom for scholars to pursue their disciplines and to interrelate them in pursuit of a unity of all knowledge, freedom to serve, and freedom from all restraint in the process. Thus, it is freedom to (pursue truth) and freedom from (interference) at both the individual and institutional level.

Each faculty among the wide variety of institutions in our society could and should contribute to a more adequate definition of academic freedom — as means rather than end — in the pursuit of truth for all contexts of a very pluralistic academy. Comprehensive review of actual cases militates strongly in the direction of academic freedom as means rather than end. For the true academic, truth is the end and academic freedom the means. For he is committed to and pursues truth, and nothing else. Truth, and its pursuit in the context of a clear worldview, is the highest value. Indeed, academic freedom as practiced exists somewhere in the moral and ethical space between an ideal for the autonomous pursuit of truth and the specific existential realities (historical, political, institutional, etc.) that limit such pursuit. If this is universally true, then it seems a vital practical matter for the academy to establish the procedures and structures that assure academic freedom as means, not an end in itself. Academic freedom is primarily a means, and a vital foundational one at that, for assuring the pursuit of truth (however defined or debated) in the academy.

Truth is the end result of using academic freedom to see reality as it should be seen. The real task is how to see reality truthfully. Academic freedom is the freedom of mind to explore alternative avenues toward a fuller understanding of reality. Truth recognizes reality as it is, but we must know how to pursue it. Worldviews (presuppositions) are every scholar's point of departure for seeing reality as it should be seen; that is, as truthfully as possible. Indeed, ultimate truth for the scholar is a pursuit, not a product. Thus, truth is best pursued from a variety of worldviews because it will result in ultimately seeing reality as clearly as possible as a unified whole — a unity of all knowledge (Neusner, 1996; Marsden et al., 1996).

Logan (1991), after a careful review of AAUP statements and selected advice in given cases, contends that the AAUP organization makes academic freedom an end, a telos, rather than a means to the kind of ends alluded to here and which characterize the mission statements of many colleges and universities (see also Nuechterlein, 1993). However, I believe the increasing acknowledgment of worldview as operational in the work of scholars throughout higher education now provides a basis for making more explicit the legitimacy of worldview as a factor in both the definition and the assessment of cases of academic freedom. Arguing in this direction, one writer has stated that his "moral position has its roots in Christian tradition, filtered through Enlightenment rationalism and existentialists' criticism of rationalism." The time is right for a comprehensive reassessment by the AAUP with the help of a valid cross-section of faculty and institutions.

Perhaps it is time for the AAUP to acknowledge, and then to enlist, a far larger and more diverse constituency to help redefine academic freedom. In any event, there is considerable discontent with the way in which specific cases have been assessed by the AAUP (Nuechterlein, 1991; Logan, 1991; McConnell, 1993; etc.). More importantly, however, it is perhaps the academy at large that needs to be chastised for negligence in this matter of definition. The AAUP simply represents the predominant mentality of the academy, not all segments of it. It is, after all, the faculties of the colleges and universities who have the greatest vested interest in the adequate definition of this concept for their own welfare and that of the institution and society they serve. The AAUP should be encouraged by both faculty and institutions to use a diverse assembly of the "best and brightest" of those faculties for the task of redefining academic freedom for the twenty-first century.

Academic Freedom as Christian Freedom

Logan (1991) points to the need, when dealing specifically with Christian institutions, for a definition that can embrace the reality of a relationship between the professor's academic freedom and her Christian freedom as derived from the Bible. This is an opportunity to also bring the biblical concept of Christian freedom more central to the discussion of academic freedom in the Christian community and context. There are many sources for the concept in the Bible, but those most often cited are found in Paul's messages to the Romans, the Corinthians, and the Galatians (Logan notes especially a point of departure in Romans 6:22).

A review of a few such passages shows striking similarity between the notion of Christian freedom and the concept of academic freedom as implemented especially in Christian colleges. It is a responsible freedom, not one legitimately used for license and selfish purposes. It is a freedom anchored in Christ and our servanthood toward the coming of his kingdom. For example, Galatians 5:1 states: "For freedom Christ has set us free." And in Galatians 5:13 we find this statement: "For you were called to freedom . . . do not turn your freedom into license . . . be servants to one another in love." Paul further encourages the Corinthians with the assurance that "where the Spirit of the Lord is, there is freedom" (2 Corinthians 3:17) To the Romans he speaks of "the liberty and splendor of the children of God" (Romans 8:21). Elsewhere in the New Testament the concept is conveyed in similar terms, as in 1 Peter 2:16, where we are mandated to "live as free men, not using freedom as a screen for wrongdoing, but as servants in God's service," and the notions of freedom, responsibility, and service are integrated. Various religious traditions have used the concept in different ways and in different contexts, but it is pervasive in the Scriptures and quite clearly drawn for all readers (Ellul, 1976; Walhout, 1999).

In the Reformed tradition this concept has usually been put in the context of Christian service. Christian freedom is a freedom to serve the kingdom of Jesus Christ and to be free to do so in every area of human endeavor. It is a responsible freedom, not one of license to do anything one pleases. It is a freedom anchored in a worldview. That worldview is anchored in the Scriptures, and so Christian freedom can be defined as a worldview source of the Christian professor's academic freedom. It is based on God's sovereignty; that is, the world belongs to God. So all truth is God's truth. The Christian scholar is called by God to explore his world. Thus, if worldview is an acknowledged ingredient of academic freedom, the concept of Christian freedom can become a part of the working definition for Christian scholars and institutions. Henry Zylstra said it concisely for the Christian scholar when he said, "Nothing matters but the Kingdom, but because of the Kingdom everything matters" (Zylstra, 1958). Advancement of the kingdom is the end, Christian freedom to serve in that effort is the means. Christian freedom is the biblical mandate to professors and scholars who embrace such a worldview to exert their academic freedom to the maximum in the service of King Jesus. So the nexus between Christian freedom and academic freedom is a part of the definition to be developed in Christian colleges and universities.

The relationship of Christian freedom to academic freedom affords to Christian professors and scholars a freedom to pursue truth to the ultimate. It is a freedom unsurpassed in any other context of the academy. It is a mandate inherent in Christian worldview that assures a lively and continuing debate on fundamental issues of life and death. Christian freedom and academic freedom are enjoined in common cause — to seek truth without interference. The Christian professor needs academic freedom as an integral part of her Christian freedom; that is, the uninhibited freedom to use God's gifts of scholarship and teaching in the pursuit of God's truth. It creates an environment — indeed, an academy — where people are involved in deep and fundamental arguments with each other and the world around them. All worldviews, including one's own and those embraced by one's college, come under intensive scrutiny and challenge. It is an environment that demands both responsible freedom and responsible tolerance. Differences and controversy become tools by which worldviews and truth are keenly honed. They are essential to sound and critical thinking. That is simply, and gloriously, the nature of the truly Christian academic enterprise.

Viewing academic freedom as Christian freedom, and taking it seriously in policy formation, can be a giant step forward in the creation of an ethos of freedom for the Christian college campus and within the church with which the college is affiliated. It instills confidence in Christian scholars as they address culturally important questions and candidly articulate their best, although not perfect, judgments on these matters for wider consideration by the church and Christian community. It provides the assurance that scholars are truly "called" to the intellectual task and that they need not fear all manner of suspicions and accusations about their Christian faith and biblical soundness. It engenders moral courage in scholars by the firmly rooted conviction that all truth is God's truth, and that the scholar's academic freedom contains a divine mandate to discover anew and learn more about the wonders of the universe. In such a community, academic freedom is quickly transformed from a technical definition to an ethos of academic life together. I am persuaded that only in such a lively and nurturing environment can the college and the church sustain a healthy intellectual vitality among believers and faithful nonbelievers alike (Wacome, 1998). Consequently, Christian colleges and universities must have a deep concern for the establishment of a sound ethos of intellectual freedom which encourages to the fullest the work of their faculties in the service of Jesus Christ.

Personal and Corporate Academic Freedom

The AAUP, an organization to which scholars often turn when their academic freedom is threatened, from its very beginning in 1915 acknowledged the strategic role of colleges and universities in protecting academic freedom. A college or university "should be an intellectual experiment station, where new ideas may germinate and where their fruit, though still distasteful to the community as a whole, may be allowed to ripen until finally, perchance, it may become a part of the accepted intellectual food of the nation or the world" (from the 1915 Declaration of Principles). For these noble purposes, then, academic freedom would be required for both the professors and the institution.

The AAUP later attempted to articulate a comprehensive statement of the principles governing academic freedom in 1940. It includes language confined to the academy and is helpful in making a distinction between individual and corporate freedom; that is, a distinction between freedom for the scholar and for the institution at which the scholar is affiliated. A portion of the statement follows:

Of the various freedoms essential if our society is to preserve itself and to promote the interests of the individuals that compose it, per-

76

haps the most nearly absolute is that of scholars to direct their search for truth and to report the results of their findings. This freedom is immediately applicable only to a limited number of individuals, but it is profoundly important for the public at large. It safeguards the methods by which we explore the unknown and test the accepted. It may afford a key to open the way for remedies for bodily or social ills, or it may confirm our faith in the familiar. Its preservation is necessary if there is to be scholarship in any true sense of the word. The advantages accrue as much to the scholars themselves.

In brief, then, the 1940 Statement stated: "Institutions of higher education are conducted for the common good, [which] depends upon the free search for truth and its free exposition" (from the 1940 Statement of Principles on Academic Freedom and Tenure).

It is important to note that precisely because the advantages that accrue from scholarship often have a "public good," the colleges and universities that are the hosts of individual scholars must preserve and protect the principle of academic freedom as a part of their role in serving society. There is, then, such a thing as corporate academic freedom — an institutional autonomy; that is, the privilege of college and university, as corporate bodies, to be reasonably secure from meddling by political or religious authorities, special interests, pressure groups, or any group that wields power in our society. In a sense, autonomy is the institutional form of academic freedom for the individual scholar. This is a freedom that parallels individual academic freedom; that is, the privilege of an individual professor or scholar to be reasonably secure against interference with his or her own work, whether that interference comes from outside the academy or from some colleagues within it. Academic freedom, then, is an immunity against arbitrary interference with the work of professor and scholar, but also with the work of the college or university which hosts them (Logan, 1991; Gordon, 1994; Habecker, 1991; Worgul, 1993; etc.).

It is especially important that individual and corporate academic freedom policies comport well with each other, for cases of academic freedom may originate either from the inside or from external sources, or both. Especially where threats to academic freedom come from the outside, it is important that both institutional and individual policies resist such interference. Also, because of the force of legal judgments in support of corporate autonomy, individual academic freedom is strengthened considerably when policies are internally consistent and mutually supportive. In cases where the interference to academic freedom comes from internal sources, the weight of AAUP influence will fall on the side of the individual professor while the weight of the law has tended to fall on the side of the college (corporate). This, too, makes compatible policies desirable.

Internal differences in academic freedom cases, especially in religiously affiliated colleges and universities, can easily pit the individual professor against the college. While these are best mediated through consideration of institutional mission and individual worldview, that often does not occur because inadequate attention to compatibility of these factors is given at the time of faculty appointment. Such internal cases often center around whether or not the individual professor may do her teaching and scholarship in ways that conflict with the parameters of the religious tradition or institutional mission (worldview). On the basis of past legal tests, the institution will prevail in most such cases (McConnell, 1993; Gordon, 1994).

Much of such internal conflict could be alleviated, even in secular institutions, if more attention were given to worldview in academic freedom definitions and in institutional mission statements. However, it seems imperative in the case of religiously affiliated colleges to do this with great care. In so doing they could possibly establish a new model for a future, and perhaps more enlightened, era in higher education. Even if the AAUP is not prepared to explore this for all colleges and universities, it must acknowledge the legitimacy of doing so within the religiously affiliated institutions. In spite of the fact that, until now, the AAUP "experts" on academic freedom cannot "discern a principled reason" for different conditions of academic freedom prevailing in religiously affiliated institutions, there are sound reasons to do so. McConnell (1993) suggests three such reasons: (1) religiously distinctive colleges and universities make important contributions to the intellectual life of their faculty, their students, and the nation, and secular academic freedom in its unmodified form would lead quickly to the extinction of these institutions; (2) the insistence on a single model of truth-seeking is inconsistent with the antidogmatic principles on which the case for academic freedom rests; and (3) even if the extension of secular academic freedom to religious institutions were desirable on intellectual grounds, it would subvert the ability of religious communities to maintain and transmit their beliefs, and thus undermine religious freedom (p. 312). Others could be added, not the least of which is the uncontestable and persuasive evidence of the rich historical record — from medieval Europe through nineteenth- and twentieth-century America — in which intellectual inquiry has flourished in religiously grounded institutions of study and higher education. Such evidence exposes the absurdity of denying the possibility of academic freedom in a religiously defined setting.

Both Logan (1991) and Habecker (1991) cite the importance of institutional mission statements for providing parameters within which academic freedom cases must be considered. While giving more prominence to institutional mission than perhaps many would grant, they do provide an idea from which the logical extension could be a kind of institutional worldview. In their own experiences in Christian colleges and seminaries, the well-developed Christian missions of these institutions provided a worldview that is intended to pervade the entire enterprise. Faculty are selected on the basis of their personal commitments to a compatible Christian worldview and their competence in the academic discipline they are called to teach and in which they pursue truth (research and scholarship). Both view the institutional mission as dominant and expect that it should prevail in academic freedom cases where there is an established incompatibility between institutional and individual worldviews. From a strictly legal perspective, as opposed to viewing personal academic freedom as an independent and special right within the academy, they are quite right. Indeed, the academic freedom statements of places like Brigham Young and Oral Roberts universities make this very explicit. Gordon (1994) makes the clear legal case for the dominance of the institutional mission in such matters. Furthermore, the Supreme Court (in a 1957 decision) has made clear the academic freedom rights of a college or university in distinction from those of the individual scholar. (See Nuechterlein, 1993; also Gordon, 1994.)

But to settle the question of the legal right of the colleges to limit academic freedom is not at all to solve the problem of prudence. It is true that colleges and universities themselves, through their various practices and sometimes patronages, give support to particular religious, political, and educational values, while opposing others. Usually these have little or nothing to do with institutional mission. So there must be a better way, and I think it can be found in the deliberate attention to the nexus between institutional and individual rights in the definition of academic freedom. Ericson (1991) rightly points out that the kind of dominance given to institutional mission by the writers cited above leaves the door wide open for institutional tyranny in the academy. He points to the significance of the "chilling effect" such potential tyranny can and does have upon faculty. Right again, and he despairs at ever finding or developing a clear policy governing academic freedom, especially at Christian institutions. On the latter point I differ with Ericson, and I strive to develop such a policy by focusing on definition. Perhaps if adequately dealt with there, it will be generalizable to all colleges and universities, not only those that are Christian. Certainly, any definition must acknowledge that the rights conferred by academic freedom also impose the obligation of responsible academic citizenship within an institutional mission. Similarly, the institutional mission by its definition of academic freedom must acknowledge the obligation to uphold a responsible tolerance for every faculty member's pursuit of truth in his arena of expertise and scholarship. Thus, at this point academic freedom becomes both the right and obligation of all parties to participate in the academic self-governance of an institutional mission. It becomes communal; it promotes covenant. It carries with it an obligation of each professor and each person carrying institutional authority to full and contributing citizenship in the academy.

To begin the pursuit for clear policy with prudence, I present a modest proposal designed to bring institutional and individual academic freedom into a context that allows for an integrated and compatible definition of each, and then establishes covenant between them by use of what I am calling a Socratic Covenant. This becomes the covenant between the professor and the institution and serves as the academic freedom component of any contract or employment agreement. It is an integrated package that from the time of initial appointment keeps both the visibility of the principle of academic freedom very high and the covenant about it soundly in place for both parties. It can incorporate tenure policy but does not require it. It makes academic freedom a principle that is not dependent on tenure. Tenure may or may not be present in such policy, but academic freedom stands independent from it and protects all scholars regardless of rank or tenure provision.

This proposal is anchored in the notion that compatibility of individual faculty worldview and institutional mission is the most critical factor in protecting and promoting academic freedom. Tenure is not a critical factor, although it may be entirely compatible; it is based on rationale independent of academic freedom. This proposal views the principle of academic freedom primarily in a moral-ethical context; that is, as covenant rather than contract. Tenure is viewed as primarily legal and contractual, although not necessarily without moral and ethical content. For example, tenure might provide safe haven for a professor even when the nexus between individual worldview and institutional mission becomes dysfunctional; the principle of academic freedom undergirding this proposal would not. Rather, it would promote mutual acknowledgment of the cause(s) of such dysfunction and a mutually beneficial resolution to it.

The proposal has three essential components, all of which are built upon the assumed existence of the two other components. The proposal assumes the existence of a clearly stated mission on the part of the college or university and a well-articulated personal worldview on the part of the professor. These are obviously necessary to determine compatibility. The college or university mission should include any required worldview components for its professor. The three components, then, include a mutually beneficial moral agreement on: (1) a definition of personal or individual academic freedom, (2) a definition of institutional or corporate academic freedom, and (3) a Socratic Covenant. Illustrations of each follow in the policy development section of this book and, of course, would be subject to whatever adjustments are viewed essential to the parties involved. These three components, taken together, can provide the essential requirements for an academic freedom policy in Christian colleges and universities.

V

Policy Development in the Christian College: Modest Proposals

The foregoing discussion of key issues in matters of academic freedom is intended to pave the way toward policy development in Christian colleges. This section of the book addresses the need for promotion of such development. I will present a series of modest proposals intended not as "final solutions" to all of the complex issues of academic freedom but, rather, as important "points of departure" for sound progress in policy experimentation and development. Although presented as modest proposals, taken seriously they will require deliberate and diligent work by all those with vested interests in the academic enterprise. I believe all are essential to the health and welfare of the Christian academy in the years ahead, for the solid promotion of academic freedom anchored in policy is imperative if Christian scholarship is to have an influence in the larger marketplace of ideas. Each will need to be developed further within the specific context of individual campuses, but the essence of these policy recommendations is articulated here. Presidents and provosts, boards of trustees, faculties, and church officials will need to interpret academic freedom in the context of their own worldviews and establish policy and procedures appropriate to their own situations. The proposals include the following:

1. That all colleges and universities establish a committee or council on each campus, perhaps entitled something like the Council for the Promotion of Academic Freedom, for the purpose of promoting campus-wide understanding of the principles of academic free-

dom and a communal will to protect it, thus creating a healthy vigilance against the threats to academic freedom and an ethos of freedom in the community. (This proposal arises from the full discussion of some predominant threats to academic freedom on pp. 11-43 of this book and is more fully articulated on p. 42.)

2. That all colleges and universities adopt the definitions of academic freedom stated in this book (as discussed and argued on pp. 6-10 and presented on pp. 84-86); distinguish between personal and institutional freedoms (as discussed and argued on pp. 76-81 and presented on pp. 84-86); and acknowledge the importance of worldviews in the academy (as discussed and argued on pp. 44-53). Furthermore, that the AAUP acknowledge the legitimacy and usefulness of these definitions, to accept worldview differences as important ingredients in the search for truth, and to assemble a broadly representative committee of its "best and brightest" scholars to reassess in this context the current AAUP guidelines for protection of academic freedom (as discussed and argued on pp. 44-53 and presented on pp. 84-86).

3. That academic freedom be assured to all faculty by the use of alternative approaches to tenure (as discussed and argued on pp. 87-99). Tenure in its current state is not essential to the assurance of academic freedom; in fact, there is increasing evidence that certain dimensions of tenure militate against academic freedom. Tenure may, however, coexist with alternative methods for assuring academic freedom.

4. That, especially in colleges and universities that embrace a Christian worldview, and view freedom as anchored within it, a "Socratic Covenant" be used as an assurance of academic freedom to all faculty and as an alternative to tenure (as discussed and argued on pp. 87-99 and presented on pp. 99-103).

5. That colleges and universities with Christian worldviews initiate a bold advance of Christian scholarship by the allocation of increased resources to such efforts both internally and in coalition with others (as discussed, argued, and presented on pp.103-14).

6. That colleges and universities with valued church affiliations (or other religious relationships) establish a covenant together with the church (or other association) for the advancement of academic freedom — a freedom anchored in the biblical concept of Christian

freedom — in both college and church. Such a covenant, while informal, can be established by a clearly articulated college mission statement that acknowledges a shared worldview and a mutual benefit with the church (as discussed, argued, and presented on pp. 74-76 and 114-22).

7. That all colleges and universities distinguish clearly between academic freedom and freedom of speech on the campus, and that they grant academic freedom only to the faculty for the purpose of assuring their unhindered task performance in the academy. Such academic freedom is a special right and security granted only within the academy, and carries clear obligation to full and contributing citizenship in that academy (as discussed on pp. 15-27 and presented on pp. 122-32).

8. That the advice given for the protection and promotion of academic freedom by each significant group — faculty, presidents and provosts, boards of trustees, students, and church officials — be taken seriously, discussed openly together, and thus be helpful and instructive in dealing appropriately with all future challenges to academic freedom (as discussed, argued, and presented on pp. 132-43).

With the exception of item 1, which is discussed on page 42, each of these proposals for policy development is discussed in this section of the book.

Definitions of Academic Freedom

The following definitions of academic freedom were developed from the research of this project and are recommended for use in all of American higher education. More specifically, however, these definitions are used consistently in guiding all of the modest proposals for policy development in Christian colleges and universities which flow from this section of the book. Furthermore, the modest proposals are based on principles which the entire academy should take seriously. All of higher education would be enhanced by the serious address and adoption of these proposals, and especially by the principles underlying them. My modest proposal, then, is that all colleges and universities adopt the following definitions of academic freedom, distinguish between personal and institutional freedoms, and acknowledge the importance of worldviews in the academy. Furthermore, it calls for the AAUP to acknowledge the legitimacy and usefulness of these definitions, to accept worldview differences as important ingredients in the search for truth, and to assemble a broadly representative committee of its "brightest and best" scholars to reassess in this context the current AAUP guidelines for protection of academic freedom. It would be especially timely and appropriate for the AAUP to provide creative leadership in the necessary restructuring of its current Statement of Principles for the twenty-first century. It should make every effort to do so.

Definition of Personal (Individual) Academic Freedom

Academic freedom is a foundational principle granted only within the academy and designed to protect the professors — whose lives are dedicated to conserving and extending the realm of knowledge — from all of those forces, both internal and external, which tend to prevent them from meeting all the obligations of the professorial office in the pursuit of truth. It includes the security and fundamental right, or cluster of rights, needed by the professors to attain truth, to teach truth, and to publish truth to the fullest extent of their intellectual powers for the good of society at large. It is that principle in the academy which, while holding to the universal merits of objectivity and reason, both acknowledges the legitimacy (and inevitability) of varied worldviews among professors and insists on the clear articulation of the fundamental presuppositions which characterize those worldviews. It is a principle that recognizes that all knowledge exists within the limits of fallible human cognition and, therefore, requires within the academy a continuing evaluation of the processes at work in the pursuit of truth. This multi-faceted foundational principle is anchored in the ethos and moral order of the academy and is protected further by charters and bylaws of those colleges and universities which embrace the principle of academic freedom and are — as corporate entities — also granted the protection of it. Finally, this principle of academic freedom carries with it an obligation of each professor to full and contributing citizenship in the academy.

Definition of Institutional (Corporate) Academic Freedom

Institutional academic freedom is the foundational principle granted only to academic institutions (colleges and universities) and designed to protect their corporate autonomy; that is, their freedom from interference by external forces in the affairs of the institution. It is the principle that protects colleges and universities, as corporate entities, from undue influence and meddling by political authorities, special interests, pressure groups, or any other entity that wields power in society. It is this principle of institutional freedom that gives anchor to, and thus parallels, the academic freedom of individual professors within it. It is also the principle that acknowledges the legitimacy of a distinctive institutional mission (worldview), thus providing direction to the college or university in its pursuit of truth and advancement of knowledge; such a mission, in turn, also is granted immunity from arbitrary interference from outside forces. Finally, this principle of institutional academic freedom also carries with it the strength of legal judgments (United States Supreme Court, 1957) which give to a college or university four essential freedoms: to determine for itself on academic grounds who may teach, what may be taught, how it shall be taught, and who may be admitted to study.

The AAUP could begin a serious address of these definitions by the continuation of what was begun at an AAUP-sponsored conference in Chicago in the fall of 1997 under the rubric of "Academic Freedom at Religiously Affiliated Institutions." Important and wide-ranging issues were initiated at this conference. Another similarly structured conferences is planned for the year 2000 on the campus of Baylor University. It is entitled "Exploring Boundaries: Academic Freedom at Religiously Affiliated Colleges and Universities." A continuing series of such conferences focusing in depth on matters of definition and principles of academic freedom would provide a logical launching pad for implementing this modest proposal. If the AAUP is to regain its stature as a significant voice in the protection of academic freedom, it must first acknowledge the need for a consistent policy that affirms the legitimacy of various worldviews (including religious ones) for both institutions and individuals. Only then will it be able to hold all colleges and universities, secular as well as religiously affiliated, to an enhanced and fair set of standards for promoting academic freedom.

Academic Freedom and Faculty Tenure

Because there has been such a strong historical tie between academic freedom and the concept and practice of tenure, I have long felt that the relationship between the two needs to be pursued and the legitimacy of their continued relationship assessed. Much has been written on the topic, and there is considerable redundancy of argumentation. There is also much in the academic freedom literature that alludes to tenure, and that comments about it in relation to academic freedom.

In the minds of American academics who were active in the early years of the AAUP, academic freedom and permanence of tenure were indissolubly associated with each other. At that time, it was said and generally accepted that tenure was necessary to guarantee academic freedom. That notion has come under increasing scrutiny in recent years and I have often been tempted to write an article questioning just how essential tenure really is to the preservation of academic freedom. That temptation was ignited anew while reading Edward Shils's article entitled "Do We Still Need Academic Freedom?" (1993). My response to Shils's question is Yes, indeed! But my current reflections on the matter of its relationship to tenure suggest a tenuous and nonessential tie at best. Indeed, what follows provides a rationale for saying No to the question of whether we still need tenure to protect academic freedom.

Shils tips his hand on the topic of tenure when, in relation to academic freedom, he says:

> Permanent tenure now has gone off on a career of its own. It has become a self-evident good in itself; it has become "job security." Permanent tenure — or plain "tenure," as it is now called — is an object of great desire among academics, especially the younger generation who are preoccupied by it. I seldom hear it mentioned as an assurance of academic freedom. Yet whenever some modification of the current practice of providing permanent tenure . . . is proposed, the argument that it is necessary for academic freedom is brought to life again. In those circumstances it is restored to its former status as the main argument for permanent tenure.

He then adds that this is rather infrequent in today's world of higher education because "the institution of permanent tenure is nowadays rather firmly established in American universities and colleges" (Shils, 1993). He later states that the AAUP has certainly changed its focus toward the direction of tenure and security of appointments while, concurrently, moving it away from academic freedom. Academics, he says, are certainly concerned about tenure or job security, but do not fear the abridgement of their academic freedom in any of the traditional senses conveyed by that term. In fact, he says that academics now take academic freedom very much for granted. Some postmodernists see tenure as essential to the attainment of power in the academy and for imposing ideologies. Furthermore, from my review of a variety of cases, I would add that often academic freedom claims can too easily become ways of defending job security (Roworth, 1997). In any event, my personal review of the literature and specific cases confirms Shils's observations.[1]

I do believe that, historically at least, tenure was granted to the faculties of academic institutions to protect them first from religious and later from political persecution. At least there is much evidence to suggest that these factors were very much present in the academic scene (e.g., Hamilton, 1995). I believe there remain significant threats of the same today — politically throughout higher education, and religiously at least in Christian colleges and universities. But tenure may not any longer be the appropriate avenue to assure faculties of their academic freedom. Tenure has never really been able to protect all members of the academy (e.g., nontenured faculty) in the matter of academic

---

1. I have included in the bibliography only those books and articles on tenure that I judged had a direct relationship to the matter of academic freedom. There is an enormous number of articles on the issues related to tenure in the academy and in our society. There is also a considerable redundancy among them. After reviewing many of them, I decided not to cite articles and books that were only tangentially, or not at all, related to academic freedom and also to exclude all articles that are found in an array of legal journals. After a week of intensive review of such articles in the Sir Robert Stout Law Library at the University of Otago in New Zealand for the purpose of familiarizing myself with the legal aspects of tenure and academic freedom cases, I decided to refer to only a few selected ones that are particularly helpful on several issues in which I was interested, and to those that have been incorporated into other books on the topic of academic freedom and tenure. While there is much of value in the legal journals on this topic, they serve best the scholar with a particular interest in the legal aspects of tenure and employment issues. A comprehensive bibliography focused on the legal aspects of academic freedom and tenure may be found in Van Alstyne's *Freedom and Tenure in the Academy* (1993).

freedom, and there is increasing evidence that tenure has even militated against it. It is surely time for the academic profession to be honest with itself on this issue and to see tenure for what it is.

There are those in the academy who are sharply critical of tenure as it functions on the campus. Some argue that it is discriminatory and inflexible. One writer describes it as "an unnecessary historical anachronism which is unfair in its application and grossly inflexible. Tenure needs removing rather than reforming." Others argue that it is a phenomenon which exists in no other profession, with the possible exception of judges, and that there is no sound rationale for it in the academy today. They contend that the demise of tenure would promptly improve the employment conditions of most academics, including the areas of workload, salary, and joint and part-time appointment. Certainly, there seems to be enough sentiment against tenure, even within the academy, to warrant serious assessment of whether tenure is more of a liability than an asset to the profession today.

The current literature, at least, calls for a redefinition of tenure. Its increasingly tenuous relationship to academic freedom (primarily because academic freedom can protect only tenured members of the faculty) calls for other rationale to justify its continuing existence in the academy (e.g., Brown and Kurland, 1993). There may be sound reasons for the continuation of tenure — perhaps reasons more similar to those for judges and civil servants of various types — but academic freedom can no longer be the predominant justification for it (see Brown and Kurland, 1993). Colleges and universities are searching for (and some are finding) alternative methods of assuring academic freedom and, in the process, expanding the protection of academic freedom to all faculty while incorporating more of the moral and ethical side of academic freedom. The mutually beneficial relationship of institutional and personal academic freedom is also enhanced. Some such alternative efforts seem to have alleviated many of the dehumanizing and demoralizing experiences of the traditional probationary period for tenure (see Sartorius, 1975; Huer, 1991). These efforts need to be carefully analyzed for the possible development of future models.

Given my assessment of the academic freedom literature and my interest in strengthening and promoting academic freedom in the future, I am persuaded that tenure is not essential to the good health and welfare of academic freedom. Indeed, I believe that with the improved articulation of academic freedom policy in the academy for all faculty we shall build both better protection for, and broad-based understanding of, academic freedom in the decades ahead. Tenure, if preserved, will need to stand on rationale other than the protection of academic freedom.

Much has been written about situations in which tenure actually militates against academic freedom. Speaking to the negative aspects of this historical relationship between tenure and academic freedom over twenty-five years ago, John Silber wrote: "Infringement by tenured professors of the rights of non-tenured faculty to develop their intellectual interests according to their own professional judgment . . . represents by far the most serious and most frequent violation of academic freedom in our colleges and universities" (1973). It is important to note that John Silber — never known for treading lightly on the sacred cows of the academy — made this assessment long before the rise of postmodernism in the academy, which I believe now blatantly enhances that risk by the unabashed use of power to attain its ends. And many others agree with Silber. Huer (1991), speaking of some of the negative implications of tenure in the academy, states: "With his [senior tenured faculty] relentless pressure for mediocrity and conformity, the senior takes away the junior's academic freedom. In no uncertain terms, the senior member has become the greatest enemy of academic freedom in America." This trend, based upon similar negative commentary receiving increased visibility, warrants careful assessment of the place of tenure in the academy and its continuing relationship, if any, to academic freedom (e.g., Parini, 1995).

Jon Huer's *Tenure for Socrates* (1991) is keenly analytical on the topic of academic freedom and, especially, its relationship to tenure. While he is exceedingly critical of the current academic environment, and of the way both academic freedom and tenure are handled and implemented in the academy, he is constructive in his suggestions for change (although not very optimistic). He is also a solid and sound supporter of both tenure and academic freedom (when rightly defined and administered). He takes a broad view of the academic scene, and as a sociologist provides a sound sociological analysis of the situation. He argues that because democracy rules in the academy, the recognized achievers are those who live by the mediocre standards that such democracy demands. Thus, professional eminence among the academic multitude is almost always associated with rather mediocre achievements. Little, he says, is a product of honest, independent, and critical pursuit of truth. Certainly not the kind of merit, he says, that Socrates, a Marx, a Veblen, or a Mills would enjoy. With a touch of cynicism, Huer summarizes his point by observing that we all know what happened to Socrates, Marx could not get a university job, Veblen never had a permanent university position, and Mills barely got tenure at Columbia University. Later, leading to suggestions for new and enlightened tenure policy in colleges and universities, Huer states: "Under present policy for tenure, what a scholar must do for his minimum attainment and maintenance is not much: he needs only to conform to the orthodoxy of views, publish a few articles of trivia, and sport a pleasing personality in regard to his posture toward seniority" (p. 185).

Huer believes tenure has been used inappropriately in the academy. His theme, for which he gives detailed and elaborate argument, is: Tenure is given to the wrong people for the wrong reasons. Those who have it do not need it, and those who need it do not have it. One of the implications of this theme and his pursuit of it might be a total overhaul of the tenure system. Perhaps tenure should be reserved, if preserved at all, for only those professors who really need it — those whose pursuit of truth has put them "at risk" of their jobs; that is, of their being able to continue their scholarship uninhibited by forces both internal and external to the academy. Perhaps it should be preserved for only those who are pursuing truth without concern for self-interest; that is, for those who are truly "called" to a life of commitment and dedication to the pursuit of truth which rises above the temptations of self-interest. Tenure should not be seen as an ordinary contract because searching for truth is not an ordinary task. My personal experiences related to the protection of academic freedom in the academy resonate with Huer's assessment. I believe there is more need for covenant than contract in the search for truth.

Huer argues that the academy is almost incurably afflicted with self-interest that, in turn, has affected the pursuit of truth in negative ways. He argues that finding truth (the ultimate, although perhaps unattainable, goal) requires freedom from self and self-interest. It requires true "calling" to a higher cause, beyond and unpolluted by self and self-interest. For Huer, self-interest makes truth impossible. Where self-interest is present in the scholar, honest pursuit of truth cannot happen. It becomes a lie betrayed by self-interest, and usually fortified in elaborate intellectualism (Huer's indictment here is very severe; see pp. 72ff.). Truth, and pursuing it, is as simple (or as difficult) as telling what one believes honestly — and that cannot be done with self-interest involved. When self-interest (as simple as concern for livelihood or improved status) becomes an end, "truth" becomes the academic's means, and we observe potentially the most corrupt transformation of a noble idea, ultimate truth. I believe that many postmodernists, by their replacement of power for truth in the academy, have enhanced the truly devastating dimensions of this corruption. It is in this context that Huer argues against tenure as now used: in it, the professor uses truth to serve his power position and economic self-interest. When tenure is used as a means, it only corrupts. This is a strong and persuasive argument which must be taken seriously. Although not his intent, I find Huer's characterization of the scholar's task as "calling," along with some of his other argumentation, comporting well with a Christian perspective on academic roles. It also resonates soundly with Durkheim's paradigm for community and moral order.

There is much in the literature about how the "seniors" abuse the "juniors" in the academy, especially in regard to limiting academic freedom. It speaks of professional orthodoxies being established over time, of senior members of the academy buying into them and gaining power from them, of professional associations in the disciplines promoting the orthodoxies and the "party line," and of ultimately impeding the academic freedom of those just entering the academy. In my own experience, I have heard a variety of anecdotes from junior faculty who felt that tenure was used to "bully" compliance from them by senior tenured faculty. Moreover, it is alleged by those who have analyzed the data that most academic freedom cases that come before the AAUP nowadays involve junior members of the faculty whose academic freedom has been violated by senior tenured members (Huer, 1991; Silber, 1997). Some senior professors of orthodoxy expect all untenured juniors to either follow their orthodoxy or get run out of the department. In this way, they make an honest and independent pursuit of truth impossible for everyone.

No scholar is free and independent unless he is released from these established and imposed orthodoxies. Unfortunately, often the professionalization of the disciplines, and thus the professions, militates against such unfettered pursuit in the discipline. The professional scholar becomes the purveyor of that orthodoxy, par excellence, which in turn has a stranglehold on the thoughts and actions of its members. But professional allegiance to such orthodoxy and to unfettered scholarly honesty cannot coexist. Tenure, then, runs the risk of actually impeding and negating academic freedom rather than assuring or enhancing it. Professionalization and orthodoxy, too, often go hand-in-hand in the academy, thus mutually enforcing each other's defensive narrow-mindedness. In the minds of some of the most severe critics of tenure, there is nothing more impossible to correct than the errant mixture of arrogance, fear, and power that sometimes goes into the making of a senior professional academic.

Some argue that tenure, or the process toward attaining it, has contributed to a pervasive "chilling effect" in the academy. They contend that the system certainly does not do what it is supposed to do in regard to academic freedom; that is, protect it. To the contrary, untenured colleagues who must endure up to seven or eight years of uncertainty before learning their fate in regard to tenure often do not feel free to speak their minds or even do the kind of scholarship they would most like to do during those years. The problem is that when these faculty have "kept their mouths shut" for that long they easily get into the habit of remaining silent. They may forsake their areas of greatest interest (and potential) for those more "politically correct." Ironically, they become socialized in such a way that makes them less than fully productive and contributing scholars. In all of this, these critics contend, politics and ideology play a part. It divides departments, and often contributes to a "we" against "they" mentality rather than one of collegiality and mutual trust (Huer, 1991; Parini, 1995). Ultimately, some critics contend that such a socialization process from graduate school through the junior faculty ranks results in what apparently is desired: nice, quiet, average, and adventureless scholars. Careful review of much anecdotal data and specific cases gives credence to some of these observations and charges. Furthermore, the rise of postmodernism — with its contention that there is no ultimate truth to be pursued, but rather only power for one's own ideology — only enhances the reality of such observations.

However, others make a strong defense for tenure on the basis of its relationship to, and critical role in the defense of, academic freedom (Brown and Kurland, 1993). Acknowledging that tenure comes at some cost to the institution, some argue that the economic security given to tenured faculty is a strength of the system because it allows them to accept lower salaries than might otherwise be the case. They also contend that tenure provides a stable faculty environment for many colleges that otherwise would have difficulty holding faculty from considering opportunities elsewhere, both within and beyond the academy. Some argue that it also allows faculty to make commitments to long-term projects, thus encouraging the academic freedom to engage in desired projects with the assurance that they will be able to see them to fruition. Stable employment, others argue, promotes efficiency by diminishing uncertainty. While all of these reasons for support of tenure, and others too, may have some legitimacy in selected cases, none are amenable to quantification. And in the end, one wonders whether support for tenure is simply a de facto requirement for leadership in the mainstream academy. Given the acknowledged costs of tenure to society, colleges and universities, and untenured faculty, most of these reasons seem less than persuasive. Indeed, if one removes the historic argument for the preservation and promotion of academic freedom, tenure must be based upon arguments that are more directly related to job security and benefits.

As I have said, my experience in several higher educational settings — two major public universities and a religiously affiliated college — suggests that tenure is rarely essential to the protection of academic freedom. Rarely today is a tenured faculty member threatened with dismissal or other sanctions due to his scholarly pursuits and truth-seeking activities. In fact, it is often the untenured who need the protection of academic freedom for such activities. Indeed, the position that John Silber takes (1973, 1997) is quite right according to my experiences.

It is quite clear from cases in the past, and in my own experience at Calvin College and elsewhere, that creating new knowledge will almost always be painful to believers in existing ideologies. I've already discussed two cases that had parallel ingredients some found threatening: The Howard Van Till issue at Calvin regarding new ways of viewing creation-science relationships (*The Fourth Day*, 1986, cited on pp. 29-32); and the Hessel Bouma challenges to the ideologies of radical Right-to-Life groups with new pro-life insights (in *Christian Faith, Health, and Medical Practice*; Bouma, et al., 1989). Experience tells us that it doesn't matter if the ideology is of the Left or the Right, or has religious, social, or cultural roots; the search for knowledge and the combination of strong ideology don't mix. It is like water and oil. The Charles Murray speech (on *The Bell Curve* cited on pp. 20-21), and the resulting fiasco at Calvin was an excellent example of an ideology that attempted for both social and religious reasons to prevent the expression of soundly researched data (Herrnstein and Murray, 1994) and its implications on the Calvin campus. For some on the campus, the college's commitment to celebrate diversity was more than adequate rationale for keeping Murray off the campus. Ironically, such wrong-headed thinking does more to demand conformity of thought and ideology than anything diversity can promote in cross-cultural understanding and variety of perspective. Ironically, too, contrary to our traditional thinking about the relationship of academic freedom and tenure, it may well be the case that current evidence points toward a "water and oil" argument; that is, academic freedom and tenure do not mix. It is an interesting thought, particularly in the context of a rapidly rising postmodernism in the academy. It is certainly worthy of serious reflection.

After all is said, of course, the "ideal professor" is something that both academic freedom and tenure should help to create and maintain. Otherwise they serve no useful purpose. The ideal professor must be a scholar devoted to pursuit of truth. Both as a scholar and as a human being, she is guided by the broad scope of a worldview that magnifies and gives meaning to her daily experience and awareness. Her worldview and her scholarship are in constant communication within her, inseparably and dynamically enforcing each other's enrichment. In the course of that pursuit and the work associated with it, she may teach her students, she may lecture on the subject to the community, and she may publish her scholarly thoughts. What she teaches, what she lectures, and what she publishes as a scholar are all the same — or ought to be the same. She cannot, upon demand, transform herself into an "objective" teacher in the classroom, a pleasing soothsayer for the community, or a good soldier for her professional orthodoxy. She is the same person in all categories; her belief in truth and her commitment to a worldview are the same in speaking to strangers as they are for her own colleagues. It is demanded of her that she be a whole, consistent person of integrity. She is a scholar at all times in pursuit of truth, both internally and externally. As a person of special privilege in society, she may offer nothing less than that in return. She must teach and profess the same truth. Does academic freedom help this "ideal professor" in carrying out her "calling"? Yes, indeed! Does tenure do the same? The evidence suggests that, of itself, it does not. Again, absent its historical relationship to academic freedom, tenure may even militate toward corruption rather than enhancement of the "ideal professor."

Much like the concept of academic freedom, the concept of tenure has been defined in a variety of ways. There is no clear consensus on any of them. Brown and Kurland, in Van Alstyne's *Freedom and Tenure in the Academy* (1993), describe two examples of the varying definitions they found in a comprehensive review of the tenure literature. One is from Kingman Brewster, former president of Yale University, who says, "The practical fact in most places, and the unexceptional rule at Yale, is that tenure is for all normal purposes a guarantee of appointment until retirement age." The other is from Duke University law professor William Van Alstyne, who defines and defends tenure as follows: "Tenure, accurately and unequivocally defined, lays no claim whatever to a guarantee of lifetime employment. Rather, tenure provides only that no person continuously retained as a full-time faculty member beyond a specified lengthy period of probationary service may thereafter be dismissed without adequate cause." I suspect both definitions are close to the truth, although one is a realistic and practical observation of what is happening throughout the academy while the other is a more cautious synthesis of the legal and technical aspects of tenure. Neither definition challenges the fact that in reality the conventions and entitlements of tenure have existed for generations and have changed little over time. Since 1940, however, the AAUP Statement of Principles on Academic Freedom and Tenure has become the yardstick for measuring adherence to proper standards of academic freedom and tenure. Nonetheless, academic tenure is seemingly always under attack from some sector of our society (Roworth, 1997).

The perks and entitlements and conventions of tenure have existed for generations and are comprehensively cited in the literature (e.g., many articles in *Academe;* Metzger, 1969, 1993; Byse and Joughin, 1959; 1940 Statement of Principles . . . ; etc.). But just two very basic goals of tenure emerge. Tenure is viewed as a means to two specific ends: freedom and economic (job) security. From the beginning, both ends were viewed as essential for the pursuit of truth in the academy. They persist to this day; yet academic tenure is continuously under attack from some segment of the academy or the larger society which it serves. The proponents of tenure seem to be constantly on the defensive (Metzger, 1969; B. Smith, 1973; Rosovsky, 1990; Finkin, 1996, 1997; etc.), while those who attack seem to come and go (Silber, 1973; Smith, 1990; Kimball, 1990; Parini, 1995; Chait, 1997; Magrath, 1997; etc.) with similar arguments. The most consistent and substantive argument for academic tenure is that it is necessary for the protection of academic freedom in the academy. The arguments against tenure are more diverse, but the most consistent one is that it is not necessary for the protection of academic freedom.

It is true that in my review of the literature I have not yet found a persuasive (or adequate) defense of the claim that tenure is necessary (and sufficient) for the protection of academic freedom. This does not suggest that genuine academic freedom cannot exist within a system of tenure, only that tenure does not assure it. There may be all sorts of other reasons why tenure may be desirable in certain settings and under some circumstances, but they are mostly related to security rather than freedom. There seem to be other alternatives to tenure for the protection of academic freedom. The idea of other methods of due process (internal tribunals, faculty courts, etc.) as a replacement for tenure needs to be pursued with the specific purpose of providing protection for academic freedom. It is the protection of academic freedom by alternative means that is at issue, not other dimensions of tenure and its benefits or liabilities. Such suggestions have been made by Silber (1973) and Rosovsky (1990) and others, but have never been fleshed out in detail as specific proposals. These alternatives have one consistent strength of argument. They would provide equal protection of academic freedom for all faculty rather than only those who are tenured. Many have argued that often the junior faculty need the protection of academic freedom more than those who have tenure, and this has always been a significant chink in the armor of those who defend tenure as the protector of academic freedom.

In their comprehensive review of this issue in the 1980s, Chait and Ford (1982) stated (citing Evergreen State University and Hampshire College examples) that "the fact remains that academic freedom can survive apart from tenure and together with term contracts." Additional alternatives have been developed in the past decade. Perhaps what is needed is careful assessment of these experimental alternatives and a longitudinal study of results, for Chait and Ford ultimately concluded from their study that — even given some of the problems of tenure — "effectively administered by a campus community, academic tenure can be an effective policy." Be that as it may, such a conclusion does not negate the argument that other alternatives — also effectively administered by a campus community — could improve on the present system. Many believe so. The fact is that most arguments for tenure — while alleging the protection of academic freedom — tend to focus on the broader issues of job security and unlawful dismissal and inappropriate sanctions of faculty. Most of these reasons, while valuable and legitimate concerns, have little or nothing to do with academic freedom, per se.

Sartorius (in Pincoffs, 1975) calls the academy back to basics on the matter of academic freedom and tenure. He cites a statement from Byse and Joughin (1959) quoting, with approval, the words of then AAUP President Fritz Machlup as follows: "Academic freedom and tenure do not exist because of a peculiar solicitude for the human beings who staff our academic institutions. They exist, instead, in order that society may have the benefit of honest judgment and independent criticism which otherwise might be withheld because of fear of offending a dominant social group or transient social attitude." Kohr (1993) makes a similar point in proposing the idea of a "Socratic Oath" to accomplish this end in the absence of tenure. It is time to consider alternatives seriously, to suspend for the meantime our defensiveness of tenure, and to enhance our full understanding of what it is about academic freedom we need to protect (e.g., Sartorius, Ritchie, Hughes, and Rorty in Pincoffs, 1975). Perhaps it is the AAUP that should assure that this be done with a valid cross-section of those who have a vested interest in the value of academic freedom for the society which the academy serves. Tenure need not be at risk in this; it can continue if warranted in a form that does not necessarily link it with academic freedom. Alternatives for the sound protection of academic freedom seem both possible and timely.

The extraordinary personal commitments to the pursuit of truth which the provisions of tenure expect, although occasionally paid lip service, have been all but forgotten by most professors. Few professors are conscious of the binding obligation that tenure imposes on them, for tenure in today's academy is normally thought to liberate them. But it is often the wrong kind of liberation celebrated entirely for the wrong reasons. The evidence suggests that the tenured professor now enjoys an unprecedented freedom without fulfilling its basic obligations. Thus tenure serves neither him nor his society and institution in a way that is mutually beneficial.

I am reminded of a cynical but humorous story from a faculty member with whom I visited during my sabbatical at the University of Otago in New Zealand. It apparently had appeared in the *Australian Campus Weekly,* and he told it roughly as follows: "There is a small sea creature — called a sea squirt — in this part of the world whose young must wander about the sea in search of a rock or piece of coral. The rock or coral selected must be suitable for the young sea squirt to attach itself to and make its home there for life. For this task the sea squirt has a rather rudimentary brain and nervous system. When it finds the right rock or coral, it takes root for life and no longer needs its brain. So it eats it. That bloody well sounds like getting tenure!"

Tenure remains an extraordinary privilege in the academy and in our society. But privilege that loses sight of accompanying obligation eventually corrupts. In today's academy both the privilege and the idea of tenure itself is taken for granted. When tenure is taken for granted, it is corrupting rather than enhancing. Reexamination of the concept of tenure, once again, is overdue. Self-examination within the academy is the place to start. And I shall next modestly propose an alternative approach that may comport especially well with the ethos and commitments of Christian colleges.

A Socratic Covenant

The idea of such a covenant began for me from a passing suggestion by Leopold Kohr (1993) that there be something similar to the Hippocratic Oath for professors: a "Socratic Oath." Jon Huer (1991) stimulated it for me by some tongue-in-cheek suggestions about an oath that might replace tenure in the academy. The longer I thought about it the more merit it seemed to have, especially in a Christian academy. Walsh and Middleton (1984), in their discussion of a biblical worldview, also rightly emphasize the importance and pervasive character of covenant in all personal and communal relationships that are anchored in a Christian worldview. It comports well with Durkheim's (1933, 1982) focus on the nature of community and moral order. So the idea of a Socratic Covenant began to take shape and substance.

While I first thought it a bit outrageous and alien in the setting of almost any academic community today, reflection on my own experiences in the academy over a period of four decades suggested otherwise. Why? Mostly, I think, because the notion of a covenant brings everyone back to basics on some vitally important principles in the academy. The relationship between a faculty member and an institutional mission is a covenant and partnership of noble stature. It is an extraordinarily important task — indeed, a "calling" to serve — for the benefit of the community and society at large. The pursuit of honest, independent, and critical truth. Scholarship designed to serve all of humanity. Security and the protection of academic freedom for scholarship. These are foundational and essential to the academic enterprise anywhere.

I contend that this is precisely what life in the academy was originally intended to be. It was a privilege granted to a select few who would, in turn, assure the larger society of honest judgment and independent criticism which otherwise might be withheld for fear of offending some dominant social group or vested interest. It was intended to be a noble covenant, a mutually beneficial partnership with society, and it often included churches and religious associations and Christian communities within society. And life in the academy was a good life. Life as a scholar was a fulfilling life, and teaching was exciting and meaningful. Service to God and fellow man through scholarly pursuits was a "calling" and a life commitment. It is this, it seems to me, that the academy today needs to be reminded of regularly.

And why the Socratic label? While certainly the reference to Socrates is not imperative, I thought it especially descriptive of the search for a covenantal model governing practice and relationships in the academy. In historical perspective and other important ways, Socrates represents for education what Hippocrates represents for medicine. Socrates and Hippocrates, respectively, represent "ideal types" in education and medicine; they provide covenant and moral order to idealized practice in both fields. They establish noble standards and "high calling."

My modest proposal is that, especially in colleges and universities that embrace a Christian worldview and view freedom as anchored within it, a Socratic Covenant be used as an assurance of academic freedom to all faculty and as an alternative to tenure.

What would such a Socratic Covenant look like? It would be based upon the mutual understanding of, and commitment to, the definitions (personal and institutional) of academic freedom previously proposed. It would be a mutual covenant about academic freedom with obligations and responsibilities for both individual (faculty) and institution (college) clearly articulated. It would be built upon clearly articulated and mutually embraced statements of worldview (by the faculty member) and mission (by the college). It would reflect a Christian ethos and social milieu. And it would obviously need to be college-specific; that is, the following model would need to be altered and revised and expanded to fit the needs of a given Christian college. But the model includes some of the essential components of a Socratic Covenant. It illustrates a path toward a greater, more civil, and more equally distributed academic freedom. It is a place to begin, a point of departure.

A Model Socratic Covenant

Upon this occasion of appointment by (CC = inserted name of the specific Christian college), I solemnly pledge the following Socratic Covenant with and in the presence of the (CC) community, for the enhancement of the Christian community, and for the benefit of the society we together serve in the name of Jesus Christ:

(1) I shall always conduct myself as a scholar-teacher in pursuit of truth and truth only. Because all truth is God's truth, I shall serve no other interests in my scholarship and teaching. I shall always pursue truth honestly, independently, and critically within the Christian worldview that I profess and have articulated. My worldview shall always be subject to self-examination and critical appraisal, and it shall be rearticulated when and as needed.

(2) I shall embrace the concept of academic freedom as a special privilege in my role as scholar-teacher at (CC). Providing me with explicit opportunity to exercise my Christian freedom to explore God's truth wherever it may lead, (CC) will assure my responsibility to freely articulate my findings — on both technically and culturally important questions — for consideration by the scholarly community as well as the wider Christian community. This responsibility is accepted by (CC) as an essential part of my role as scholar-teacher, and will be carried out with special sensitivity when new and disturbing questions are engaged in the context of contemporary life and current vocabulary.

(3) I shall to the best of my ability as a scholar-teacher avoid partisan issues, personal political views and ideologies, and single-issue and sectarian interests that serve only limited segments of society and Christ's kingdom. My scholarly activities will always be designed to serve God, the students of (CC), and all of humanity. None shall be intentionally excluded or favored.

(4) I shall seek no pecuniary rewards from commercial or contractual agreements which detract my primary duties as a scholar-teacher or which might be presented in lieu of my scholarship. Such non-scholarly activities shall not be presented as scholarship; rather, when present they must be in a supportive relationship to my scholarship. I shall be content with the intrinsic value of any reward as a scholar-teacher and with the security and protection of academic freedom that my scholarship and teaching has been accorded by (CC).

(5) I shall, when called upon to judge my fellow scholar-teachers, consider only the quality of their scholarship and teaching. Neither the approval of established orthodoxy nor the quantity of standardized output shall be considered evidence of scholarly accomplishment or teaching excellence. Only originality of conception, enhancement of knowledge and its transmission, benefit to mankind, advancement of Christ's kingdom, and intellectual integrity shall be considered primary criteria.

(6) I shall teach and publish, or otherwise express, only those ideas that are worthy of wider attention. I shall neither write nor present works only for the sake of routine professional productivity. I shall seek and respect the advice of my peers in cases of dispute over ideas generated by my scholarship. The ideas I express in classrooms and in writing shall be only those that comport well with the Christian worldview I have articulated and, when they are ideas or worldviews arising from others, those that I truly believe will benefit students, community, society, and humanity as a whole.

(7) I shall always do my best to support and enhance the scholarship and teaching of my faculty peers, and to protect their academic freedom in scholarly endeavors no matter how unpopular or unorthodox. I shall always recognize the supremacy of sound scholarship and the honest search for God's truth over all external forces and administrative or ecclesiastic imperatives. I understand that (CC) shall support me and my faculty peers toward this end.

(8) I shall avoid involvement in activities, both on and off the cam-

102

pus, that may be inimical to the scholarly and academic community. I shall consider my life and thought bound by a special covenant with (CC), the Christian community, the academy, and the larger society to be employed wisely, frugally, and fruitfully on their behalf.

(9) I shall always recognize and uphold the right of academic freedom in the pursuit of the truth at (CC), which freedom is a Christian freedom that is unconditional and inviolate before God. (CC) will strive always to develop and enhance an ethos of freedom that upholds this high calling. I shall, in the event that pursuit of truth is no longer the purpose of my life or the Christian worldview that I now profess changes in ways which may no longer comport with the stated mission of (CC), voluntarily revoke my scholarly privileges and resign from my post as a faculty member at (CC). In the latter case, and if necessary, (CC) will provide me with assistance in seeking a position more consistent with my worldview, or in pursuing alternative professional roles.

The world today, and especially our society, lives by contracts rather than covenants. The academy has followed that pattern too, so what is proposed here may be viewed as countercultural and radical to some. In truth, however, it is a modest but specific proposal to bring trust and mutual respect to the stature it deserves in college-church-community relations. I can think of no better way to do that than to consider a solemn and public commitment to such a "calling" at the time of appointment to the faculty of a Christian college or university. And why not make it a public ceremony so that everyone can be reminded of the "calling" and the partnership and the mutual benefit? Perhaps in an opening convocation there might be the official and public "inauguration" of all newly appointed faculty with the Socratic Covenant being a central part of the ceremony. Returning faculty would be reminded each year, students would get a sense of the ethos of the academy at each new beginning, trustees would feel the full weight of their role in the partnership, and all would be renewed in their roles in this truly noble venture. Invite everyone: alumni, church leaders, community, parents . . . everyone! Ceremony has great value in such circumstances.

Academic Freedom and Christian Scholarship

Academic freedom is an essential component for promotion of scholarship everywhere, but especially for the advancement of Christian scholarship in Christian colleges and universities. As has been noted by a variety of writers on the topic, some of the early efforts of the AAUP were directed specifically to protect faculty against the intrusion of ecclesiastical bodies and church officials into their pursuit of truth and scholarly activities (e.g., Shils, 1993). It certainly is true that the early efforts of the AAUP sought the immunity of the individual academic from actions that would drive him away from the path toward discovery and disclosure of truth. The AAUP judged, I suspect, that if individual academics could be protected, all would be well and truth would be advanced wherever scholarship was directed. But it is clear today that much more is needed if Christian scholarship is to take its rightful place both in society and in the church. And much of what is needed falls directly in the arena of responsibility of the Christian colleges and universities as corporate entities and communities of Christian scholars (Walsh and Middleton, 1984; Marsden, 1997).

It has become increasingly clear during the last two decades that Christians have to take greater responsibility for the careful articulation of Christian thought in the broader intellectual world (Walsh and Middleton, 1984; Hatch, 1989). This means providing a Christian presence among those for whom a Christian worldview and conviction are not givens. It means that Christians need to do much more than simply raise the red flag about the pervasive secularism of today's intellectual life. To simply wring our hands over the resulting implications of this condition in almost every area of our society — law, medicine, business, social services, family, and church, to mention a few — is not enough. The Christian community must acknowledge that it has not addressed the roots of the problems, and then further recognize that Christian scholarship must play a significant role in addressing them. In turn, then, Christian colleges, as corporate entities and as communities of Christian scholars, must take major responsibility for leadership toward that end (Diekema, 1995; Marsden, 1997).

The battle for the mind cannot be waged adequately by political efforts, or public demonstrations and denouncements against prevailing secularism, or by pious retrenchment into small Christian enclaves

104

(Noll, 1994). Recent efforts by the Religious Right have demonstrated that (Thomas and Dobson, 1999). Rather, it must be waged in the intellectual life of our society, of the churches, and of the schools — in the learning and nurturing centers of classroom and curriculum. If Christians are to help preserve even the possibility of Christian thinking for their children and grandchildren, I am persuaded they must begin to nurture first-rate Christian scholarship.

It won't be easy. It means, of course, that Christian colleges will need to free up some of their "best and brightest" to undertake what is always a painstakingly slow and arduous task. It means finding the resources to recruit more of such scholars to their faculties, and to be sure that the full protections of academic freedom in the conduct of that scholarship is firmly in place.

Academic freedom is so vital for the pursuit of Christian scholarship simply because such scholarship is carried out by the "best and brightest" of the Christian thinkers among us, and it is exactly those persons who will be on the frontiers of new and creative findings and interpretations in their fields of endeavor. Because they are Christian in worldview and committed to the Christian faith, they will always be assessing their findings in the light of Scripture and will be the most likely to challenge traditional ways of thinking and behaving in the Christian community. It is especially at such times that Christian colleges must provide the academic freedom necessary to protect the Christian scholar from the intimidation that may deter him from his scholarly work. Christian scholarship is at the same time both the most essential and the most "dangerous" for the established church and the ecclesiastical establishment. It requires a pervasive ethos of freedom in Christian colleges and in the churches and religious organizations that support them.

The Christian community and our society at large needs such first-rate scholarship to bring fuller understanding to our world and to our Christian worldview and biblical mandate, but it is exactly that kind of scholarship that will most likely and most frequently challenge old and established ways. Christian colleges, then, must be prepared to grant soundly grounded and clearly articulated academic freedom to its most productive scholars and to those it attempts to recruit to its faculty. At the same time, it must constantly seek the support and understanding of the ecclesiastical and church leadership in this vital enterprise, and help to educate the constituencies of the Christian mission of the college in this regard.

I have addressed elsewhere some of the threats to academic freedom generally, and especially those which have special relevance in the Christian college. Because of the long history of concern in the academy for the intrusion of religious groups and ecclesiastical bodies into the scholarship conducted by faculty, there is widespread suspicion of Christian colleges and their ability or willingness to grant truly sound academic freedom to their faculty. There is good reason for such suspicion, not only in the early history of cases in the archives of the AAUP but also in more recent and widely publicized cases (e.g., Kurland, 1996; Curran, 1993; Withham, 1991). There are many more cases, especially in smaller Christian colleges and seminaries, only a few of which get broad attention in any of the media.

All of this understandably has made it more difficult to bring some of the best and brightest Christian scholars to the Christian colleges that should be providing the leadership in this important arena of Christian life and mission. There has been a significant "chilling effect" operative among Christian scholars, both those currently in Christian college faculties and those who should be recruited to them. There are simply too many "horror stories" in the pipeline of Christian scholar scuttlebutt to deny the reality of this chilling effect among them. I learned of a variety of such instances during my tenure in the presidency, and such cases continue. A recent theme issue of *Christian Scholar's Review* (26, no. 4 [Summer 1997]) was dedicated to the topic of "Christianity and Homosexuality," and articles were solicited broadly. It is a credible publication addressing what the guest editor calls "perhaps the most controversial issue confronting the evangelical Christian church in America today." It is, at least, a start toward giving the topic more legitimacy within the churches and the broader Christian community. But I am aware of at least one first-rate Christian scholar in a respected Christian college who would not submit an excellent article on the topic because of the potential "grief" it could cause him by the negative reaction of his institutional administration and board. Even the encouragement of respected colleagues did not convince him otherwise. The chilling effect, in this case, led to self-censorship. One can only speculate on how many others may have done the same, and on the frequency of such occurrences on a variety of controversial issues in the churches and Christian college constituencies. In any event, correcting that chilling effect must be given priority attention by Christian colleges in the days ahead.

Christian colleges will have a special challenge, then, in not only protecting the pursuit of truth for those scholars already there, but also to bring in those Christian scholars who are zealous in their commitment to pursue truth in a Christian context. The latter, especially, will be scrutinizing carefully the commitment of the college and its leadership to the principles of academic freedom. For this reason, the process by which Christian colleges recruit and select future faculty will be a precondition for the Christian college's continued existence as a viable communal entity in the pursuit of truth. Life within a Christian college — if it is a good college — strengthens the desire of individual faculty and students for truth. But this can only be strengthened by the faculty, and especially those faculty who already possess the disciplined propensity for scholarship and who have given evidence of it. The process of recruitment and appointment must discover such persons; they are the future faculty who truly merit a place in the really sound Christian college as teachers, scientists, and scholars.

Many Christian colleges are not as attentive to this process of appointment as they should be, and generally the quality of the college and its faculty have suffered accordingly. In some a superficial piety and spirituality takes precedence over sound Christian scholarship, and such slipshoddiness has diminished the quality and stature of those colleges. While piety and spirituality are desirable for all faculty, these characteristics are brought to bear on a community in many different ways, including the way of rigorous Christian scholarship. Piety and spirituality are positive characteristics, but they must never constitute an excuse for disregarding the essential criteria of achievement and promise of achievement in scholarship and teaching. Those Christian colleges that rise to positions of greatest influence and significance in the years ahead will be those that make parallel progress in the strict application of academically relevant criteria for Christian scholarship and spiritually relevant criteria for Christian living.

Recruitment and appointment, of course, are not matters to which academic freedom in the specific sense applies directly. But they are processes intimately connected with academic freedom because they are determinants of the primacy given to the attainment of Christian truth

107

toward which all academic activity must aim and which academic freedom must protect. If persons who do not care deeply for truth as sought out in Christian scholarship are appointed, the Christian college enlarges the part played by faculty who care little for the very objectives which merit the sound protections of academic freedom. As I have said often during my twenty-year tenure as a college president, the faculty is the heart of any college. As the faculty goes, so goes the college. So academic freedom and Christian scholarship are both important ingredients of the faculty recruitment and appointment process.

I have mentioned earlier that academic freedom is not high on the priority list of most faculty when considered collectively. Unless their own freedom is impinged upon, most are silent on the matter, and often on the "cases" that surface in the media. Although seemingly ironic, there may be good reason for this. The majority of college and university faculty are not active scholars in the true sense; that is, they do not have ongoing scholarly projects of research and writing. Consequently, many of them have not even dreamed of doing any of the things which might be the object of sanctions and for which the protection of academic freedom would need to be adduced. For many of them, it has never been an issue. And for some, even the infrequent "cases" are a nuisance they would prefer not to have "rock the boat" of their own college or professional discipline. Unfortunately, for the academic profession taken as a whole — all fields, disciplines, and departments included — academic freedom is not a significant concern.

The situation is a paradoxical one, indeed, because for the "best and brightest" of the faculty the sentiment is entirely the opposite, and especially so for those who are addressing some of the keen issues of society and the church and Christian community. Matters of right and wrong, of ethical behavior, of social and political consequence, of religious tradition and practice; all fall in the arena of the kind of truth-seeking that demands strong policies of academic freedom for the active and productive Christian scholar. And it is this, after all, that matters most in the fulfilling of the Christian mission of the college and, consequently, must be protected by academic freedom. Academic freedom is both needed and justified in the Christian college because it serves as the means toward the continuing discovery and transmission of God's truth through the methods and procedures of Christian scholarship.

Christian college presidents and boards must take this challenge very seriously. They must acknowledge that if a Christian voice is ever to be heard on the great issues that trouble our society — issues of life and death, of global responsibility, of morality and justice — the Christian colleges must take a leading role. They must develop communities, led by Christian scholars, that cultivate intellectual life, that anchor it in the gospel, and that articulate it to the larger culture. They must take responsibility for bringing Christian alternatives to the marketplace of ideas and into the public square. They must do so by establishing clear policies in support of Christian scholarship, and by providing the resources to implement them.

There is some evidence that the current lack of faculty engagement in scholarly dialogue and activities is even inhibiting the teaching task which is such a vital part of most Christian colleges (Hatch, "Christian Colleges," 1989). Creating and promoting a climate congenial to lively Christian scholarship must be a top priority for college leadership. If they fail to do so, they will certainly fail to attract the best talent to the enterprise, thus diminishing the quality of both scholarship and teaching. Students at Christian colleges must have the opportunity to see a Christian scholar at work, and to work side by side with her, in bringing faith and Christian worldview to bear upon important intellectual issues. Nothing will do more to assure the future supply of first-rate Christian professors at our Christian colleges and first-rate Christian thinkers in our churches and in society at large. That must be the objective of presidents and boards who want their colleges to be first-rate places in the development of God's kingdom.

None of this comes without risk. Christian scholars must recognize at every turn the reality of the antithesis — the fact that daily we face the "powers and principalities" of evil in the world — while acknowledging the reality of common grace — the fact that God's goodness extends beyond the walls of the Christian community and that we learn from it in secular settings of all sorts. The Christian academy — the coalition of individual Christian scholars all over the country and the world — will need to engage in regular communal, as well as individual, introspection to insure that Christian scholarship is measuring up to its own high standards. It must constantly guard against endowing fundamentally secular ideas with Christian verbiage and calling them Christian. This is a practice far too common in the Christian community today, including some of our Christian colleges and universities.

Some of what has passed for Christian scholarship is, at base, not Christian in its fundamentals. This need not deter or detain us; it should simply keep us vigilant. Christian worldview discussions and debates will be helpful in sorting this out and finding it wanting. But we may also need to institutionalize ways to help in the professional socialization of current and future Christian scholars to this vital, yet precarious, task.

As a graduate student in sociology and anthropology during the late 1950s and early 1960s, I was exposed along with all other graduate students — and I do mean everyone — to John Henry Newman's *The Idea of a University* and John Stuart Mill's *On Liberty*. Both were intended to give us a classic yet clear vision of some of the ideals we would be pursuing as members of an academic community and how very fundamental those ideals were to the future of our society. I shall never forget the lively debates we held in graduate seminars and in the coffee shop over the issues that these little volumes raised. In retrospect, what was most important for me and others in those debates was the resulting realization that we were part of a very important enterprise and that the responsibility for the future of the college and university was in our hands. I don't remember whose idea it was to make this a part of our academic socialization process, but I do know it was effective. Somehow I have the feeling that we have lost some of that communal sense of responsibility in our faculties today. Perhaps because of the increasing fragmentation of knowledge, the increasing departmentalizing of the disciplines, and the increasing specialization of our fields of endeavor we have lost an essential ingredient of Christian scholarship in the Christian college and university.

The modern dilemma for the Christian college as it relates to first-rate Christian scholarship is how to insist on the true integration of faith and learning in the context of a Christian commitment to the unity of all knowledge while surrounded by a secular academic environment that is militating toward just the opposite — that is, the rigorous separation of faith from learning and the increasing disunity across the disciplines and their various specializations. But it is exactly in the midst of such a dilemma that the Christian college, by its nurture of first-rate scholarship, can make a contribution. I am persuaded that it is precisely because so many secular scholars are unaware of their worldviews, and use no guiding paradigms, that there is so much academic superficiality in much of what is called scholarship. What is needed in the chaos of

110

the profoundly secular sea of disjointed and unconnected knowledge is a model that leads toward a unity of it all. It does not need to be a model that everyone embraces, but rather a model of how it can be done. This is the role, it seems to me, that can be played by the serious introduction of a worldview paradigm into our discussions of curriculum and scholarship.

Taking this challenge seriously and making a contribution will be exceedingly difficult. The academy today seems dominated by celebration of the disunity rather than the unity of knowledge. It applauds the use of concepts like deconstructing and decentering and subverting; and it accords virtue to such efforts. There seems to be almost no room for the virtues of Newman's idea of a university — virtues that are essential to his foundational belief that all knowledge is connected and ultimately unified. This interconnectedness of all truth is woefully out of favor in today's modern university (Hamilton, 1995; Neusner, 1996).

No one in the academy needs to be persuaded that knowledge now lies around us in scattered and unconnected pieces. They are confronted with it each day, and many are on the brink of despair at being able to do something constructive about it. Much of what we observe in postmodernist thought today not only devalues any unity of knowledge, it champions its discontinuity (Wilson, 1998). It has impoverished our public discourse and emaciated much of the learning we convey to our students. An increasing number of faculty no longer care about the unity of knowledge. All universities and colleges, not just Christian ones, face the challenges and dilemmas of unifying and remapping the world of learning. Christian colleges — especially the first-rate ones — may be called to a special role in this very difficult but common task.

Worldview — with its perspectival confidence that there is an ultimate unity of all knowledge — matters a great deal if we are ever to resolve this common problem of the fragmentation of knowledge. It can provide, I believe, a model in which we can find some common ground for addressing shared questions and engaging in coherent debate. In a sense, postmodernism not withstanding, the use of worldview as a legitimate expectation for the introspection of all scholars and their scholarship could provide the common ground for constructing a new intellectual tradition that we all can share, and which may lead us toward building anew the lost unity of knowledge. Indeed, it may be the utter chaos left in the wake of a failed postmodernism — which I believe

111

to be inevitable — that creates the window of opportunity for such a worldview thrust in the academy. While this may sound like some utopian adventure at the outset — and it is — the first-rate Christian colleges and universities among us may well make a natural home for this experimentation while they are building their own strength in Christian scholarship.

Christian scholars, like most other Christian intellectuals and academics, retain the traditional mark of a Christian worldview by holding the conviction of dual faith in a Creator God and in human reason as a reliable God-given tool for understanding his creation. It is exactly on such a worldview that a unity of knowledge can most comfortably rest. In my own worldview tradition — that of the Reformed perspective — there is already considerable advantage brought to bear by a commitment to and living memory of an actual unity of knowledge, by a continuing experience of working intellectually on a common ground with a significant portion of our church leadership and constituency, and by an extraordinarily strong philosophical and theological tradition on which to build new connections and interrelationships. There remains a strong Dutch reformers' confidence that even secular knowledge will ultimately be brought into unity with Christian religious beliefs, and that there is nothing to fear in the exploration of every corner of God's creation. In such an environment, even the faithful nonbeliever can make a significant contribution during the journey toward reasoned belief and worldview (Wacome, 1998). Christianity needs no special protection anywhere, only the Christian and academic freedom to explore openly every crevice of God's universe. The words of Abraham Kuyper often become the call to arms for rigorous and bold Christian scholarship: "There is not one square inch of this universe about which God does not say; 'It's mine!'" Worldview mattered then and it matters now.

Not all Christian colleges have been blessed with such a tradition and commitment to worldview. Certainly not many have a history of building the theological and philosophical framework for bringing Christian scholarship to bear on all of life. Consequently, and to the contrary, many have built bulwarks against modernity and the secular world of scholarship so as to protect and preserve their religious character. Unfortunately, most of those bulwarks have militated against an ethos of courageous Christian scholarship and the academic freedom to promote it. And most have paid a heavy price. They cut themselves off from any real hope or possibility of influencing the larger world of knowledge and scholarship, and in most cases created an environment on their campuses which even prevented the molding of their own Christian scholarship. But many have come to recognize the folly of that strategy, and they are articulating a desire to chart another course. For them, as well as for all of the academy, a focus on worldview may be a methodology worth pursuing.

For most Christian colleges, this bold advance of Christian scholarship and worldview is a precarious walk. It places new demands on already scarce resources. It inevitably leads to charges, none of which seemingly need any evidence in support, that the college is selling its Christian birthright for a very messy mess of secular porridge. It will hear charges that the college is already on the slippery slope to rampant secularization. But these are the methods of the "bulwark mind," the closed mind, while the issues of today's "playing field" are of a different sort. The question to be addressed is more like this: How can the Christian college restructure itself to bring the best resources of the Christian tradition to bear on our common task of rebuilding the house of learning? What can the Christian college and its "best and brightest" Christian scholars bring to the effort of raising the state of knowledge from what one writer calls the current "undignified heap of squirming confusion" to one of unity around well-constructed worldviews? It is a watershed era for these colleges, and the jury remains out as to whether such refocusing of effort can really take place in most of them.

My modest proposal is that colleges and universities with Christian worldviews initiate a bold advance of Christian scholarship by the allocation of increased resources to such efforts both internally and in coalition with others. It must be given high priority in annual operating budgets. Endowments restricted for Christian scholarship must be built.

There is much in higher education today that would facilitate such a concerted movement in Christian colleges. Not only is the need acknowledged by the academy, but the communication technology is now available to bring together various communities within the academy, which formerly was not possible, or extremely costly and difficult. The new technology now makes it possible for the Christian scholar to be in direct communication with other Christian colleagues around the world. New and expanded collaborations among Christian scholars is made simple and productive. It also allows Christian scholars to make

113

their way into largely untried conversations with secular scholars all over the world. It gives them the means to persuade in new and improved ways that knowledge forged within a Christian worldview illumines problems of universal import. In fact, Christianity has often generated a broad and complicated set of ways of understanding reality in worldview terms. Christian scholars now have the means to show that all this matters, and that worldviews are essential tools in the scholarly enterprise.

For Christian colleges and scholars to pull this off, however, they need to rediscover and reapply the intellectual resources of Christianity in previously unimagined ways; that is, they must do so with the constant thought that they are speaking to all scholars, not just Christian ones. They have the opportunity to make their daily intellectual climate a pluralistic one without necessarily having secular scholars on the Christian college faculty. This allows them to be effectively Christian in the larger arena of scholarship without actually being "in residence" with secular scholars. It prevents the isolation and intellectual impoverishment of the past by living more fully in the modern academic world, living by universal scholarly standards, and wading with renewed confidence into the debates over new methods, new directions, and new canons. Indeed, what makes their contributions as Christians most distinctive is not their methods but the kinds of questions they favor and bring to bear in intellectual interchange.

The Christian tradition raises some kinds of questions more urgently than others, and these no doubt would be more prominent in Christian college research programs. That is a strength. The questions asked would be more fully informed by Christian worldviews, not constrained by them. These would tend to raise issues and suggest interpretations that secular researchers might overlook or play down. It would enhance the interchange and make significant contributions to the larger mosaic of intellectual activity both within and beyond the Christian college (Marsden, 1997). But I fear we shall not see this day so long as many Christian traditions flounder intellectually in malnourished isolation from the mainstream of scholarship. Modern technology can now begin to lead the way out.

Academic Freedom: College and Church

There is perhaps no place where academic freedom is more misunderstood than in the church and religious communities. But academic freedom, when correctly defined and understood, need not be a threat to religious commitments and worldviews. Academic freedom is simply the logical extension of Christian freedom in the context of the Christian academy. Colleges which are affiliated with churches or denominations should assure that there is a Christian presence, a pervasive Christian voice, in the discussions and debates that are carried on in the campus environment. The church and its worldview deserve a distinctive place in the intellectual conversation of the campus.

This acknowledges that one perspective or worldview may have a privileged place in the discussions on the campus, but that it is not the only one present. While the dialogue centered around the dynamics of faith and learning in the classroom is entirely appropriate and proper, it should never be intended to indoctrinate or coerce a single perspective in the mind of the student (Hardy, 1995). Thus, the privileged perspective of the church's worldview does not give it the final word, but rather it provides an open and acknowledged presence in relationship with every discipline on campus in whatever way seems appropriate to the faculty responsible for each course. In that context the church's worldview should be critiqued and evaluated for its value and truthfulness along with any other perspectives on life and thought that are addressed. The college must uphold a responsible tolerance of other than the privileged view, and faculty must enjoy the responsible freedom to honestly critique it. Mutual respect for the privileged view and the legitimacy of others is essential. Where such respect is present, faculty will enjoy the academic freedom to openly and honestly present, critique, and pursue the merits and deficiencies of all perspectives.

It is important to see the role of the college in this broader perspective. Much of the tension that tends to arise within the college's constituency is caused by a too limited focus. For the college to focus exclusively on the repetition of faith commitments and Scripture may be a good catechetical device, but it would not encourage necessary and healthy theological and worldview development. New circumstances and situations, qualitative changes in society, and the problems raised by contemporary technology require the attention and study of the col-

115

lege. In this process, the college provides an indispensable service to the church; it sustains the faith tradition of the church in dynamic interrelationship with contemporary life and thought. While leaving catechetical instruction to the role of the church, it provides an intrinsic relevance to the church's perspective without giving it some unwarranted divine priority. Furthermore, to see all life and thought within the context of God's law and governance provides the student with a basis for holistic integration at a time in society when fragmentation is the norm. A Christian worldview of this sort provides invaluable assistance to both students and faculty in seeing that "in him [Christ] all things hold together" (Colossians 1:17). This is precisely what worldview is intended to accomplish in any intellectual dialogue. A worldview helps to advance our understanding of truth. So whatever the worldview, it enhances the ability of the scholar to order truth about the world — to make sense of it and hold it together intellectually.

So it is an entirely legitimate expectation that academic freedom in the college be supported and upheld in the church. This kind of expectation built on mutually beneficial understanding of the role of the college in the task of the church is not unreasonable. Indeed, maintaining trust, accountability, and understanding between a college and the church with which it is affiliated requires that the mission of the college be entirely compatible with the ministry of the church. The task of the college is different from that of the church, to be sure, but keeping faith with the church and its religious heritage means, above all else, sharing religious beliefs and worldviews. Antagonism between the church and college, when it exists, tends to be caused by losing sight of their different yet complementary tasks. I believe, for example, that the continuing controversy between the Vatican and the leadership of many Catholic colleges and universities can, at least in large part, be attributed to confusion over different tasks. Even while including substantial and sound statements of academic freedom, the 1990 papal directive *Ex Corde Ecclesiae* ("From the Heart of the Church") has the leadership of Catholic higher education scurrying to limit its potential impact on policy development within their institutions (Allen, 1999; Monan and Malloy, 1999). More sensitivity to the different, yet complementary, tasks of college and church — and clearer articulation of these differences — could avoid much of this controversy.

It is also important to understand that church leaders, and the

116

church as institution, need freedom to fulfill their roles. That freedom is entirely compatible with the academic freedom required by the Christian college and scholar. Imposing orthodoxies on church leaders has essentially the same negative effect as it does on college faculties; it forces unnecessary choices, which militate toward confrontation rather than covenant. Neither church nor college, as institutions, can bear having the motives of its leaders and faculty constantly scrutinized for heresies or its decisions judged by their immediate contributions to the creation of a flawless church or a perfect world. Both institutions are, by their very nature, vulnerable and fragile. An ethos of freedom is essential in each. We have noted in an earlier section of this book that such necessary freedom comports well with the biblical concept of Christian freedom. College and church need each other in matters of freedom (Neuhaus, 1996).

Viewed positively, then, colleges and churches keep faith with each other by sharing a belief system and maintaining trust (Brandt, 1996; Van Harn, 1992). The college confirms this in a clearly articulated mission statement that acknowledges such vital relationship (see the Appendix, pp. 167-210). The church, by its embrace of this mission as an extension of its own belief system and worldview, supports the college in its activities and entrusts it with the academic freedom to complete its task faithfully. The role of the college is distinguished from that of the church, and vice-versa. Both entities live in two worlds — the ecclesiastic and the academic. The church primarily in the ecclesiastic and the college primarily in the academic are strengthened by the interplay and interrelationship. As long as both acknowledge and cherish the mutual benefits of such a relationship, it continues to grow and gain strength.

Unfortunately, the story of college and church relationships in the history of American higher education is not exemplary of such acknowledgment of mutual benefit. Indeed, the literature is filled with commentary that attributes this to the abdication of church relationships in the drive by colleges to be fully accepted in the academic and intellectual world (e.g., Marsden, 1994; Burtchaell, 1991, 1998; Lutz, 1992; Allen, 1999; etc.). They describe the history of secularization of most early Christian colleges as primarily driven by perceived contradiction in religious and academic goals, resulting in the compromise of religious beliefs in favor of secular worldviews. But it remains unclear as to what the active role of the church might have been in allowing such abdication to go on with almost no resistance. The history of secularization in church-related colleges was, I believe, much more of a two-way street than those commentaries suggest. Much of the cause, as I suggested earlier, was related to limited focus and, thus, a blurring of the differences in roles toward common and mutually beneficial purposes. In most cases, I would contend, churches failed to keep the mutual benefit of these relationships clearly before their constituencies and, consequently, often found themselves in the position of managing antagonisms and then actively encouraging the breaking of faith with their colleges. In most cases, churches could have done much to prevent such breaking of faith but had neither the heart nor the grassroots support to do it.

To understand better the mutual responsibility of both parties in the breakdown of this vital college-church relationship, one needs to look at the exceptions to the rule as portrayed. Why did the relationship among those exceptions continue and, in some cases, thrive? What explains the deviations from what has been portrayed as the norm? I believe the answers are evident in the "survivors." They can be found in the mutual nurture and appreciation of the historic and continuing benefits of the college-church relationship. In most cases, this is reflected in the active efforts of both parties in the mission of the college and the worldview of the church. Burtchaell (1998) provides extensive analyses and assessments of some of the vital factors necessary for healthy church-college relations.

The church and college must covenant together that, whatever the formal or legal affiliation, the essence of their relationship is an interdependence based upon common mission. Mere agreement is not enough; there must be sufficient benefits accruing to each party to warrant a meaningful covenant. There must be a sense of mutual dependence shared by the leadership and constituencies of both. The covenant is much more important to the relationship than is any legal contract (Brandt, 1996; Van Harn, 1992). Indeed, these relationships tend to thrive more readily without a focus or concern for the formal relationship. The mutual dependence often centers on many important things: the preparation of future leadership for the church as well as the college; the maintaining and strengthening of the faith and learning nexus which is essential to both the church and the college; the promotion of values and moral order in the larger society; the serving of public good by the preparation of future generations oriented toward altruistic social service; and the development of faith in God and dedication to seeking his kingdom. There are others, of course, but even this list provides more than an adequate number of areas of mutual concern and interest for the enrichment of the college and church relationship. Many of them have been articulated more fully in other places (e.g., Brandt, 1996; Van Harn, 1992; H. Smith, 1980; Horner, 1992).

I am persuaded that we can learn much from each other in this mutual task of covenant-building between church and college. One wonders, for example, how much more acceptable the *Ex Corde Ecclesiae* would be to Catholic colleges and universities if there had first been a clearer differentiation of tasks between colleges and churches, and then a greater mutual respect for the unique challenges of each. One wonders whether, after years of intensive consultation between representatives of the universities and the Vatican, they were simply "talking past each other" and missing the mutual trust and understanding so essential to covenant-building. How many of the subtle suspicions could have been allayed and how much more mutual embrace of the different tasks of the churches and the colleges could have been attained? One can only speculate, for example, whether the leadership of places like Notre Dame and Georgetown and Boston College could now be promoting the autonomy and academic freedom granted in *Ex Corde Ecclesiae* rather than decrying the inclusion of "the university's care for the poor and underprivileged" (among other matters, of course). Role differentiation and ongoing communication between college and church are key factors in covenant-building and mutually beneficial statements of compatible missions.

My modest proposal, then, is that colleges and universities with valued church affiliations (or other religious relationships) establish covenant together with the church for the advancement of academic freedom — a freedom anchored in the biblical concept of Christian freedom — in both college and church. Such a covenant, while informal, can be established by a clearly articulated college mission statement that acknowledges a shared worldview and a mutual benefit with the church. Such an expanded mission statement is presented in the Appendix. It belongs to Calvin College, one of the notable "survivors" in sound and covenantal relationships between college and church. There are others, of course, but I know Calvin College and its intellectual heritage and church relationships most intimately.

In summary, it should be said that the vitality of college-church relationships is found in a mutual dependence to accomplish some of the shared goals articulated here. This is promoted by a shared belief system and an unwritten covenant to be accountable to each other in meeting these shared needs. A close relationship is best maintained by faculty and administrators at the college who are loyal to the church and embrace the mission in those matters that relate to both institutions. While tensions in the relationship are almost inevitable because college and church have different tasks, they are best overcome by focus on shared mission and the keeping of faith toward the accomplishment of those things most dear to both. At base, Christian college faculties and church leaders, in spite of their different roles in the church, are solid allies because they alike are committed to exploring the truth of God's revelation in Jesus Christ. The freedom enjoyed in their respective offices of teaching and leadership has its roots in Christ, who is himself the truth that sets us free. Such an ethos of freedom and mutual trust is essential to the mission of both college and church.

The tensions that seem inevitable between Christian colleges and their church constituencies, then, are largely due to lack of understanding of the different roles performed by each and the limited focus of some voices within the church and Christian community. For a variety of reasons, not the least of which is a hermeneutical one, there are always those in the church that seemingly need to have closure on God's revelation to his people. While these may often be a minority in the church or constituency, they tend to be a very aggressive and noisy minority of zealots. They have often solidified their interpretation of Scripture and are easily threatened by almost any pursuit of alternative views, or even ambiguities, in the meaning of scriptural passages. They become "guardians on the walls" of both church and college, and can find threats to orthodoxy in even the remotest events and utterances. Tolerance among these people is nonexistent; and warfare metaphors abound. They often see themselves as called to protect the integrity of the Scripture as they have come to know and interpret it. It is not difficult, then, to understand that this mentality also is strongly anti-intellectual and often leads attacks on the Christian college. Because they see themselves as defenders of the faith, they are inclined to see all tactics and methods as legitimate in carrying on the "battle for the Bible." Often by use of innuendo, distortion, and blatant untruth, they move to create unrest in the church and constituency in efforts to gain supporters to their "cause." Indeed, the pattern of a small radical fringe in the church and constituency trying to hold a Christian college hostage while they fight their battle is well-known within the Christian community. Horror stories abound. This phenomenon is a travesty in the church as well as in the Christian academy, and it militates against the potential influence that a Christian college and Christian scholars can have in the larger secular academy. It certainly promotes the continuing intolerance of religion in the academy at large (Hamilton, 1995; Marsden, 1997).

Anyone exercising leadership in the defense of academic freedom in Christian communities should, unfortunately, expect the use of such common and predictable tactics by the zealots. I experienced them frequently, although with varied intensity. Several instances from my personal experience — some alluded to earlier — comport well with others observed in the academic freedom literature and may be illustrative here. Any defender of academic freedom for a faculty member who has allegedly spoken "heresy" against any prevailing orthodoxy will promptly be accused of holding the same heretical views. Whether presidents, provosts, deans, trustees, church officials, or faculty peers; the "tarring by the same brush" of heresy or secular humanism is inevitable. During the heat of the Van Till controversy (cited on pp. 29-32), full-page advertisements in the public press identified four of us as the "Four Horsemen of the Apocalypse" amongst a host of blatantly false and libelous allegations. Several science faculty peers of Van Till were drawn into the controversy by their associations with Van Till, and by their alleged sympathy with his views. The defense of Hessel Bouma's right to publish new and enlightened perspectives on pro-life practices in health care delivery (cited briefly on pp. 21 and 94) saw the systematic unfolding of identical tactics by the radical right-to-life zealots. George Marsden describes his experiences with the fundamentalist creationists (1997, pp. 38-41), which also included similar tactics toward the college (and me as its president) for the defense of his academic freedom to take a contrary view. In the case of the allegations against the college by Mr. Robinson and the Young America's Foundation (cited on pp. 18-19) over "Leftist leanings" and the boycotting of "conservative speakers" on campus, the use of deceit, innuendo, distortion, outright falsehood, and fear-mongering in widespread written communications was morally outrageous; yet it was intentionally continued irrespective of the facts and any ethical sense of truth-telling. And because the zealots are always motivated by an incontrovertible "higher morality," I am persuaded that prudence demands moderation and civility, and a non-confrontational stance even in the face of outrageous charges. These incidents often provide opportunities to explain anew the meaning and importance of academic freedom for the college and Christian community. Straightforward presentation of the facts in the matters at issue, without responding directly to the zealots' allegations, can also do much to keep the controversy in proper perspective and to expose the zealotry by non-confrontational methods.

A certain amount of intolerance and zealotry will perhaps always be found in religious communities. Religious feelings and convictions are deeply held, and it is the zeal for them that leads to less tolerance of alternatives than might be desirable for both the proponents and those not so convicted. But the Christian college and church must recognize that such zealotry is not limited to the Christian community. I have alluded earlier to the fact that zealotry in the support of feelings and convictions about political, social, economic, and other issues often results in the use of similar tactics in the secular community. It has been demonstrated to be operative in the secular academic community throughout the history of our country (Hamilton, 1995). A review of academic freedom cases over time shows a remarkable presence of intolerance surrounding other than religious issues. Much more typical in academic freedom cases are issues surrounding intolerance for reasons of political and social "violations" in the culture of academic disciplines, prevailing campus ideologies, and interpersonal "power-brokering" of various sorts. Except for the early history of religious dogmatism in the academy, there is little evidence in the annals of academic freedom cases to account for the pervasive intolerance of religion in most of American higher education today. And while that may be small comfort to the Christian scholar, the evidence for religious intolerance seems much more profound in the overall secularization of our entire society, especially during the past half-century. The academy, then, is not distinguished from other segments of our society by its religious intolerance (Whitehead, 1995).

Academic Freedom and Freedom of Speech

Unfortunately, in the minds of most of our publics and some academics, academic freedom is no longer thought to have any particularly close relationship to the search for, or the affirmation of, truths discovered by study and reflection. It has come to be perceived as part of the more general right of the freedom of expression or speech. Expression understood in that way, of course, excludes rather than includes the measured expression of reasoned and logically and empirically supported statements that are demanded by academic freedom. In the minds of many, however, academic freedom is quite synonymous with expression of any desire, any sentiment, any impulse. Indeed, that leads to the "anything goes" mentality many have about the academy.

This perception is not without substance (Shils, 1993; Veith, 1994; Hamilton, 1995; Marsden, 1996). Indeed, there is much in the current postmodernist movement in the academy that aggressively advances ideas and objectives that essentially deny the value of academic freedom as traditionally understood. These ideas deny the view so foundational to academic freedom — that truth can be achieved by scholarly activity governed only by the standards of evidence and argument that can be openly and honestly addressed within the academy. The value of such academic freedom is replaced by the value of no criteria at all — that is, no statement can ever be truer than any other. Thus, it replaces the criteria of truthfulness with the denial of any governing criteria within the academy. Radical relativism is the obvious result, and the search for truth is replaced by a search for power among the equally deserving values of gender, and race, and culture, and sexual preference, ad infinitum. The objective for each value is to gain power, that is, to have one's value and viewpoint prevail in the academy. The objective is to dissolve the traditional consensus around the value of truthfulness in the academy. Partisanship replaces it. Much more could be said about this current movement, but suffice it to say that it provides an adequate and legitimate basis for concern within the academy as well as among our important publics.

I remain optimistic that postmodernism will be short-lived, because such a movement cannot long survive as a community of scholars. It can only exist as a parasite on an existing community (the current academy) — reaping the benefits of that community while willy-nilly attacking its moral order and contributing little or nothing to it. It takes, but gives nothing in return. Again, using the Durkheimian paradigm of community, the postmodernist movement does not contain the essential components for a true and lasting community of scholars. The movement does not have a moral order; nor does it have an inclination to establish one. Without moral order there can be no standards; hence no assessment, no evaluation. Indeed, its orientation toward unbridled tolerance, and its attribution of equal value to all and any voices or ideas, can only lead to disorder and chaos. And, ironically, if its single most cherished value continues to be the pursuit of power, any success in that pursuit would automatically demand intolerance of anything except a radically relativistic worldview. Its unbridled tolerance, in the context of power, would become rigid conformity. Indeed, any ultimate victory for this movement would mean chaos for the academy and death for academic freedom.

A recent personal experience comes to mind as a useful illustration of some of my concerns about postmodernism. I read a very comprehensive and first-rate response to (and critique of) a symposium in *Sociological Theory* on "queer theory" (July 1994) that was intended to bring sociologists into dialogue with a postmodernist intellectual movement that has been neglected by the discipline. The critique was submitted as a response to the symposium but was rejected for publication. The reasons from readers (reviewers), all queer theorists or QT sympathizers, are revealing.

Because the critique used traditional theory and methods in the discipline for evaluating the symposium, the readers essentially rejected it out of hand. Indeed, one reader rejected it even though he or she confessed to not having read the symposium articles to which the critique was a response. Another reader rejected it because the response used "traditional Aristotelian logic" rather than a "supplementary logic" that is more acceptable to queer theorists because it allows for apparent contradictions. Most consistently, however, readers argued that the critique should not be published because it included "relatively minor questions of logical consistency" (not acceptable to postmodernists) and because it "represented an effort to police the boundaries of the discipline" (also not acceptable to postmodernists). Furthermore, readers seemed consistent in arguing that because "there is an enormous intellectual gulf between the responder and the queer theory writers," the responder should not use traditional social science premises to do violence to the premises of postmodern theory. The responder, knowing well the "gulf" between them but not himself a queer theorist, was faulted for simply "measuring" and "evaluating" the queer theorists "according to the disciplinary and intellectual protocols" of traditional social science. Hence, according to one reader, the responder "fails to provide an intellectually productive model" for opening up issues. The critique was rejected, at least in part, because "one can see the issues being developed as a clash of traditional (pro-empiricist) vs. postmodern (anti-empiricist) paradigms." Even more revealing, a reader stated that "an effective critique would have to be informed by the premises of postmodernism." In essence, a critique, to be acceptable, must be written from a set of premises that queer theory shares and embraces.

Ultimately, the bottom line of the readers' assessments was that queer theory can only be critiqued by proponents of queer theory, that postmodernists can only be critiqued by postmodernists. One reader even queries: If this is not the case, "what conclusion could one then possibly come to except that queer theory has failed to make its case?" Since when did the burden of proof rest with the acceptable and acknowledged standards of the academy (its moral order) rather than with the new, untried and untested? Of course, it doesn't take the proverbial rocket scientist to see that such argumentation turns the traditional pursuit of truth and discovery of knowledge "on its head." No matter how illogical, this line of argument gives postmodernists temporary safe haven, and avoids all of the pain which normally accompanies rigorous assessment. I find this argumentation revealing, indeed; and one wonders how often this sort of power-brokering and intimidation is used by postmodernists in today's academy. In any event, I am persuaded that it is exactly this wrong-headed mentality that allows events like the Sokal hoax in *Social Text* — the satirical article suggesting that the laws of physics are merely a social construction — to expose the intellectual vacuity of the radical postmodernists (Sokal, 1996).

The postmodernist idea that the liberal intellectual system can be a kind of "anything goes" pluralism in which all ways of believing are created equal is seriously and, I believe, fundamentally flawed. The lack of a set of criteria of truthfulness, and the denial of any governing criteria for establishing one, leaves the entire academy without the essential tools of evaluation and assessment. Without such tools, the academy cannot fulfill its obligations to itself and to the society it is called to serve. In its logical extension, this idea removes all notions of quality differentiation among students, faculty, writing, research, and ideas — even the one we are here discussing. It can only mean chaos for the academy and, ultimately, for our society. On the other hand, academic freedom as it has functioned historically will continue to call for the essential nature of criteria and standards within the academy. It will continue to call for civility of discourse in the pursuit of knowledge, but totally reject the notion that those pursuits will be without pain; that is, knowledge claims will always be subject to constant checking in the pursuit of new and improved knowledge. This checking process is often painful, offensive, and not nice to those whose truth is being questioned. This will be especially true for those, often the postmodernists, who hold strong ideologies. Most postmodernists will resist all such pain, I believe, arguing that their avoidance of pain is more important than the advancement of knowledge by such a process. Consequently, critical reviews of their positions are resisted, and when they do appear are quickly judged as "doing violence" to their cherished ideologies. Academic freedom, on the other hand, will insist on the continuation of the essential tools of evaluation and assessment.

While the distinction between freedom of speech and academic freedom is important, so is the relationship between them. Because freedom of speech is such a critical element in a democratic and free society, this very freedom in a college setting takes on a special character and is especially protected through the avenue of academic freedom. Because of this close relationship, the courts and governmental agencies have tried to keep some distance from academic freedom cases in the academy. Indeed, Justice William Brennan has written: "our Nation is deeply committed to safeguarding academic freedom, which is of transcendent value to all of us and not merely to the teachers concerned. That freedom is therefore a special concern of the First Amendment, which does not tolerate laws that cast a pall of orthodoxy over the classroom. . . . The classroom is peculiarly the 'marketplace of ideas.' The Nation's future depends upon leaders trained through wide exposure to that robust exchange of ideas which discovers truth 'out of a multitude of tongues, (rather) than through any kind of authoritative selection'" (Brennan, 1993). Thus, academic freedom is given special status and strong (but not statutory) support by the existence of and its relationship to the freedom of speech.

Free speech in the college and university setting then does have special status, at least from the perspective of the law and the courts. Consequently, colleges and their faculties need to take special care that free speech on the campus is not abused, and furthermore, that it is not confused with the academic freedom extended to scholars. Freedom of speech is always limited to some extent, but the college must be sure that free speech is responsible speech, particularly as it relates to the college mission. Freedom of speech, too, like academic freedom, has been misunderstood by some of our important publics and has given the concept negative connotations in the academic setting.

In reality, of course, no speech is truly "free"; it is not separate from intended results or behaviors. Communications theory has told us that for a long time. Simply stated, "free speech" is often just the name we give to verbal behavior that serves the substantive agendas we wish to advance. We want all of our speech to have an effect of some sort, otherwise we wouldn't speak. There is specific motivation for our speaking. Considered in this way, all speech is intended to have consequences of some sort regardless of the significance placed on those consequences, so speech cannot be "free" from some intent or impact.

Given such a definition of all speech, and thus the unlikely existence of truly free speech, the college is faced with the monitoring or regulating of speech in ways that are consistent with its educational mission and are viewed as responsible in the academic setting. This is especially complex in the campus setting because of widely varied "political" views about almost everything. Furthermore, the speech-action relationship only adds to the complexity of the issues arising from so-called free speech on the campus. Speech always seems to be crossing the line into action, where it becomes, at least potentially, consequential. So it is common for persons and groups to argue, for example, that a speech or some forms of speech may have the purpose of inciting violence or will include "fighting words" — words that will likely provoke persons to retaliation and thereby cause a breach to the peace.

Nowadays there is the deep concern on many university campuses that "hate speech" will result in consequences that violate the mission of the institution as well as the intent of the free speech statutes of the law (Smolla, 1993). Consequently, colleges and universities must find ways to limit free speech to the extent of being faithful to educational missions as well as the laws of the land. This, like academic freedom, places special responsibilities on the institutions because free speech has special status in the educational and academic setting. Taking this argument to its logical extension, then, all and any speech on the campus may be a candidate for regulation of some sort. Those regulations, I believe, are best developed in two distinct categories: one governing academic freedom for the faculty (the academy), and the other governing the speech of those not covered by the academic freedom provisions. In essence, the latter category would govern all public speech by other then faculty on the campus. Because such speech often challenges the college more frequently, we should briefly assess its potential regulation. This may also help to distinguish it from our primary concern; that is, academic freedom.

It is often said that history shows that even a minimal restriction on the right of free expression too easily leads to ever-increasing restrictions; and to the extent that this is true, there is usually some comfort and protection to be found in campus speech codes and other guidelines that help to determine what speech(es) can stand. But in most cases these codes cannot make the judgments that are called for in the tough cases. For example, I am persuaded that at the present time the risk of not attending to hate speech on some of our major university campuses is greater than the risk that, by regulating it, we will deprive ourselves of valuable voices and insights or slide down the slippery slope toward tyranny. This is a judgment for which I can offer reasons but no assurances. But those whose judgments come down on the other side carry no assurances either. They usually urge us to put our faith in apolitical abstractions, but the abstractions they invoke (e.g., "free speech," marketplace of ideas, etc.) usually come in political guises.

It is not that there are no choices to make or means for making them; it is just that the choices as well as the means are inextricable from the din and confusion of a partisan struggle. And postmodernism, which gives every view and idea and ideology equal value, has only added to the chaos of such power struggles, resulting in even more risk, for there is no safe place to stand. Consequently, there are occasional tough choices to make — and when all else fails (that is, the best of the guidelines, codes, and processes put in place for making them), the president must be prepared to make them. The buck must stop somewhere. Some will always be upset by that, but none should be surprised by it, for in a very real sense the mission of the entire enterprise is at stake. It is precisely in such instances that the president is called to lead, and such leading often comes to making the "tough calls" which can have long-lasting impact — for either good or bad — on the future of the college. Incidents which put at risk the rights of academic freedom and freedom of speech on the campus often fall squarely into the president's sphere of influence and decision. And the president should cherish the right and the opportunity. Especially with the role of the president changing rapidly to primarily that of external public relations and fund-raising leadership, such opportunity provides a place for real moral leadership by the president without violating the democratic processes of decision making in the academy.

In my personal experience such "tough calls" on freedom of speech issues, while always important and usually troublesome, never reached the level of significance of academic freedom issues. For example, the Charles Murray *(The Bell Curve)* and David Noebel (gay rights) free speech controversies cited earlier (pp. 17-21), even if these speakers had been denied the podium, would have been far less harmful to the college than would have been an action of censorship denying academic freedom to the faculty. In the cases of faculty members Howard Van Till and Hessel Bouma, also cited earlier (pp. 29 and 21, respectively), the long-term damage of denying them academic freedom would have exceeded by far any damage caused by the denial of "hate speech" or any other infrequent incident of speech control for explicit cause related to institutional mission. Only if the infringement of free speech becomes commonplace on a campus will it begin to approach the significance of a single incident denying academic freedom.

So the distinction between academic freedom and the freedom of other speech on campus is important to make, and both must be carefully protected, albeit in quite separate ways. Freedom is the common ingredient in both, but beyond that they must be seen and addressed as quite different dimensions of the educational mission. Both are important because they have a direct relationship to a cherished value in the academy; that is, the high value placed on open discussion and debate in the learning environment. Both need principles, policies, and procedures that will protect the academy against both inside and outside forces which are constantly looking for ways to limit the freedoms so essential to the fulfillment of our educational and scholarly mission. Mission must be the ultimate guide.

These distinctions are often confused in academic freedom discussions and debates. For example, one such source of confusion arises because of the keen issues now being debated in the public press and in higher education journals about the desirability of campus speech codes (often interpreted as "hate speech" codes because of recent incidents). Speech codes are not related to the concept of academic freedom in the academy. Rather, they are related to constitutional and legal issues centered on the concept of freedom of speech and/or expression.

So what about speech codes, or regulations generally, on the campus? Based upon my own experiences with attempts to impose severe restrictions on given speakers at Calvin College, and upon my review of cases on other campuses, my preference turns to broadly stated guidelines and codes for the use of students and campus organizations and any others who have responsibility for the invitation of outside speakers. Such codes must include factors of civility, credibility, knowledgeability, pedagogical soundness, and similar qualifications. These should be thoughtfully and deliberately constructed. Given these, then, I much prefer the pragmatic approach of considering each situation as it emerges; and in each case assess the situation in the context of the college's mission and fundamental purposes. These deliberations and experiences should also be the basis of revised guidelines and codes because the question of whether or not to regulate, and by what standards, should always be an internal and local campus one. I have learned not to rely on abstractions that are either empty of content or filled with the content of some partisan (and usually single-interest) agenda to generate a "principled" answer. Instead, I much prefer that we consider in every case what is at stake and what are the risks and gains of alternative courses of action in the context of the college mission. I have learned that absent the given situation and the mission of the college, free speech principles on the campus don't work, and they don't exist — except as a component in a weak argument in which such principles are invoked (usually in desperation) to mask motives that would not withstand close scrutiny in the context of the college's mission. The best process, even preceding the individual judgment on a case by case basis, would perhaps be a mandated procedure that requires the sponsoring organization or individuals to jump through some hoops — that is, do some intensive argumentation work on any potentially controversial speaker — before an invitation is allowed to stand. This would bring both sound educational merit and deliberate judgment to the process before pressures from other interest groups mount. Such a process should be monitored by a faculty mentor or a member of a discipline with special expertise, such as a speech or debate professor.

Finally, we should ask why speech, especially from those invited from outside the campus community, takes on such significance in an educational setting. On the face of it, free speech seems entirely compatible with the learning environment (O'Neil, 1997). The answer, of course, is found in acknowledging that, as we have said, speech is rarely, if ever, really "free." That is often the case with so-called "hate speech"; it usually includes an exaggerated description of an oppressive situation needing immediate action. "In your face" expressions tend to be the norm in such speech, followed by calls to action. Now while such expressions may be the way of "hate speech" and television talk shows, it is not the way of sound educational process. It is not the way in teaching or in public discussion where one hopes to have some helpful effect on those who hold other views, and vice-versa. Rather, a learning environment, such as the college campus, seeks to find some common ground, regardless of how controversial the topic, from which differing views can be discussed and assessed in a civil manner. Criteria of reason and evidence are cherished and upheld. Shouting matches and "hate" themes are rarely, if ever, compatible with an educational process or college mission.

My modest proposal, then, is that all colleges and universities distinguish clearly between academic freedom and freedom of speech on the campus, and that they grant academic freedom only to the faculty for the purpose of assuring their unhindered task performance in the academy. Such academic freedom is a special right and security granted only within the academy, and carries clear obligation to full and contributing citizenship in that academy.

Academic freedom, in distinction from freedom of other speech on campus, is a freedom designed to liberate the faculty from any forces that would limit their primary task — the pursuit of truth and its related tasks. Furthermore, academic freedom also protects the college, as a corporate entity, from all forces that would limit the fulfillment of its institutional mission. To facilitate the careful protection of academic freedom, then, we must always acknowledge that academic freedom is a security against interference in the pursuit of truth by those persons

131

whose lives are dedicated to conserving and extending the realm of knowledge, and by those colleges and universities whose missions include the pursuit of truth and the advancement of knowledge. It is the right, or cluster of rights, which are intended to make it possible for certain persons and certain institutions to teach and do research and scholarship truthfully, and to employ their intellectual power to the fullest extent for the good of society at large. Academic freedom can best be granted, and in the appropriate degree, where it is an integral part of the ethos that is congruent with task performance. Thus, it is a security and right granted only to the academy. That security and right, in turn, carries with it an obligation to full and contributing citizenship in the academy.[2]

Protection and Promotion of Academic Freedom

The literature on the topic of academic freedom includes the review of many cases and the use of those cases to illustrate the principles and dynamics of sound policy surrounding the promotion of academic freedom. Thus, the literature is rich in observations and experiences that can be helpful to those who are in positions which can be influential in the future of academic freedom in our colleges. Rarely, however, is specific advice given to those who generally play major roles in the conduct and resolution of academic freedom cases. My experience in the presidency suggests that specific advice taken seriously prior to the time difficult cases need to be adjudicated can be very helpful. Preventive maintenance is usually well worth the effort. What follows here is my attempt to glean from the literature and my personal experience with

2. While this distinction between academic freedom and freedom of speech is sufficient for the purpose of limiting discussion in this project to only academic freedom, it should be acknowledged that there is a rich and extensive literature in the freedom of speech and related matters. Because there is some overlap with academic freedom in specific cases, this entire area is worthy of more attention. Indeed, college presidents, using their college legal counsels, should be encouraged to conduct periodic campus discussions entitled something like "Freedom of Speech and Academic Freedom Distinctions: A Legal Perspective" for those most likely to be involved in the adjudication of academic freedom cases. Pursuing such discussions would require familiarity with the wealth of legal literature and case studies in this area.

such cases some rather general advice to selected players. Some of these suggestions are more universally applicable across all colleges than are others, but I think all have relevance in most cases and may be altered to fit local situations. In any event, this advice is offered in the hope that it may be helpful to those who are, or very likely will be, facing an academic freedom case at their institution.

My modest proposal is that the advice given for the protection and promotion of academic freedom by each significant group — faculty, presidents and provosts, boards of trustees, students, and church officials — be taken seriously and discussed openly, so that the institution will be adequately prepared to deal appropriately with all future challenges to academic freedom.

Advice to Faculty:
1. Be confident upon initial appointment that your own view of the world (worldview) is consistent with the mission of the college. Review the mission statement and discuss it with colleagues who have been at the college for a time. Do a "reality check" every two or three years to determine that your worldview and the college mission are still compatible and mutually supportive.
2. Be open and honest about any perceived differences in your worldview and the mission of the college. Discuss these differences with your department chair, dean, or president. Some differences can create a positive tension and stimulate a lively intellectual environment. If they seem irresolvable, look for other opportunities. Don't remain at a college where the nexus of your worldview and the college mission becomes (or is already) dysfunctional or fundamentally incompatible or inconsistent.
3. Be especially introspective about your own personal and professional development as a scholar-teacher in your present institutional environment. Act on your best judgments after consultation with those you trust and who know your workplace. Do not pursue or accept tenure at an institution whose mission is contrary to, or significantly inconsistent with, your view of the world. If necessary, look elsewhere; be patient and deliberate in pursuing other opportunities in a more nurturing environment.
4. Review carefully the academic freedom policy of your college or university, and determine as clearly as possible the expectations of

133

the institution (and your faculty peers and colleagues) for your creative scholarship and teaching assignments. Expectations provide important clues to the importance of academic freedom safeguards at a college, and about the general character and quality of the academic environment. Be confident that you can thrive academically and professionally in such a place.

5. View your relationship to a college as a partnership where trust and covenantal relationships are the "glue" that holds the mutually beneficial association in place. Your task is not to change or transform the college and its mission, but rather to join as a full partner in an educational enterprise with common ends.

6. Both in scholarship and teaching, keep a healthy and open "testing of ideas" mentality with colleagues and peers both within and beyond your academic discipline and area of expertise. Cross-disciplinary insights and observations often enhance an already comprehensive worldview and even promote a more fully orbed one. It also helps in the establishment and continuing assessment of your "fit" within the college mission.

7. Keep in mind your obligations to important "publics" of the college as you carry out your tasks in teaching and research. Seize opportunities to explain and describe your work, and to set forth your perspective on critical issues in your areas of expertise. Alumni, church members, professional associations, and various lay audiences provide useful feedback and observations often absent in the academy. They can also be important partners in the advancement of your work.

8. Be deliberate, yet prudent, in your discussion of sensitive findings of your research and scholarship in the public arena. Especially when findings challenge traditional practices and values, it is important to carefully distinguish between what is plausible scientific speculation and what is factual. Be prepared to articulate your personal worldview and how it may influence your findings and perspectives on those findings. Humility is a virtue in such a setting, regardless of how "right" you may be.

9. Avoid the temptation of using the classroom as a "soapbox" for your own political views or to advocate your own political causes. Organize lectures and class time around the substance of the course, knowing and presenting well the research findings and

empirical data upon which the topics are judged worthy. When deemed appropriate, don't hesitate to state an opinion about a topic under discussion. But also try to state opposing positions accurately in the same context. Be sure students know it is an opinion, and invite them to differ. Distinguish carefully between real data and the varied opinions about it.

10. Be able to articulate the meaning of academic freedom and how it is promoted in your institution. Show its relevance to your task of teaching and research, and personalize how it comes to bear on the way you do your work. When academic freedom cases arise on your campus, be equipped to focus and articulate the critical issues involved, especially for those beyond the campus environment. Be prepared to justify and support the "due process" procedures governing the adjudication of such cases.

11. Develop a keen sense for the dynamics of "political correctness" on your campus and articulate any concerns you have about it. Especially avoid some of the common pitfalls of worthy causes taking on the character of an ideology. Be prepared to openly discuss the threats to academic freedom that come especially through the dynamics of "political correctness" and ideological imperialism. Be wary of single-issue movements.

12. When for you, personally, there arises even a glimmer of "trouble" related to an academic freedom or "political correctness" matter, keep accurate and comprehensive written records of every encounter or conversation related to it. Keep your department chair and dean fully informed of developments each step of the way. Remain calm and thoughtful, explaining carefully your position at every opportunity and tracing its legitimacy to your research and study. Avoid ad hominem attacks on your critics at all costs. Sound evidence and the civil manner in which it is presented will gain the support of colleagues and others in the important "publics" of the college. Even your critics will ultimately be more likely to be persuaded by a person of integrity and decency. Stay the course.

Advice to Presidents and Provosts:

1. Know the meaning of academic freedom (or develop it) for your campus, appreciate its significance for the health and welfare of the college, and promote it openly. More than anything else, aca-

demic freedom protects the very essence of the academic enterprise. It gives integrity to institutional mission and purpose. Be prepared and have the courage to "stand alone" in the defense of academic freedom when circumstances warrant it.

2. As soon as an academic freedom case surfaces, or a potential one is noted, be the first to know the facts in both the substance and the circumstances of the matter. Be in a position to make an early personal (and usually private) judgment about the merits of the case and its importance to the character and ethos of the campus. This will equip you well to make a variety of decisions along the way that have the integrity of your own judgment as foundation and will free you from the temptation of accommodation to influence and pressures that tend to come from a variety of campus constituencies. However time-consuming this may be, it will be the best preparation for strong presidential leadership in matters that have the greatest long-term effect on the college. This is an area where only the president can lead, and that leadership is absolutely essential.

3. Be sure that you have prepared your board of trustees for such academic freedom cases. The best way to do so is to see that all the "Advice to Boards of Trustees" (see below) is accomplished and operational. Work closely with the board leadership to have this happen as a total board effort that is ultimately approved by the full board. Because the substance of most academic freedom cases tends to divide boards, this is an essential process. The president of the college or university, along with the board chair, must lead this process, but it must result in a product that has had full board participation and effort.

4. Recruit and appoint as many established and promising young Christian scholars to your faculty as resources will permit. Lead your board in establishing policies congenial to first-rate Christian scholars and in finding the resources to appoint them. A strong cadre of active and lively Christian scholars will establish an ethos in the campus community which promotes the zealous search for truth and anchors the commitment to academic freedom so vital to that search. Identify, nurture relationships, and finally appoint the "best and brightest" Christian scholars to your faculty. This should always be a top priority throughout the campus.

5. Appoint outstanding Christian academics and scholars as chief administrators in academic affairs and curricular matters. Scholar-provosts and scholar-deans make excellent role models for young faculty. They also bring scholarly discernment to appointment and promotion decisions by bringing to bear sound judgment about intellectual and scholarly achievements. They are best equipped to lead lively cadres of first-rate scholars toward institutional as well as personal goals.

6. Establish policies and programs that bring the best and brightest students into collaborative scholarly projects with outstanding faculty scholars. This will do more to generate an ample supply of outstanding future faculty, as well as superb Christian thinkers in our society, than any other initiative in the college. It will also help to create an ethos in support of Christian scholarship in the student community. It will also provide unique opportunities for bringing to bear the spiritual dimensions of Christian scholarship on both faculty and students.

7. Promote the perceived value of Christian scholarship among the entire community by initiating programs and policies which enhance it. This would include differential teaching, advising, and research loads that recognize scholarly gifts and productivity; sabbaticals and grants for scholarly activities; special recognition and merit stipends for scholarly awards and productivity; and rigorous accountability for scholarly activities at times of promotion and reappointment. These, too, do much to create an ethos of strong support for Christian scholarship in the entire community and enhance the recruitment of first-rate scholars to the campus.

8. Be sensitive to the "chilling effect" that academic freedom cases can have on the faculty at large. Strive to prevent it by openly promoting through your words and actions the creative and progressive scholarship of all faculty. The chilling effect can only have a long-term negative impact on the health of the college.

9. Develop a healthy working relationship and a covenant-building ethos with church leaders and constituents. Articulate regularly the differences in roles between college and church, and demonstrate the mutual benefit of covenanting together to attain common and compatible goals. Meet periodically with church leaders and "influentials" in key constituent communities. Promote a

sound understanding of academic freedom among these colleagues and constituents before the occasional crises occur.

Advice to Boards of Trustees:

1. Acknowledge openly that the board of trustees has ultimate responsibility for all policy established by the college. It has fiduciary obligation to protect the academic as well as the financial well-being of the institution. Boards must protect academic freedom from both internal and external threats; it is a most important duty. Trustees must ensure that an ethos of intellectual freedom is maintained on the campus. They must also win support for such an ethos among the college's important publics, even while such freedom may at times promote ideas that are anathema to many constituents.

2. Insist on the existence of a comprehensive statement of mission (or the development of one) for your college or university. This should be an expanded and unified statement which serves as a guiding document for everyone in the college. It should include, or refer specifically to, statements on academic freedom and institutional worldview. Be confident that the procedures for "due process" in academic freedom cases are clearly and precisely outlined and approved by the board.

3. Know the legal implications of trustee statements and actions in academic freedom cases. Have qualified legal counsel address the board periodically about these and related matters, but always in the early stages of any academic freedom case that arises on the campus. Be especially sensitive to rules of strict confidentiality on personnel matters which are always operative in academic freedom cases. Follow precisely all "due process" specifications.

4. Be confident that the board of trustee handbook cites the appropriate and expected behavior of board members in personnel matters, especially during academic freedom proceedings. Boards should be prepared to take prompt and strong actions in the case of violations by any of its members. A single spokesperson for the board should be appointed in advance, especially for all matters pertaining to confidential personnel issues.

5. When academic freedom cases become public, keep the institutional rudder firmly in the hands of the president and the board.

Be patient with the process, and especially vigilant that due process be meticulously observed. Be supportive of the president in managing the campus dissent and stress that usually accompanies academic freedom cases. Resist the urge to settle cases quickly. Take time. Be deliberate. Good order is especially vital in such cases. Keep your heads and stay the course.

6. Use the president in making any necessary public statements on academic freedom cases. Most statements should be limited to the process and procedures being used and focused on the time required to adjudicate the matter. The substance of the case should be rigorously avoided in all public statements.

7. Insist that the "accused" (usually a faculty member) be adequately supported and affirmed in his or her work while the due process is taking place. With the president and chief academic officers, be sure the "accused" has tangible evidence of an institutional "sense of justice" that is prevailing over any criticism from the broader community, constituents, peers, church leaders, alumni, and other common sources of concern in academic freedom cases. Care for the "victim" in the midst of frequent "rush to judgment" efforts by such groups is essential.

8. Understand the distinctive role of the college in relationship to the church and the broader Christian community. Along with the president and provost, promote a sound understanding of academic freedom and the important role it plays in covenant-building with church leaders and constituents. Stress the importance of clear role differentiation between college and church, and be able to articulate those differences and their mutual benefit in key constituencies. Support the president and provost in keeping open lines of communication with church leaders and other constituent groups. Participate, when possible, in meetings and activities designed toward that end.

Advice to Students:
1. Academic freedom cases provide excellent opportunities to gain knowledge about important intellectual topics and issues, as well as some dynamics of human behavior. Use such opportunities to enter the dialogue on critical issues in the academy. Engage in the conversation in whatever way seems most comfortable to you, but

do the necessary homework on the issues to make your engagement in them as intellectually productive as possible.

2. Avoid taking "hard and fast" positions on specific academic freedom cases. Rather, try to understand the rationale for different positions and understand the various perspectives which are brought to bear in these cases. Recognize that such cases often become highly emotionalized, so try to avoid being caught up in the emotion and, rather, analyze why that is so. Learn the principles of debate and analysis that often are the essential ingredients of the ultimate resolution. These principles have significant carry-over value for almost any case of conflict resolution in other environments.

3. Observe and discuss with faculty some of the human behavioral manifestations of controversy and disagreement. Identify some of the universal characteristics, as well as any unique and valued approaches, found in conflict, criticism, and negotiation. You have an excellent opportunity to learn from such cases; so seize the occasion of a "real life" laboratory. Engage professors, administrators, and other students on the issues involved.

4. Learn about what it means for a professor to pursue the truth. Most academic freedom cases involve in some way the pursuit of truth in the area of the professor's expertise. Be willing to participate in discussions centered on the importance of "pursuing the truth" in an environment that is free from forces of oppression; and equip yourself to do so intelligently. Distinguish between the closely related concepts of "academic freedom" and "freedom of speech." Learn how each affects you as a student in the academy and as a participant in a community.

5. Arrive at your own independent thought about such cases of academic freedom, but do so only after careful and deliberate discussion with others, and preferably in communal discourse. Develop your understanding in areas of tolerance for differences of view, empathy, and communal judgment.

6. Distinguish between the "pursuit of truth" from the perspective of the professor and that of the student. Identify the responsibilities which accompany the freedoms in the "pursuit of truth" for both the professor and the student. The freedom to profess as well as the freedom to learn come with associated responsibilities; identify and define each to your own satisfaction and understanding.

7. Be vigilant against the power of political correctness and manipulation by various forces within the campus community. Resist thoughtlessly following the "crowd mentality" of the community, and don't succumb to manipulation by faculty or student proponents of single-issue and politically correct causes. Think carefully about the issues involved, test your ideas in consultation with others, and keep your own deliberate and discerning mind.

Advice to Church Officials:
1. Develop and nurture an understanding of the meaning and place of academic freedom in the Christian college. Know the policies which govern academic freedom in the Christian colleges most closely related to your church or larger ecclesiastical body. Be prepared to explain it to your constituencies and to describe why it is important for the advancement of understanding and truth in the Christian community.
2. Be an advocate for clearly articulated academic freedom policies in the Christian colleges within your arena of influence. Support and promote the deliberate use of due process in the adjudication of academic freedom cases. Keep a clear distinction between church and college as separate corporate entities in such proceedings, and be able to explain that distinction to church constituencies.
3. Avoid official ecclesiastical declarations or pronouncements about academic freedom cases in your related colleges. Where statements are required, be sure they recognize the role of the college in the pursuit of truth and make them positive in tone so that the relationship of the church and the college is enhanced rather than diminished. Avoid adversarial approaches, especially in the public media. Where negotiation with affiliated colleges is necessary, keep such proceedings as private as possible.
4. Withhold judgment on all charges in academic freedom cases, regardless of their source, until the issues in the case have been fully adjudicated in conformity with approved due process procedures. Advise other church leaders and vocal constituents to be patient and deliberate in reaching personal decisions in such cases. Try to avoid any movements in the church that apply individualized or personal "tests of orthodoxy" and discourage "rush to judgment" inclinations in the church. Assure the church that appropriate pro-

cedures are in process, and express your confidence that fair and honest conclusions will be reached.

5. Acknowledge openly and confidently the Christian commitment of the college and "the accused" in academic freedom cases. Describe and affirm the vital partnership between church and college in carrying out the communal enterprise in Christian education. Insist on carefully reached communal decisions, and denounce the personal application of quickly contrived "tests of orthodoxy" which militate toward individualistic judgments.

6. Since academic freedom cases often touch on issues of vital significance to the church and society, encourage constructive discussion of those issues within appropriate church bodies and organizations. Cases often give attention to issues that need to be addressed in the context of mutual trust and respect, even when positions differ radically and emotions run high. Seize the moment that academic freedom cases often present for productive discussion and mutual understanding of complex issues. Done well, this will promote harmonious relationships between already existing factions in the church, and often between the college and the churches.

7. Remind the churches and their leaders that the colleges with which they are affiliated are called to a very special role in the Christian community. The colleges are called to bring to bear the Word of God in every sphere of life and in every area of human endeavor, and that gives cosmic dimensions to the colleges on behalf of the churches. Encourage the churches to honor this special role of the colleges, and to acknowledge that the colleges can lead the churches to a growing Christian maturity in their witness to a secular society, and thus help the churches in living up to their God-given mission in the world. Help the churches to understand that the colleges and their faculties have a common mission with that of the churches in this regard, and that both are bound by the Word of God in all things.

8. Encourage the churches to use the faculty (including those who have been controversial from time to time) of their colleges in leading discussions of keen issues in the church and the world. College faculty have considerable expertise to bring to bear on key issues, and this can be used on a continuing basis to keep the church communities well informed and more understanding of

the complexities of such issues. It also serves to promote mutual trust between church and college.

Vigilance in all matters related to the protection and promotion of academic freedom is essential for the future of the academy. I am persuaded there is no better way to attain such vigilance than to develop a community that both understands and cherishes the central role of academic freedom in the fulfillment of a college mission. That community — through the enlightened leadership of faculty, provosts, presidents, boards of trustees, students, and church officials — will soon develop an ethos of freedom on the campus. Such an ethos, nurtured and allowed to thrive, will develop a culture of healthy and civil disagreement and debate on critical issues. Education will be enhanced. And together, all of this will insure the fair and deliberate adjudication of any academic freedom issues that arise, albeit with less frequency.

VI

Reflections:
Toward an Ethos of Freedom

A cademic freedom is an extraordinary phenomenon in the world to-day. Indeed, in most of the world academic freedom is denied in both theory and practice. Its life in the United States is even rather short by many standards of tradition and heritage. But it is a principle that now stands at the very essence of what an educational institution must be in a democratic society. Most of the essential functions of the modern college and university cannot be sustained at the present level of quality, and certainly cannot be enhanced, without the existence of academic freedom. It is a principle that must be protected and enhanced in the decades ahead. And it must be better understood by all.

Yet the evidence demonstrates that it is clearly a mistake to believe that academic freedom is fully protected anywhere. From four decades of experience in both public and religiously affiliated colleges and universities, I am persuaded that there are orthodoxies everywhere: a professor who feels silenced in the classroom in order to prevent the charge of advocacy of a personal ideology; a student who feels intimidated in the classroom for a personal (albeit minority) point of view; a graduate student who feels constrained to pursue a dissertation project more in line with departmental orthodoxies than her own interests; or a faculty candidate who is not hired because colleagues believe his research does not fit the department's ideology. Eternal vigilance seems essential to freedom's survival. But even though academic freedom must fight for its survival today amid a minefield of contradictions and dilemmas, it nevertheless remains the essential foundation of intellectual life in our colleges and universities. As such it is, in turn, an indisputable anchor of our free society.

Even in the United States, where it perhaps has a greater impact than almost anywhere else in the world, academic freedom is a principle that is not supported or widely shared outside the academy. And, ironically, even within the academy it is often misunderstood, taken for granted, unappreciated, and often undefended. And throughout its century-old history, it has been an idea threatened almost constantly both from inside and outside the academy (Symposium, 1997). Yet academic freedom is a principle that has served our society very well, for it has assured the seeking, discovering, and disseminating of both old and new knowledge — without restraint of vested interests and political ideology — to the entire society. It has helped to keep our society truly free and democratic. It has kept open discussion and discourse of any issue in the academy readily accessible to the public and for the public welfare. Without the protection of the principle of academic freedom, such open discourse would not be possible and colleges and universities as we know them would be compromised in their basic missions.

In the light of history and experience, then, it must be acknowledged that a large part of the world (and many within the academy itself) resists the central premise upon which academic freedom rests; that is, the premise of a liberal intellectual system that all knowledge claims are revisable. The predisposition to censor in the name of all sorts of higher moralities is extremely strong. And contrary to prevailing opinion, such predisposition is no greater in religiously affiliated colleges than in any other academic institution. The entire academy and all of its members are particularly exposed to this potential for censorship, both from within and without. So it is doubtless the academy must find new ways to preserve this central premise on a constant and continuing basis. Hofstadter and Metzger (1965) stated the problem well over forty years ago when they said: "No one can follow the history of academic freedom in this country without wondering at the fact that any society, interested in the immediate goals of solidarity and self-preservation, should possess the vision to subsidize free criticism and inquiry, and without feeling that the academic freedom we still possess is one of the remarkable achievements of man. At the same time, one cannot but be appalled at the slender thread by which it hangs . . . and one cannot but be disheartened by the cowardice and self-deception that frail men use who want to be both safe and free." To be sure, vigilance is essential if we are to preserve this remarkable achievement of humankind; there must always be some faculty, and presidents, and provosts, and board members who will enter the fray publicly to protect academic freedom for the sake of the colleges and universities committed to our historic liberal intellectual system. One of the greatest contributions they can make is an open and honorable defense of the principles on which both the academy and our society have stood and must continue to stand in the years ahead.

But I am persuaded that it must also become a beacon for all. It is an ideal we must pursue constantly and hold up for all to see, even though we may never quite fully achieve it. Academic freedom must move from that small and almost unseen "light under a bushel" it has been over the past century to become a towering beacon of freedom within our society. Academics — those who have the most to lose and whose very purpose in society depends upon it — must become much more involved in its protection and welfare in the years ahead. For the academy to have legitimacy and our society to be served in the cause of freedom, academic freedom must not only survive — it must thrive as a centerpiece in our free society. I believe there is no greater contribution that the academy can make to our society than the courageous defense of the principle upon which most of the other essential contributions of the college and university ultimately must rest — the principle of academic freedom.

Academic freedom, then, is clearly worthy of the attention called for in the proposals of this book. It is the foundational principle of the intellectual enterprise, yet it is not fully protected anywhere. It is the anchor of our free society, yet misunderstood and widely unappreciated. It is under constant threat from both inside and outside the academy, yet too often undefended by too many faculty. Now it must become a beacon of freedom — the ideal — toward which we move for the sake of truth and understanding in our entire world. It is so important that it demands constant vigilance and enlightened policy development toward an ethos of freedom on our campuses. And it demands that such an ethos of freedom be shared with the constituencies we serve, thus promoting a clearer sense of academic freedom and its importance throughout our society.

The modest proposals of this book are designed to promote an ethos of freedom on our campuses. An ethos of freedom within the academy embraces the complex of fundamental beliefs, standards, ideals, and values surrounding the scholarly pursuit of truth in an academic setting. It is the tone and style and character of an academic community's life together. While seldom fully articulated, it guides and directs those who live within a community of scholars. It acknowledges the existence of standards of reason and evidence, of varied worldviews, of presuppositions, and of moral orders. It undergirds and permeates the methods and patterns of behavior that a given "community of scholars" uses and reflects. It helps to actualize and free that community's major patterns of thought. It provides the positive spirit which motivates the community and the individual scholars within it. It holds up freedom as an essential core component of any academy which wishes to fulfill its foundational commitment to truth. It permeates and pervades everything about the academy and its purpose. It embraces all responsible freedoms bounded by moral order; it despises the reckless "anything goes" freedoms which destroy community at its essence. It demands continuing nurture in order to thrive in a community, but it returns and assures a renewed vigilance for freedom.

For many in the broader academy, these modest proposals are not modest at all; indeed, some will be seen as radical and even ridiculous. Given the present state of the larger academy and its leadership, these modest proposals are countercultural at best and revolutionary at worst. But not to worry. The case can be made that, even while this book is directed primarily toward Christian colleges and universities, the principles underlying the discussions are generally applicable to the entire academy. They are intended to sharpen our understanding of academic freedom, to protect it from the ever-present threats, to keep its essential character under continuing debate and discussion in the academy, to enhance its acceptance among our important publics, and to foster deliberate progress in the development of institutional policies by which academic freedom is advanced in the twenty-first century. We shall need to create "common cause" among faculty, administration, and boards of trustees to create an ethos of freedom which both embraces and nurtures a healthy academic freedom.

So the modest proposals are intended for all colleges and universities. They should be taken seriously, and then considered for selected applications within varied settings. I also contend that Christian colleges and universities are very well equipped to provide some of the cre-

147

ative and innovative change that is needed in an academy that has lost its way from the foundational principles of academic freedom. Increasingly, and regrettably, academic freedom is sought by contract rather than covenant, and it is used for the pursuit of power rather than truth. Self-interest increasingly overshadows mutual goals and the idealism which ignites communal effort. The larger academy has moved from a community to a collection of scholars; it has lost its "common cause." It has created an ethos in which intellectual freedom does not thrive. Unfortunately, and too often, chaos does. And an ethos of freedom is almost impossible in a badly ordered academy.

Christian colleges and universities and their assembled faculties have special gifts that may be brought to bear in this endeavor. They tend to have a sound grasp of the Durkheimian model of community (see pp. 39-41) and its accompanying concept of moral order, and they embrace its importance in a "community of scholars." They work well with worldviews and appreciate their value for providing order to knowledge and the pursuit of truth. They resonate well with the notion of covenant over contract, and tend to be committed to the pursuit of truth over power. They often see academic freedom as having sound foundation in the biblical call to exercise Christian freedom. These gifts, among others, have extraordinary potential for creating and nurturing an ethos of freedom in which academic freedom can thrive.

But for many Christian colleges and universities, taking full advantage of these opportunities for leadership will be a "tough call." It will require renewed commitment and reallocation of resources. Some will need to shake off elements of intimidation, parochialism, and isolationism. It will demand new ways of seeing and doing some things; it will take a broader vision of their role in the larger academy. It will call for "common cause" with others in developing and articulating a fully orbed Christian worldview. It will mean developing a tolerance for risk, and for the scorn that some intellectual guilds reserve for new ideas and experimentation. For they must now, together and individually, determine whether there is the courage and the will to make such an effort. Their faculties, along with Christian academics everywhere, will also need to join hands and muster the intellectual stamina and personal commitment to "stay the course" toward intellectual freedom and integrity in an academy which seems only to be moving deliberately in an opposite direction. But once begun, I am persuaded there are many in the larger academy who will embrace the effort as healthy for all of higher education. They will lend a hand and a voice in support of academic freedom as newly defined and implemented in strategic segments of the academy. They will embrace the goal of establishing an ethos of freedom throughout the academy.

Given the present "state of things" in the academy, how realistic is it to expect that the modest proposals of this book can make a difference? Frankly, I don't know, but I do have hope. Perhaps that is because I am reminded of German sociologist and social theorist Georg Simmel's (1950) haunting description of the function of "the stranger" in providing new hope and threat to a community. Because the stranger presents unexpected responses and new ways of being and perceiving reality, she offers the threat and opportunity of breaking through tacitly assumed patterns, comfortable but uncreative and unproductive styles of living and perceiving the world.

This stranger, however, is not conceptualized as the wanderer who comes today and goes tomorrow. Rather, she is the stranger who comes today and stays well beyond tomorrow. She is a potential wanderer, of course, but she has chosen not to move on. Her position in the community, then, is determined by the fact that she has not belonged to it from early on, and that she imports qualities into it which do not and cannot stem from the community itself. She is, at least in part, what Marsden (1997) and others have called a "resident alien" when considering the role of the Christian scholar in the secular academy. To be such a stranger is to be in a positive relationship to the community and fosters a unique form of interaction with it. This stranger takes on the positive role of being a quasi-member of the community while simultaneously an outsider to it. She both cares about the community and confronts it with new ways of perceiving its life together and in interaction with others. She is more objective and introspective in the sense that she carries less cultural baggage than those members who are fully committed to the unique ingredients and peculiar tendencies of the community. In a word, the stranger enjoys a special freedom in the community; she is not tied down in her actions and perceptions by the habits, pieties, and precedents of the community. The stranger, in a sense, is both near and far, both inside and outside, yet she can lead a community to new levels of understanding and development. The stranger can bring new vision to a community and be a prophetic voice.

The academy today desperately needs a stranger — one with the high qualities of rigorous thought, of patience for deliberation and civil debate, of charity and fairness toward differences, and of an unerring sense of direction for the pursuit of truth. I believe that worldview can be such a stranger in the academic community today, and that Christian scholars can and must play the positive roles of strangers in the broader academy. Both are well equipped for the role. Over the past two decades, modernists, perhaps inadvertently, have moved the academy to acknowledge that cognition, or knowing, is subjective, mediated, and contextual. They, along with the academy as a whole, have essentially established the impossibility of doing scholarship that is value-free and pursuing truth from an entirely neutral perspective. Consequently, the legitimacy of worldview and the Christian scholar has been acknowledged at the theoretical level, but not yet at the practical level. And although some postmodernists have unfortunately carried this acknowledgment to an extreme relativism, it has paved the way for the strangers — worldview and Christian scholars — at the practical as well as the theoretical level in the academy. Perhaps — just perhaps, postmodernist excesses have paved the way for a moderating and reasonable voice.

A large proportion of the professoriate today sees the pursuit of truth as conditioned by worldview, even though few have assessed its impact on their scholarship or its implications for academic freedom. Most have acknowledged that all intellectual endeavors begin somewhere — with first principles and worldviews — and that it is more honest and more freeing to say so openly rather than pretend otherwise. They may now be ready to openly and more explicitly integrate both into the practical fabric of all scholarship and intellectual interchange. The Enlightenment is past, and the academy is ready for a stranger.

The world is in many ways a technological wasteland today, not because the Enlightenment objectivity or scientific methods are worthless, but because they by themselves reveal nothing about values or the meaning of life, or what it means to be human. And to me this is not only a call for worldview and faith considerations at the religious and philosophical levels, but a new emphasis on perspectival assessment at all levels of scholarship and education. The academy must come to appreciate the centrality of worldview for human and humane understanding, and for providing meaning in life and faith for eternity upon death.

For centuries, secular humanism and Enlightenment fervor have held that moral and religious and spiritual questions can only be resolved by reason alone. Some still believe that (Wilson, 1998). But it has become increasingly apparent that such a belief is just that — a belief, a faith, a kind of religion of its own. It no longer provides answers that seem adequate even to many who tried hard to be faithful to them. It has not defended itself well against the onslaught of nihilists and postmodernists. And, interestingly, today it is often the brightest and most able who are acknowledging that we have come to the edge of a failed Enlightenment, and that we must be stepping beyond into something new and untried but not yet transparent. Indeed, they seem ready for a stranger.

Enter worldview and Christian scholars. Christian scholars, equipped with a growing understanding and appreciation of the practical value of the worldview concept, can provide leadership in coming to something new and productive. They can embrace the value of Enlightenment contributions while asserting the legitimacy and utility of worldview considerations. The empirical findings of science and the philosophical reflections of worldviews can be converged in a scholarly frame of mind, rather than adversarially, and scholars can begin to search out fruitful hypotheses on a new frontier of research and scholarship. Mutual respect will replace automatic hostility. In such a context, even conflict and disagreement will be dealt with civilly and can bear great intellectual fruits. All parties will struggle to go deeper and start anew in a fresh and productive way. Academic freedom can thrive in such a setting, where everything is subject to rigorous inquiry. The pursuit of truth within such an ethos of freedom will be an altogether fitting and fruitful response to a new alliance of science and worldview in the academy.

I believe that we in the academy can come once again to understand that educational statesmanship and sound scholarship are not the craving for power we see so much of today but, rather, because ideas and truth matter dearly, are a high calling of self-denial and self-sacrifice for the cause of truth. These characteristics arise out of community and covenant, not chaos and contract, and they thrive within an ethos of freedom. Only such statesmanship and scholarship, nurtured within an ethos of freedom, will embrace and protect the unstinting pursuit of truth and the courage to tell it. Such statemanship and scholarship will speak to the heart of things with integrity and conviction, and they will enhance our common cause toward academic freedom because they will come from statesmen and scholars who are servants, not rulers, of the greater good.

An Expanded Statement
of the Mission of Calvin College:
Vision, Purpose, Commitment

October 7, 1992

PART I:
SHAPING A COLLEGE MISSION

Introduction: Bridging Traditions

Calvin College's mission originates in the commitments that have shaped the college's identity since its beginning. These commitments are well expressed in the quotation from John Calvin inscribed on the college seal: *"I offer my heart to you, Lord, promptly and sincerely."* Our mission begins with faith and the call to serve God.

At Calvin, the Reformed tradition of Christian faith has been and continues to be our guide to hear God's voice and to respond obediently

---

Note: Following are abbreviations and titles of four major Calvin College documents referenced in this report and cited in the bibliography:

CLAE — *Christian Liberal Arts Education*
PECLAC — *Professional Education in the Christian Liberal Arts College*
ACE — *Adult and Continuing Education at Calvin College*
GRADS — *Graduate Education: A Report on Advanced Degrees and Scholarship*

to God's call. It is a living tradition of Christian faith that draws upon historic confessional statements of the Church, both past and present, in a continuing effort to understand God's redeeming purposes toward creation. This confessional identity informs all that we seek to do. It shapes our vision of education, scholarship, and community.

Enduring confessional traditions are realized in the faith and practice of specific communities of God's people. The Christian Reformed Church is the community that gave birth to Calvin College. It continues to be the confessing community that immediately supports the college as its covenantal partner in mission. The college and church draw strength from one another as we engage in the work that God has given us to do.

These two interconnected aspects of the college's identity, our confessional identity as a Reformed Christian college and our covenantal identity as a partner with the Christian Reformed Church, provide a framework within which decisions about the implementation of mission can be made. Our confessional identity encourages and directs us as we reach out to form ties with those who share the substance of our commitments and vision. Our covenantal relationship with the church secures our commitments and vision and reminds us to nurture, challenge, and draw wisdom from the family whose history we share.

Calvin College in Relation to the Reformed Tradition

Among the different genres of Christian colleges, Calvin identifies itself as a confessional college related to the Christian Reformed Church. This distinguishes it from many evangelical Christian colleges which historically have developed around theological reactions (e.g., fundamentalism) or approaches to Christian living (e.g., pietism) that cross over confessional traditions. And although a college of the Christian Reformed Church, as a confessional college Calvin is also distinguished from those institutions whose Christian identity lies chiefly in their formal ecclesiastical ties to the denominations of which they are a part.

What does it mean for Calvin to maintain a confessional identity or, more particularly, an identity as a Reformed Christian educational institution? Primarily, it means that our approach to education is set within a tradition of biblical interpretation, worship, and Christian practice expressed in the creeds of the Reformed-Presbyterian churches having their roots in the Protestant Reformation. Calvin embraces the expressions of this tradition in the Heidelberg Catechism, the Belgic Confession, and the Canons of Dort as authoritative historic guides to our understanding of scripture and its claims on our lives. A contemporary testimony of this tradition, *Our World Belongs to God: A Contemporary Testimony*, demonstrates the continuity and flexibility of these historic faith-claims.

The creeds represent the work of the church as it sought to give obedient witness to God's Word in response to the challenges, sufferings, and opportunities of its day. Confessions, then, are formed by historic actions of a community of faith when it listens to scripture anew and recognizes current cultural realities in order to shape obedient discipleship. At their best, confessions provide a community of faith with a prophetic voice that the world can hear. Used appropriately, they are guides in a continuing common effort of reexamining the scriptures to hear God's call.

Calvin's confessional identity arises from a specific community of faith, a particular people of God who continue to seek obedient discipleship in this confessional way. This understanding provides the foundation for Calvin's relationship with the Christian Reformed Church. The Christian Reformed Church is the community of faith that gave birth to the college out of its desire to practice Christian discipleship more effectively. While a part of a broader confessional community, this denomination forms the confessing community whose life of faith continues to uphold the college in its mission.

Calvin College is a part of a broader Reformed confessional tradition from which it draws strength. The collective experiences of other Reformed and Presbyterian denominations in the United States and abroad provide resources which can enrich, and in some cases constructively challenge, our understanding of the Christian identity we bear. It is with a concern for Calvin's place in all of these communities that we attempt to identify some of the distinctives of a Reformed confession that may guide our understanding of mission today.

Characteristics of a Reformed Christian Confession

It is difficult to try to organize Reformed belief around any single concept or motif. Nevertheless, there are distinctive themes that characterize the Reformed expression of the Christian faith. These include the following. God is sovereign over all of creation. The scope of humanity's rebellion against God is total, affecting every aspect of creation, including every area of human life. In divine grace God acted unconditionally in Jesus Christ to redeem humanity and all creation from sin and evil. We receive God's salvation through faith alone, which is a product of divine grace. The Bible is our only infallible guide for faith and practice in the Christian life. All believers stand in direct relationship and communion with God through the Holy Spirit. We are called to experience God's grace regularly conveyed in the preaching of the Word and administration of the sacraments. All believers are called to serve the Lord as witnesses to Christ's love in every area of life and as agents of renewal in the creation.

These confessional elements may be brought together in the affirmation that we live in a covenantal relationship with God through Jesus Christ. The concept of covenant implies an agreement between consenting parties. But God's covenant with us has a special character, being initiated by God alone in sovereign grace. We have been formed in relationship with God and this intimate relationship is upheld by God's promise. Although divinely initiated and upheld, God's covenant requires our grateful response in lives of faith expressed in service to the Lord. Thereby the covenant establishes our relationships with other persons, forming us into a people who practice God's covenantal love with one another.

The Reformed confessional vision identifies this covenant pattern through the four great moments of human history: creation, fall, redemption, and fulfillment. In creation God initiated a relationship of love with everything created, manifested in the very order and pattern of what God made.

Yet humanity is unique among the objects of God's love, having been created to represent God on the earth. We are the stewards of God's whole creation with the responsibility to help the creation flourish while we also respect and preserve what God declared good.

Created to acknowledge God's claims and enact God's purposes in created reality, human beings have an innately religious character. Life cannot be divided into sacred and secular realms. Right human action begins in worship of our covenant Creator; wrong human action begins in ignoring or rejecting God's authority.

The tragedy of our human existence is that men and women, created to live in responsible freedom as God's children, exchanged God's truth for a lie, and served created things rather than the Creator. Humanity replaced its worship of God with the worship of idols, setting personal desire over devotion to God's revealed will. The effects of this disobedience are total in scope. Since we are covenantally bound to acknowledge God's rule in all areas of life, all of human life suffers the effects of denying this worship. Sin penetrates the deepest desires of our hearts, affecting the way we believe and the things we believe. Because our covenantal responsibilities extend to the physical as well as the human creation, scripture teaches that the entire creation has come under a curse. A universal illness has been unleashed and is directed toward undoing our covenant life.

The relationship between creation and the Creator was marred, but God's covenant promises were not broken. Throughout history God intervened in human life to redeem it. Finally, God became one with us in the person of Jesus Christ. Jesus lived in obedient covenant love with God, fully revealing the design of God's image in human life. He fulfilled God's covenant promises in his death, liberating humanity and all of creation from its enslavement to sin. He restored creation's relationship with God in a new covenant by his resurrection victory over death.

Through the Holy Spirit, God in Christ continues this covenant relationship today. In the midst of all creation's brokenness, God continues to uphold the order and pattern of creation, which reveals the divine claims to all humanity. At the same time God chooses a people to receive Christ's forgiveness by faith, live in renewed covenant relationship, and enter into eternal life. God's people are to live as the visible embodiment of the covenant promises. They manifest the universal scope of divine love; drawn from every tribe and language and people and nation, they become one body, one priesthood, one church.

Through this people God declares the restoration and completion of the creation. The church calls men and women to faith in Jesus Christ, and as agents of covenant renewal the people of God work to see God's reign over the whole creation. We are called to correct the exploitation and oppression of people, to alleviate pain in the world, and expunge evil from ourselves. The confessing community forms the principal witness to the awakening reign of God, and provides a vision of spiritual liberation that also requires liberation from injustice and bondage.

Confessional Themes and Calvin's Present Mission

If the preceding is taken as a summary of the major elements of a Reformed confessional vision, then certain themes may be singled out to guide our consideration of Calvin's mission. Remembering that we are called to obey God as whole persons in every area of life, we believe that education should explicitly connect the way we think with the way we live. We recognize the importance of leading students to identify their own idols, whether materialistic values or selfish individualism or secular ideologies. We encourage them to see the actual faces of human suffering and need.

We view the challenges and opportunities of scholarship confessionally. Remembering that God preserves a creational order which may be witnessed in theories that are not explicitly Christian, we also remember how this is God's world, upheld by divine grace, and revealing of God's will. Therefore, we also recognize the importance of developing theories and programs of research based upon a clear acknowledgment of God's covenantal claims.

We view the challenges and opportunities to develop community relationships at Calvin confessionally. Our life together as students, staff, and faculty should be organized to promote mutual trust and accountability, responsible freedom, friendship, and Christian love. Christ's church is characterized by the unity of diverse persons, who contribute different formative experiences to our understanding of the faith. We affirm the goal of seeking, nurturing, and celebrating cultural and ethnic diversity at the college. Remembering that the church of Jesus Christ is to live as one people by his power and command, we also encourage the development of greater dialogue and cooperation with individuals and institutions of various Christian denominations.

To place oneself confessionally in the Reformed tradition is far more than to place oneself in a particular church or denomination or even a mode of worship. The uniqueness of the Reformed understanding of the institutional church inheres in its assertion that the church is a living organism comprised of believers with Christ as their head. As we form alliances with other expressions of the Christian faith, we do so as a living body of God's agency, knit together with other believers on the basis of our common confession.

Calvin College in Relation to the Christian Reformed Church

While Calvin College is allied confessionally with other educational institutions and ecclesiastical bodies in the Reformed tradition of the Christian faith, it maintains a special relationship within that tradition with the Christian Reformed Church. As it looks toward its future, the college affirms its continuing relationship with the denomination that formed and governs it. Especially when seen in terms of a covenantal relationship for mutual service in God's kingdom, the benefits of this historically-proven relationship guide the future mission both of the college and of the church.

In a piece of ecclesiastical committee work cautiously labeled "Pre-advice," the Synod of 1898 considered the "endeavor to organize a College in conjunction with the Literary Department of our Theological School, so that our young people, who received advanced education, no longer have to wander in various institutions outside our circles, but can be molded by our own reformed interests" (Acts of Synod, 1898, p. 57). The supporting rationale registered arguments familiar to nearly any Christian college today: the need for a "well-rounded" or liberal arts education, and the need for training in a particular tradition of the Christian faith. The notable distinction lay in the explicit sense, appearing often in random qualifications, that such training was ultimately directed toward seminary training and eventual service in the ministry of the denomination. Nonetheless, the concept of a liberal arts education from a Reformed perspective lay there in embryonic form.

Financial quotas were established and paid, buildings acquired and erected. The college itself matured as a Reformed institution of the liberal arts. Issues concerning ownership or privatization seemed to disappear into the background; as long as they stayed there, all seemed well. The world of Calvin College and the Christian Reformed Church prospered apace, despite upheavals in both American society and American higher education. Until 1957.

The considerations of the 1957 Synod on the state of the college occurred at a crucial moment in the college's history, for they were tied to the purchase of and move to the Knollcrest campus. As the physical plant of the college underwent change, the very foundation of the college's relationship to the church came into question. If separation were to occur, surely this seemed the propitious moment. The heady excitement of change charges nearly every word of the 1957 Synod's dealings with college matters. That this same synod saw fit to affirm a bedrock relationship during such momentous change seemed to strengthen the foundation of church-college unity. It recognized a living relationship between two separate parties interested in a mutual mission in God's kingdom.

Showing the influence of Kuyperian[1] thinking, yet without a compelling warrant for complete separation of the two spheres, the study committee of the 1957 Synod distinguished between the proper tasks of church and college. The tasks of the church, for example, include (1) training of young people, (2) preparing members for Christian service, and (3) bringing the truth of scripture to bear upon learning and Christian living. The tasks of the college are (1) to provide a liberal arts education, (2) to engage in Christian scholarship, and (3) to apply the truth to "the present situation," or the world at large.

Church and college, then, constitute distinct spheres of kingdom service with their separate and largely autonomous tasks. Yet, the college is also a ministry of the church, effecting a mission in the world by means of higher education that the church in its specialized ministry is not equipped to do. Despite their separate identities and functions in God's kingdom, a covenantal relationship unites them. Under the dispensation of grace, this covenantal relationship should be construed as a mutual pledge of fidelity, service, and support between partners, in which the distinct activities of each work for the betterment of both.

---

1. After Abraham Kuyper, the Dutch church and political leader (1837-1920), whose ideas and vision of the cosmic lordship of Jesus Christ shaped Christian thinking in the Netherlands and beyond.

Why the Church Needs the College

To state that the Christian Reformed Church and Calvin College hold a covenantal relationship is not to suggest that the relationship is therefore always harmonious. Church and college are both, after all, human institutions, and have at times exhibited the fallenness of their humanity in uncongenial ways. While it seems inevitable that tensions might arise between two closely allied parties, pursuing different means to a common end, such tensions are not necessarily bad. Indeed, tensions often provide opportunity for reassessment and growth; a lack of tension may simply signal decay.

In an arena of potential conflicts, the questions of why the college needs the church and why the church needs the college acquire renewed urgency. Either for principle or for pragmatic reasons, it would appear to some to be a fairly painless procedure to sever the church from the business of ownership and the college from ecclesiastical control. To do so, however, would also risk stripping the college of a vital tradition and the church of an agency of mission. The benefits of maintaining the relationship may be understood by asking why the church needs the college and why the college needs the church.

Reformed Higher Education

The Christian Reformed denomination does not locate itself in a posture of separation from the world, but seeks to be an agent of change in the world. This world belongs to God, so Reformed people confess, and, although fraught with evil, this world may be reclaimed under the dominion of Christ. Thus the task of Reformed believers is to bring a redemptive message to bear everywhere and in all things of this world.

Under this principle of a vigorous redemptive mission, the Christian Reformed Church has committed itself to Christian education, believing that in all areas of education the task of God's people is to engage the world in order to change and redeem it. Thus, Reformed believers see education as a ministry, a means through one particular channel of appropriating, forming, and redeeming knowledge and culture. Out of such a vision Calvin College was born.

Calvin College continues to be the capstone in the denomination's commitment to higher education. Here the denomination says that

Christian higher education is important to us. It accords with our tradition and our faith. It is a living organism effecting a historically tested vision.

In founding the college, the church declared that it was to be a training ground in doctrine and faith. Such was not to abrogate the task of the church to train in doctrine and faith, but to expand the task that the church begins. The college trains in doctrine and faith by engaging the world, by educating Christians beyond simple belief to effective belief, by equipping Christians to transform the world in their individual areas of calling.

Intrinsic to the Reformed tradition has been the sense of the significance of each calling — Christians called to serve God in their vocations. The college shapes that calling by finding areas of integration between faith and vocation, an effort that remains a primary educational objective of the college. Through the college the church demonstrates that the life of the mind is important to Christian living.

Outreach to Academic Communities

Calvin College has always been gifted with inventive scholars and creative intellectuals as well as fine teachers. As such, the college has achieved a position of respect, both in the community of Christian colleges and also in the larger academic world.

Whereas once the faculty saw its primary task in scholarship as educating the church, largely through such avenues as denominationally allied journals, over the last twenty years the faculty has increasingly turned its scholarship toward the broader academic community. Faculty members have served in influential leadership positions in learned societies. They have conducted seminars and presented scholarly work in diverse ways that reach all levels of academia. They have served in editorial positions on numerous journals. Research publications have become valued in the general academy as in the Christian community.

In view of its contribution to scholarship, the college represents one powerful branch of mission of the church. The church requires an academic community to effect this ministry, and to build bridges to the intellectual community of North America and beyond. This ministry best occurs from the college, where scholarship is kindled daily in the classroom, and where new generations of scholars are being formed.

Curator of Heritage

While scholarship that is influential upon the larger academy has become a mainstay of the college's mission, that task is not accomplished at the expense of a scholarly mission to the church. One area that has always distinguished Calvin College from other colleges related to the denomination has been this special task of serving as the curator of the denominational heritage. Traditions are seldom lost through tension; they are easily lost through neglect. The scholarly work at Calvin College and the teaching that derives from it provide a lively interchange with the cultural and theological legacy of the denomination. Through the teaching and scholarship of Calvin faculty, that legacy is both assembled and interpreted for the church.

Calvin College is equipped to do so in special ways. The agencies of the church are designed to do the business of the denomination, but not to maintain its curatorship. The college, on the other hand, has established specific centers of scholarly research devoted to the denominational heritage — the Meeter Center and Heritage Hall collections in particular. Furthermore, the college provides the scholarly activity of assembling, analyzing, and assessing such materials through the labor of librarians, archivists, and professional directors.

Such materials are intrinsically worthy of sustained scholarly interest. In the present case the college and church work in concert for the preservation of a special but common heritage, with the recognition of the clear gifts of the college to administer and enact that preservation.

Preparing Church Leaders

This special relationship is supported, furthermore, by the fact that a primary task of the college has been and remains today the education of people of the denomination. That relationship between church and college is affirmed by the fact that the sons and daughters of the denomination constitute the greatest percentage of students at the college. While respecting the broader mission of the college to higher education and society in general, there exists a special relationship between denomination and college.

That fact implies certain things about the education students receive. While it is no longer possible to assume that all Calvin students

163

enter with a fundamental knowledge of Reformed traditions and creeds, it remains the task of the college to educate in the context of those traditions and creeds. A specific, rather than general, shaping of theological contexts and Christian beliefs influences the teaching of instructors at the college.

The college thereby provides training in leadership for the church. It instructs people in ways of analysis and in forming a vision for Christian living. It guides people toward vocations by instruction in decision-making processes and by providing the acquisition of a base of knowledge that will enable a person to act wisely and well in a chosen profession.

Christian Leadership in Culture

Calvin College also provides a training ground where believers are becoming Christian leaders of society. The college serves the church by developing the Christian mind, one that investigates freely, analyzes carefully, and judges by biblical standards. The Christian mind grapples with the world at large; the Christian college trains that mind to do so.

Especially important in this regard, for example, is training students to engage modern cultures. The classroom is a context for looking outward, for equipping students with an understanding of the world in which they live and for bringing a redemptive message to that world. The college thereby serves as a mission by the church to modern culture.

That training also, however, informs the church itself. If the college is a bridge between the church and culture, the traffic on the bridge is two-way. In the classroom, students also achieve an understanding of the way God is at work in the world generally. Through the college's interims abroad, for example, students may experience first-hand the religious activity in other cultures and various expressions of faith. As they bring these different expressions from a world community of believers to bear upon their own religious experience, the effect is often a revitalizing one for the local congregation.

The college serves as a kind of window both to modern culture and to the larger Christian church. Through this window, the denomination may observe an entire dimension of life not readily observable simply in the context of the local church. Thereby the denomination itself can grow spiritually in its understanding of the modern age, its mission to modern culture, and its partnerships with other Christian communities which share in the task.

The college, then, remains a necessary and effective instrument of mission for the Christian Reformed Church. To the church the college represents not merely support for, but a deeply-rooted commitment to, Christian higher education. By means of the college, the church reaches out to other academic communities, establishing relationships impossible apart from the college. Moreover, as it values its own heritage, so too should the church value its college, for the college functions significantly as a curator of that heritage. Finally, the church needs the college for its important role in forming leaders, inspired by Christian belief, nurtured in a Reformed world and life view, tutored in intellectual practices, both for the church and for our larger culture.

Why the College Needs the Church

The close relationship historically maintained between the college and the church has bestowed a sense of special identity upon the college that is enjoyed by few other Christian colleges. Calvin College is not simply one more Christian college. While Calvin College maintains a leadership position in the Christian College Coalition, and while the college maintains ties with a larger network of Christian colleges, the college also cherishes a distinctiveness based to a large degree upon its being the college of the Christian Reformed Church. This relationship with the church provides specific benefits to the college.

A Community of Faith in the Reformed Tradition

In an age of spiritual relativism, the Christian Reformed Church provides the college with a community of faith which is larger than the college itself. Any Christian college may have its own confessional standards, guiding values, and lists of prescribed and proscribed activities to effect its beliefs and values. The denomination provides an orderly community for establishing the expression of the historic faith in the contemporary world. While the college is an educational community, albeit one in which faith may be enacted in curricular pursuits, the church provides the core of a religious community of faith that supports the educational ministry of the college.

In reflection on the value of the Reformed tradition to educational pursuits, Nicholas Wolterstorff observes in *Keeping Faith* that "What ultimately binds us together is not allegiance to a certain hierarchy, as in the Orthodox and Roman churches; nor adherence to liturgical prescriptions, as in the Anglican Church. What binds us together is the declaration: This we do confess" (p. 17). The value of the Christian Reformed Church to the college lies precisely within the pale of an orderly, unified community that provides the basis of "This we do confess."

A Community of Values

College students find themselves at a critical point in shaping and confirming the values that will guide the rest of their lives. The avowed purpose of Calvin College is to educate in such a way that those values will be Christian ones, in accordance with biblical revelation. Such a view provides both the coherence of our curriculum and a goal for our curriculum. The church provides the college with moral authority.

Over the years Synod has enacted many such decisions that guide the teaching, scholarship, and daily living at the college. For example, Synod investigated and established a position on life issues well before the landmark Roe v. Wade case of 1973. Synod established decisive moral views on how we are to consider people of other cultures and racial backgrounds, and thereby has identified and condemned the racism prevalent in our culture. Synod adopted a resolution on pornography and sexuality that addresses a major moral concern in society. These positions grant a common reference point for the frequently more pluralistic views found at the college. Thereby Synod has established a structure for the college within which further debate may occur.

A Community of Loyalty

The college needs the special base of loyalty, support, and direction from a dedicated constituency that the church provides. While the tensions that exist between both parties often receive the greater share of attention, the loyal support evidenced by so many church members should be nurtured.

The tasks of the college are education and scholarship — revealing and investigating. Frequently that two-fold task is a daunting, even lonely, one. It is less so when it is done in the context of a loyal, supportive constituency, one committed to spiritual intercession for the college. In an age of increasingly pragmatic considerations about the work of the college educator, that common bond of spiritual support becomes ever more precious.

As in the past, the college continues to rely upon a common vision and a common spirit to effect its calling. The dominant historical pattern has been the Pauline concept that we are members of one body, each performing special tasks, each united in a common purpose. In contrast with the specialization and fragmentation that marks higher education generally, the spiritual unity that our church and college have enjoyed in the past has been a blessing and a formidable witness.

That unity has received special emphasis under the covenantal relationship of church ownership. To the church, the college is one part of *our* body, one requiring devotional intercession and spiritual support.

The church, then, provides the college with a definitive Reformed legacy, an articulation of one tradition in the exercise of Christian faith. It brings this distinctiveness to the college in a theological heritage that antedates the founding of the college, that has shaped the history of the college, and that continues to provide a framework for the activities of the college. Moreover, within biblical authority and in its interpretation of Reformed distinctiveness, the church supplies the college with a moral framework for Christian living and ethical decision-making. Above all, perhaps, the church supplies the college with a supportive community of faith, a sense that the college is not alone in its high mission of Reformed education but is nurtured by the prayers of its constituency, by the grace of God, and by the vigorous direction of the Holy Spirit.

Conclusion

While noting the benefits of covenantal relationship between church and college, the college also bears a responsibility to its broadened constituency and its changing educational mandate. In this case, the sense of tradition upheld and valued must also be flexible enough to permit the college a certain latitude in meeting the challenges of the future. Calvin College now draws a substantial proportion of its student body and faculty from various Christian constituencies. Similarly, its sphere of influence extends far beyond the parameters of the Christian Reformed Church to other Christian and educational communities. Having a well-defined place to stand in its own religious tradition, Calvin College bears the responsibility to join with these allied communities to achieve its primary objective of reclaiming and transforming all creation in service to Christ and under the guidance of scripture. Our task is not to transform the world to *our* view, but to engage partners to transform the world to God's intent.

In a history of higher education in America replete with dissolved church-college relationships, the legacy of the Christian Reformed Church and Calvin College is a powerful and enviable one. That unity has served, and will continue to serve, both parties well.

PART II:
ENACTING A COLLEGE MISSION

Introduction

In the coming years, Calvin College must continue to live by the best features that have marked it from the start. Maintaining its character in changing times might require altering various policies, but its salient ends and means continue. Several such traits have characterized the college from the outset and remain guiding principles for engaging the future.

From the start, Calvin has aspired to provide formal education marked by rigor and excellence, infused in whole and in every part by a vital Reformed Christian vision. The guiding commitment and the quality of education are not regarded as options, as separate, or as being subordinated one to the other. Calvin's religious commitment undergirds its dedication to uncompromising quality of teaching, learning, and scholarship.

From the start, Calvin College has combined liberal arts and pre-professional education. It has not layered these two nor run them along parallel tracks, but so thoroughly intertwined them that education in the broader, fundamental issues of human endeavor culminates in an enriched, responsible, Christian understanding of work and vocation. Education at Calvin College aims at developing that Christian wisdom which envelops knowing *and* doing, which compels perspective and praxis to enrich each other.

Calvin College has long been egalitarian in culture, faculty-run in governance, and communal in sociology. Calvin promotes a structure and atmosphere which equitably divide burdens and opportunities, which encourage the development of gifts of individuals and groups, and which make mutuality in service of God and to neighbor the means as well as the end of its education.

Calvin College has always participated in broader trends in higher education, yet has also served a community that for much of its history felt alien or separate in North American society. For its own well-being and the fulfillment of its calling, Calvin maintains both sides of this tension. It genuinely responds to — also learns from — cultural demands and social needs but out of its own set of loyalties. It maintains a critical distance that arises from a clear identity, kindles keen education, and empowers true Christian service.

While different constituencies expect different qualities from the same college, and while different cultural pressures place their demands upon the college, Calvin College continues to testify particularly to Christian education based upon a liberal arts curriculum, to scholarship that shapes the Christian mind and that demonstrates the engagement of that mind with the world, and to a life of community that acknowledges each person as made in the image of God.

The Mission of Calvin College in Education

Firm convictions about the task of Christian education lie at the heart of learning and teaching at Calvin College. As stated in CLAE (pp. 27-38) and reaffirmed in this report, three convictions have special status among us. First, the aim of Christian education is to let faith find expression throughout culture and society. Second, the life of faith, and education as part of that life, find their fulfillment only in a genuine community. Third, the Christian community, including its schools, is called to engage, transform, and redeem contemporary society and culture.

Accordingly, the college sees higher education as a God-given vocation, to be enacted on behalf of the Christian community, for the benefit of contemporary society, and to the praise of God's name. Christian learning and teaching at the college level are not optional frills but essential contributions to Christ's work in the world. Without Christian higher education, the body of Christ would lack much of the careful reflection it needs to be a thoughtful and effective agent of renewal.

Calvin College seeks to engage in vigorous liberal arts education that promotes lives of Christian service. This mission in education affects the goals that the college sets for its programs, the contexts in which various fields are studied, and the pedagogical techniques used to fulfill those goals and to examine those fields.

Educational Goals

To ask what are the goals of education is also to ask how we should live. As Christians we offer our hearts to the Lord. In so doing, we recognize purposes and goals for education that go beyond simply knowing about reality or simply acquiring competence in some academic or professional field. Knowing entails responsibility and competence includes caring. Accordingly, we acknowledge several, interlocking, educational goals at Calvin College.

At the heart of our programs lies the pursuit of *knowledge* of our triune God as revealed in scripture and creation, and as expressed through religious traditions in general and the Reformed Christian tradition in particular. Along with such knowledge come an understanding of God's world and critical inquiry into its problems and potential. We need to understand the structure and integrity of nature, discern the cultural and social forces that shape our world, and address the needs and issues of contemporary life. We also need to know ourselves — our nature, gifts, and callings — as we engage this world.

So that such knowledge responsibly guides Christian living, we encourage insightful and creative *participation* in society. Our programs aim to foster sensitivity to the working of God and creation and respect for the variety of gifts that are offered by people of different gender, race, age, and ability. We strive to learn an appreciation for diverse cultures, an attentiveness to the religious meaning of life's events, and an awareness of ways to renew the world for God's glory.

Our educational goals include the development of abilities and *competencies* that enable people to be effective in the tasks of knowing and caring. Gaining competencies, however, is not enough; they should be used in ways that honor God in the tasks for which they are intended. Competence is not only a skill; there is a moral purpose as well as a technical purpose for the competence. Competencies that are emphasized at Calvin College include reading and writing standard English well, listening and speaking effectively, employing graphic and numeric forms of communication, exercising valid and sound reasoning, making discerning use of technology and popular culture, and maintaining personal health.

In order for knowing to include responsibility and for competence to include caring, the mind and heart must be one. To do this in a way that is faithful to Jesus Christ, we need to foster *commitments*. A goal, then, of education at Calvin College is to foster a thoughtful and compassionate commitment to Christian faith and to such values as stewardship, justice, truth, and gratitude. These commitments include a joyful trust in the triune God, an attachment to a Christian worldview, a strong desire to connect theoretical understanding with Christian conduct, a willingness to contribute to the church and society in various careers, and a dedication to the cause of Christ's renewal of the earth and human life.

Christian education at the college level needs to be seen as a dynamic process in which all of us continually try to get our deepest commitments, educational activities, and life practices headed in the same direction. Goals, however, remain abstractions until fulfilled by someone, and fulfilled in a particular program rather than by educational accident. Our educational goals carry certain implications about students at Calvin College, about the academic programs offered to them, and about pedagogical methods used to educate them.

Students at Calvin

Students at Calvin College are engaged in the mission of the college. They participate in the mission of pursuing vigorous liberal arts education for lives of Christian service, producing solid works of art and scholarship, and caring for one another in the performance of tasks. For this reason the college seeks students who are eager to learn, value learning as a gift of God, are curious about creation and culture, and strive to develop individual and communal gifts for leadership and service. Given its mission, the college seeks to serve any student interested in higher education that is shaped by the Christian faith.

While the qualities common to all students at Calvin College are important, both the nature of the church and the nature of education require that the college serve an increasingly diverse student body. Diversity, however, is not only an accident of birth, nor simply a matter of gender, race, or ethnic heritage. Diversity also occurs in ways of thinking and worshiping. The challenge for Calvin College in education is to inform, encourage, and affirm these diversities. The guiding premise for such education is that God's revelation is not restricted to one mindset or worship form, nor indeed to one curriculum or pedagogical method.

The college wishes to serve persons from Christian traditions different from the college's own. This affirms our commitment to being a confessional college and recognizes that Christian traditions are gifts to be strengthened through sharing. Students from other Christian traditions will enrich the community and through their contributions enhance the education.

Moreover, the college strives for ethnic diversity, while also acknowledging its own ethnic roots. The goal of an ethnically diverse college community recognizes that the Christian community transcends cultural and geographical boundaries and we live in a world community. Moreover, a multicultural community will assist in the educational goals of understanding different cultures and promoting understanding between people.

Similarly, the college also seeks to serve students from a variety of socioeconomic backgrounds, from a range of intellectual abilities, and those with disabilities that do not prevent them from the task of learning. Not only does this honor our commitment to being a diverse community, it also recognizes the diverse educational needs that the body of Christ must meet and the diverse ways in which leadership in society occurs. Our academic programs should enable people with different intellectual abilities, socioeconomic backgrounds, and gifts to prepare for positions of leadership and lives of service.

Finally, because of its strategic position among Christian institutions of higher education, the college wishes to serve students of diverse ages and walks of life. It does not restrict its mission to undergraduate students of traditional college age, but seeks to attract and benefit adult learners and graduate students.

The challenge to cultural, social, and academic diversity constitutes an important part of the future mission of the college. The college is not content simply to confirm students in their traditions and prejudices. In order to achieve its goal of leadership the college desires graduates who make a difference in their cities, countries, churches, and places of work. This challenge, moreover, bears implications for the academic programs and curriculum of the college.

Academic Programs

Calvin College currently offers three types of programs: undergraduate, graduate, and continuing education. The oldest, best established, and most heavily enrolled is the undergraduate program, which divides into either disciplinary or professional degree programs. About half the undergraduates pursue disciplinary majors in the humanities, natural sciences, and social sciences. The other half are enrolled in professional programs, with over a third of these students being in education. All undergraduates take a liberal arts core.

Graduate programs and continuing education are relative newcomers at Calvin. The college has stated three purposes for its graduate programs (GRADS 21-50). First, these programs are to train Christian leaders at the graduate level, with particular emphasis on the areas of public service, church work, and education. Second, graduate programs should enhance the teaching, scholarship, and alumni support of Calvin's undergraduate programs. Third, Calvin's graduate programs should serve to develop advanced Christian scholarship aimed at academic, professional, or public audiences.

173

The purpose of the continuing education program at Calvin is to help adult learners understand and address issues of the Christian life in society (ACE 13-15). The primary audience are alumni of the college's undergraduate programs who wish to deepen their reflection on cultural and social issues and become more effective agents of renewal. By serving these students, the college not only recognizes their continuing part in Calvin's mission and community but also seeks to benefit from the insights they gain through engagement with contemporary society.

With such a wide range of programs and students, questions inevitably arise regarding unity, balance, and character of programs. Unity comes from the conviction that in creation and in Christ all of reality coheres and finds meaning. Unity in curriculum and community in education also require a balance in programs offered; a few programs with many students and faculty should not dominate the college curriculum. A full range of disciplinary courses is necessary, and enrollment levels should not serve as the sole guide to whether a course remains in the curriculum. While we affirm the conviction with Abraham Kuyper that "every square inch in the entire cosmos Christ claims as His own" and, as a result, that all of creation is worthy of investigation, the liberal arts, with emphasis upon contextual study, remain central to education at Calvin College. Since the liberal arts are basic to all the college programs, they should also be the most prominent feature of a Calvin College education. Professional programs, graduate programs, and continuing education as well as undergraduate programs should reflect an emphasis on contextual study in the liberal arts.

Contextual Education

The fundamental premise of a contextual view of education is that objects and events do not appear randomly or independently, but rather that they exist and occur within such contexts as the natural, cultural, societal, and spiritual. Moreover, information and ideas about objects and events should be understood within their larger contexts. The aim of such education is to capture a living heritage of information and ideas, rather than seeing them as isolated events stripped of contextual implications and ultimately of contextual reference.

Contextual education seems particularly well-suited for a Christian college. Such education helps one see the working out of God's revelation and redemptive plan in creation, in culture and in the patterns of society. Furthermore, the contextual approach provides a practical means of integrating faith and learning as one discerns the revelation of God in all areas of life and learning and begins to employ Christian beliefs in the relevant contexts of one's own time.

To call attention to contexts requires both an appropriate curriculum and effective pedagogy. The contextual approach should not be relegated to certain disciplines or courses, but should permeate the entire curriculum, at every level, whether undergraduate, graduate, or continuing education, and in every type of program, whether disciplinary, professional, or practical. At the same time, the core courses in Calvin's academic programs should be those which best enable all students to study and understand the wider contexts of their lives and learning.

With the adoption of CLAE in the 1960s, Calvin's curriculum focussed especially on religious, historical, and cultural contexts. To be more precise, it has emphasized Reformed Christianity, Western civilization, and the academic disciplines. Since the 1980s the college has also directed attention to the study of world religions and other Christian traditions, internationalizing the curriculum, and addressing additional areas of culture such as popular art and entertainment. Furthermore, the societal context requires greater attention, along with issues such as poverty, sexism, racism, and the destruction of the environment. Such emphases affect both the core curriculum and the design of majors.

Core Curriculum

The challenges confronting Calvin College in the area of core curriculum resemble those facing most other colleges and universities in North America: fostering common learning, promoting upper-level engagement in the academic disciplines, engaging current world issues, and addressing interdisciplinary subject matter including non-Western or minority cultures. In order to meet these challenges appropriately, the college must achieve as much clarity as possible about the character and role of its core curriculum, and must not let departmental interests and

175

professional certification requirements set its curricular agenda. Every proposal for revision of the core curriculum must demonstrate in detail how it will serve the college's educational goals and give renewed vigor to contextual education.

In contrast to the major, study in the core will usually be more general than study in the major, and the competencies learned will be those basic to the life of an educated person generally rather than for a specific vocation. The goals of the core curriculum extend beyond those for the individual student; they are goals that help shape the educational community of the college. Calvin College students should be part of a vibrant Christian educational community, and they should be prepared for a Christian life in society. The core curriculum, while directing individual students toward the educational goals of the college, contributes significantly to shaping the character of the educational community in both its practices and commitments. It prepares students for a life of Christian citizenship in the world.

Majors

The CLAE document recommends major concentrations and group concentrations, but provides little rationale for this recommendation and leaves the details of concentrations to various departments. PECLAC gives even fewer aims and guidelines for concentrations in professional programs, choosing instead to argue broadly for the legitimacy of professional programs and for their recommended relation to general education requirements. Presumably there was not sufficient debate about the character and role of disciplinary and professional majors to warrant more detailed discussions in CLAE and PECLAC.

Since the adoption of CLAE and PECLAC, two developments have made such discussions more urgent. One is the proliferation of undergraduate majors. The other is the growing conflict between careerism, or the use of an education as a springboard to a career, and vocationalism, or the discovery of one's life calling through education, as the goals of a Christian college education. Taken together, these developments often result in the nature of the academic major being dictated by external forces — professional concerns and accrediting agencies, for example — rather than being shaped by the internal mission of the college. With in-

176

creasing external demands upon a major, one finds a very real danger of the unifying educational goals of the college paling in significance.

These developments affect Calvin College no less than they affect other North American colleges. Indeed, careerism is not restricted to students and departments with professional majors. It also prevails in attitudes toward majors in the disciplines, which in the past were seen as preparations for graduate study leading to academic or learned professions, and now are often measured as training grounds for potentially lucrative careers. The danger in this kind of thinking is that colleges lose sight of their educational goals as various majors are pitted against each other in terms of their potential payoffs. One corrective approach is for all majors, whether professional or disciplinary, to place their fields of study in the larger contexts of culture, society, history, and religion. This approach recognizes the importance of proficiency in a field, but gives equal importance to the way in which one achieves, holds, examines, and assumes such a proficiency.

General education, anchored in the core curriculum, serves to equip all students to live the Christian life in contemporary society. The major should do the same, but equips students to assume specific positions in society and to show expertise in shaping contemporary culture and social institutions. The major is a study in depth: its later courses build on previous courses, and it gives preparation for service with expertise. Through such cumulative and preparatory study in depth, students gain more detailed and complete understanding of a particular field; they come to terms with a definite range of traditions and institutions; they learn to make creative use of specialized methods and techniques; and they gain a concrete vision of how to serve the church and society in a vocation. Since the body of Christ needs many different members to accomplish its work, the major should enable people to respond to Christ's calling by finding suitable vocations through which they can make contributions to the church and society.

As well-educated members of Christ's body, students need specialized expertise, but they also need to serve the body with discernment regarding the place of that expertise in the contexts of life. Calvin's commitment to contextual education calls for innovative approaches to the entire curriculum, together with appropriate strategies of instruction.

Pedagogy

One of the hallmarks of Calvin College has been its steadfast and enduring commitment to excellence in teaching. In accordance with the assertion of the *Faculty Handbook* that "effective teaching is expected of all faculty members" (Appendix I), and in order to maintain and further that excellence, the college appointed a Committee on Faculty Teaching (1987) to examine all areas of pedagogical concern, from methods of instruction to peer and student evaluations of those methods. The mandate to the committee, furthermore, is to provide careful training of new instructors, and ongoing assistance to regular faculty to develop pedagogical effectiveness.

Pedagogical techniques are often closely associated with an instructor's subject matter, the number of students in a given environment, and the tasks at hand. Instruction techniques will probably differ between a laboratory and a lab theater. They will likely differ between a survey course and a seminar. Similarly, pedagogical techniques will differ according to an instructor's personality, prior models, and training. Even the traditional mode of college-level pedagogy — the lecture method — will vary widely depending upon how an instructor delivers the material.

While respecting these variables, Calvin College challenges its teachers to employ pedagogical techniques that quicken the interest of students, recognize the varying learning styles and capabilities of students, and actively engage the student in learning. The teachers also aim to make the subject matter of the disciplines relevant to the lives of students and encourage students to take responsibility for their learning. Teachers are also encouraged to reflect systematically on their pedagogy and to ask whether it achieves the college's purposes.

The college also supports the use of instructional materials and technologies that are appropriate to learning and are within the available resources of the college. Such materials and technologies enhance learning and prepare students to use new approaches in their chosen vocation. The employment of technology should contribute to the pedagogical pluralism which is important to effective teaching and learning.

Faculty members, therefore, are encouraged to a pedagogical pluralism, a willingness to employ a variety of pedagogical methods befitting subject matter, classroom context, and student abilities. One such variation, for example, is the concept of collaborative learning whereby an instructor outlines a problem or question and organizes the students into groups to find solutions or answers. The concept involves several types of peer tutoring and evaluation, as well as group discussions, student-run group presentations, and team projects. Collaborative learning requires students to participate actively in the educational process and to appropriate the materials as their own.

Flexibility of pedagogical methods can also encourage and strengthen connections between the curriculum and co-curriculum. The co-curriculum includes a wide range of events, programs, and organizations outside the classroom setting. This larger network plays a crucial part in the learning of students. It has great potential for helping students test the personal, social, and religious implications of their education.

The most desirable institutional culture at Calvin is one which best accords with our deepest shared convictions about the task of Christian education: that Christian education should let faith find full expression; that genuine community is essential to such faith and education; and that Christian colleges are called to help transform contemporary society and culture. Taken together, these convictions point toward an institutional culture where students take wide-ranging responsibility for their learning, experience their learning as part of a communal undertaking, and direct their learning toward the renewal of contemporary society and culture.

The Mission of Calvin College in Scholarship

The Historical Development of Scholarship at Calvin College

The emphasis upon excellence of teaching at Calvin College should not diminish the importance of scholarship in the college environment. Indeed, this very emphasis, which sees research informing teaching, which sees the classroom as a stimulating arena for the interchange of ideas, and which sees the college as a whole engaged in a communal search for knowledge and in a committed effort to bring knowledge to bear redemptively upon this world, has proven an invigorating stimulus to scholarship.

The scholarship practiced at the college has, nonetheless, undergone substantial change during the college's history. From the 1930s to 1960, it spoke by and large through elite but non-technical journals to educators and the educated laity in conservative Reformed circles, and in critique of the secularistic worldviews that dominated American culture. This effort aimed at establishing, reaffirming, and legitimating the cardinal premises of a "Christian mind" in contradistinction to those of "secular minds." Such efforts were generally undertaken by gifted faculty members on their own time and at their own initiative.

In the past thirty years, without closing off those channels, scholarship among faculty members has turned to more conventional academic and artistic outlets and has taken up issues within the academic disciplines, including both the theoretical foundations in the disciplines, and applied, thematic, or specific case analyses within disciplinary parameters.

During the 1970s and 1980s in particular, a concerted effort has been made by the college to nurture faculty scholarship, particularly as it accords with such objectives of the college as the investigation of religion and culture, faith and learning, the history of the Reformed tradition, and the nature of creation. This emphasis has resulted in several documents to guide and to support scholarly research. The first is the "Constitution of the Calvin Center of Christian Scholarship" (1975; revised 1978 and 1992), which established a center to study a variety of practical and theoretical topics in Christian perspective. The second and third, "Proposal for the Establishment of a Program of Faculty Development Seminars" (1977), and "On the Promotion of Scholarship at Calvin College" (1980), expanded programs of institutionally supported study and research opportunities for the faculty. The fourth, "Report of the Calvin and Calvinism Center Study Committee" (1981), established a study center with opportunities to do advanced research in the history and character of Calvinism. Additionally, the GRADS document (1988, revised 1990) defined certain expectations in scholarship of Calvin faculty. Such documents constitute a serious commitment by the college to fulfill its mission to scholarship.

This time of growth and transition, during which Calvin College scholars have increasingly reached out to a larger audience, has also necessitated attention to issues of academic freedom. In its respect for scholarly and creative work, Calvin College follows a more generous definition of academic freedom than do many Christian colleges (see *Handbook for Teaching Faculty,* Appendix A, Section I, Parts C and D). Essentially faculty members are free to exercise their talents with only three restraints: the confessional standards of the college, the professional standards of the discipline, and the prohibition of propagandizing in the classroom for causes unrelated to their profession as Christian teachers of a discipline. These restraints are not without risk and may be enforced only via due process and by communally accepted standards. Still, they are and should continue to be required in order to maintain the confessional, professional, and educational integrity of Calvin as a college in the Reformed Christian tradition.

At the same time, this very integrity demands a positive, supportive, expansive vision of academic freedom. The integrity of any educational institution resides in a process of free postulation, inquiry, interpretation, and conclusion. While the task of scholars at any college is to keep alive, develop, and pass along the root ideas of a culture, and while the task of scholars at a Christian college is to engage those ideas, to examine them, and to challenge or affirm them as consequential for the Christian faith, the Reformed Christian academic especially feels obligated to engage alternative points of view in order to learn from them, to be challenged by them, and to bring a Reformed and Christian witness to bear upon them.

The Current Situation

Two items in particular have marked the history of scholarship at Calvin College and continue to affect our current scholarship. First, the college has attempted to be egalitarian in its faculty structure. Seeing each member as of equal value, the college strives for equality in terms of rank, compensation, teaching, and advising responsibilities. Moreover, each member has an equal voice in running the affairs of the college. Within this egalitarian structure, scholarship has been seen as an individual gift among many other gifts necessary to the profession of education and the intellectual life of the college. This structure has fostered a rare collegiality and sense of communal purpose at the college. But, second, in its communal purpose to examine ideas, to exercise the life of the mind, and to engage modern culture in all its manifestations, Calvin

College has also acquired and supported a faculty that does a considerable amount of scholarship. The life of the mind that is cherished in the classroom frequently expands beyond the classroom in articles, books, workshops, conferences, and performances for larger audiences.

Scholarship at Calvin College is expressed primarily through four avenues of effort and production. First, individual faculty members have developed their areas of professional expertise through publications and presentations. Many such efforts have achieved prominence on the national academic stage, and bear evidence of an individual's engagement of, mastery over, and contribution to an academic discipline or professional field. Second, Calvin faculty have also assumed leadership in national affiliations of committed Christian scholars and artists within various fields. Such faculty have brought a direct influence to bear upon national and international organizations, some of them specifically concerned with the challenges of integrating faith with learning, others of them predominantly secular organizations dedicated to a certain field. Third, in-house support of individual projects by means of a sabbatical system and Calvin Research Fellowships encourages individual projects of faculty, broadening their professional expertise, providing time for concentrated research yielding significant results, and contributing to classroom teaching. Finally, ventures through the Calvin Center of Christian Scholarship and the Meeter Center have established ties with other communities by bringing their representatives to our campus. Thereby, we benefit as a college by receiving fresh points of view, by stimulating classroom teaching and lectureship opportunities, and by testing our particular premises in the company of others.

Calvin now faces new challenges to continue its achievement and new opportunities to broaden its leadership role in scholarship. For example, other evangelical colleges are joining with Calvin in pursuing perspectival issues. We now work in a spirit of communal scholarship with many institutions, particularly those in the Christian College Coalition. As a result of Calvin's recognition in the broader academic world, some of its scholars have been hired at major research universities. We welcome the extended range of influence that these scholars have had, but we are also challenged to maintain the scholarly excellence of our institution. Furthermore, increased interaction with broader evangelical and secular networks may begin to erode communal loyalty on the part of present and potential faculty members and on the part of the college's supporting constituency. While we welcome diversity and aggressively seek scholarly partnerships with other institutions, we cannot risk losing the clearly identifiable voice of the Reformed tradition.

Before outlining how Calvin might work to meet these challenges and opportunities, we need to define the nature and proper role of scholarship in our Christian academy.

The Nature of Scholarship

Scholarship is not just needed in the Christian academic community for intellectual vitality, prestige, or adornment, but is needed for that community to do its part in the church's larger mission of being God's agent of witness and reconciliation in the world. Preserving the beauty of the world and redressing its pain do not proceed from scholarship alone; neither do they proceed far without it. Scholarship is not just a registering or responsive activity but a shaping, driving force, particularly over the long run and in the echelons of power and authority. Without seeking to dominate the world coercively, Christians must work persistently, intensively, and communally to make their voice heard in the world: as a witness against secularistic pretensions and idolatries, as a witness against their own perversions of the faith, and as a witness for that reconciliation among the peoples and between God and humanity which is offered in Jesus Christ. Committed Christian scholarship is vital to forming, guiding, correcting, and forwarding that witness.

Purposes of Scholarship

Within the Christian community, scholarship may be considered to serve three purposes: *conserving, transforming,* and *enriching*.

Conserving scholarship promotes understanding of the various Christian traditions in order to provide the Christian community with the integrity, vision, and wisdom needed both to frame and to energize its ongoing work. An example of such would be the college's role of curator of historic church documents. Fundamental to conserving scholarship are the research skills of ordering materials, observing significant patterns, and interpreting patterns for the community.

Transforming scholarship may establish Christian criteria for knowledge or for its application, or may implement those criteria in a particular field in such a way as to challenge the wisdom prevailing there or to show the critical, redemptive, or reconciling power of the Christian faith. Transforming scholarship brings to research materials a method for applying analytic skills to a given body of material and theorizing about the significance of that material.

Enriching scholarship brings the insights or methods of the arts and sciences to bear on Christian thought and the understanding of creation and culture. Such scholarship can enhance appreciation for God's creation and human experience, expand the fund of human knowledge and wisdom, help Christians engage in proper self-criticism or self-understanding, and enrich the testimony of the Christian message. The primary focus here is the scholar's engagement of materials of his or her discipline, or the expression of a creative gift. It includes a range of scholarly endeavor from scientific work in the laboratory, to the writing of a book on a literary figure, to the presentation of a creative performance. Such work is marked by its originality and by its contribution and significance to a field of study.

Definition by Audience

Scholarship, which for our purposes we define as concerted, persistent intellectual reflection in a field of study or of creative endeavor, the results of which are communicated to an audience within appropriate conventions, appears in different forms among Calvin College faculty. And while faculty members are called to be scholars, it is nonetheless clear that not all members will fulfill all categories of scholarly endeavor. While we are all members of one body of Christ, we prize the fact that we are highly diverse members, gifted in different ways for different callings. As there is no superiority of gifts in the biblical analogy of the body of Christ, so too no superiority is implied by these categories. Their purpose is to clarify the ways in which research and scholarship are carried out.

By the criterion of audience, scholarship may qualify as *personal*, *applied*, or *advanced*.

Calvin College currently requires *personal scholarship* of all its faculty and defines it to be "that active life of the mind . . . in which the faculty members are engaged as they continue to learn" (Faculty Development Task Force, July 1987, p. 7). This includes staying current in one's field, remaining inquisitive about the world, and interlinking those two qualities in creative and challenging ways. The primary audience of such scholarship is for the professional integrity and improvement of oneself, though it will be communicated quickly to others in — and remains absolutely necessary to — the college community as well; for only through the vibrant intellectual life of individual faculty does teaching stay fresh, collegiality exciting, and community service distinguished.

Applied scholarship is that intellectual reflection which is communicated beyond the college or beyond one's academic-professional circle strictly defined. It can include such work as consulting, counseling, advising, or speaking on topics of extra-collegiate or -academic interest to the extent that these draw from or are informed by one's reading, research, and reflection.

Advanced scholarship can be defined as the generation, interpretation, and evaluation of knowledge or of performance/creative activity for and before one's professional peers, whether these be within or without one's special field of endeavor. Advanced scholarship receives detailed analysis in the GRADS report as a foundation for graduate study (pp. 58f.).

Commitments

To fulfill its mission in scholarship, Calvin College should take concerted and innovative measures to improve scholarly research and exchange within its own house and in broader academic networks. The priorities in this mission may be viewed according to the purposes and audience for scholarship.

Calvin should encourage scholarship to achieve the three purposes of scholarship outlined above. These three feed, correct, and drive one another, and thus go forward best together. They seem to be equally needed for the construction of Christian scholarship and for its address to the broader academic world.

In terms of the criterion of audience, however, different categories need different measures.

As indicated above, *personal* scholarship is already required of Calvin faculty but does not seem to be practiced equally or adequately throughout the faculty. The canons of personal scholarship must be clearly noted at the time of hiring and more strictly enforced at the time of promotion and at subsequent reviews. Every faculty member must be held accountable to the standard of *personal* scholarship, as each member diligently engages the intellectual life of a discipline and brings it to bear upon the classroom and the larger college environment.

Any glimpse at faculty activity will find the practical area of *applied* scholarship in abundance. These efforts should continue to be encouraged in order to reduce the risk of scholars losing touch with the broader audiences that also need their insight; the risk of the college losing some vital, nurturing ties with its constituency; and the risk of scholarship losing "real world" insights and stimulation for its own projects. In particular, the college must make sure to maintain its historic strength in serving the denominational community while broadening the scope of that service to include more civic, professional, and other religious organizations. Applied scholarship is the readiest avenue for such service. To qualify as scholarship, it must reflect persistent intellectual engagement with the substance of the arts and sciences; to qualify as service, it must challenge, instruct, and learn from its audience.

For the next few decades, the promotion of *advanced* scholarship deserves particular attention and new initiatives on the part of the college. The college should provide material, moral, and structural support to those conducting advanced scholarship. This can take any number of forms from flexible contracts (which might reduce teaching or advising loads in exchange for clearly accountable scholarly work), to stipends for summer research equal to those awarded for summer teaching, to the creation of new institutes for Christian scholarship or the re-tooling of current institutes toward advanced rather than only applied research, and to the development of new graduate programs.

In all areas of its scholarship, finally, Calvin must give keen attention to nurturing the resources that have helped distinguish its efforts thus far. These include the concern for forthrightly Christian scholarship that has set Calvin apart from most other institutions. While scholarship is often an individual enterprise, it becomes communal in that Christian scholarship depends fundamentally on the collegial solidarity of purpose and perspective that has marked Calvin historically.

This collegiality has been manifested at the college in many ways: departmental seminars, collaborative research among colleagues, student research participation, lectures by fellows of the CCCS, lectures given by faculty on the occasion of publishing a book. Such mutual support certainly merits continued encouragement and should include the support and exchange of scholarly research across disciplinary and departmental boundaries on campus. Colleagues within and across departments should stimulate, encourage, and hold one another accountable for scholarship.

Such collegiality, however, extends beyond the campus environment as well. One of the foremost means of bringing together scholars in like-minded pursuit of knowledge and direction is through conferences. In recent years individual departments have sponsored conferences that have drawn national and international participation. As Calvin College's leadership in scholarship increases, some administrative channel must be established at the college for the encouragement and conduct of such conferences.

All these efforts require patience and perseverance over the long term, concern for quality above quantity, and conviction of the importance of knowledge and ideas — all of which good scholarship requires and all of which Calvin, by confessional and ethnic heritage alike, has manifested in the past.

The Mission of Calvin College in Community

To have a sense of community is a laudable goal for nearly all groups of people working and living together; to state precisely what constitutes a particular community, however, may well be the most challenging and divisive task for the members of any community. The very elusiveness of the term poses dangers for including the building of community as a mission of the college. The danger is heightened by the dramatic transformation of Calvin College from a small institution serving almost exclusively the sons and daughters of the Christian Reformed denomination to a large and complex institution involving a diverse student population, an increasingly diverse faculty, and also a multiplicity of concerns extending beyond the classroom. Because of that very diversity, earlier assumptions about community have proven inadequate.

187

At Calvin College we seek a specific kind of community — a learning community. The nature of community should grow out of our educational tasks as well as the principle that learning is done communally. Students and faculty together acquire knowledge and insight. Members should help one another cultivate aspirations, nurture commitments, and practice what we profess. In this community learning goes well beyond the classroom, making it possible and necessary that all campus life promote the educational tasks.

The Making of Communities

The college's commitment to community affects its internal life — the way in which students, staff, and faculty work together — and its external relationships with other institutions — the way in which it forms partnerships to work with others toward common goals.

The making of an internal community appears, at least superficially, an easy task. People gather in different capacities at Calvin College because of a common commitment to educational aims, spiritual values, and religious beliefs. Bound by these things we hold in common, we have, perforce, a community: a gathering of like-minded people. This view may serve as a basis for a mission statement of community. It begins, for example, to define the needs of community as larger than any one individual's personal satisfaction of needs. It suggests that community consists of more than just being together or knowing everyone, more than simply harmonious co-existence, more than gratification of individual needs for companionship. Similarly, community is more than simple like-mindedness on issues of moral values, more than spiritual gratification through modes of worship that the individual finds personally satisfying. All of these items may remain important qualities for the individual in a community, and they may even constitute the reasons why an individual joins a community. But they do not fully inform the shaping of a community.

A Purposeful Community

The fundamental principle for community resides first of all in a cohesive *purpose*. However like-minded or diverse its members may be, the community exists to enact a purpose; in the case of Calvin College that purpose is to shape hearts and minds through higher learning for Christian living. Therefore, the end of individuals working in community is always larger than any individual self-interest. Purpose, moreover, consists of more than tasks; purpose entails the mutual holding of common confessions that direct individual tasks. In this sense, the purpose of all participants in Calvin College's mission arises from our sense of being agents of God's plan. The particular expression of that agency is the individual task to which we are called. Purpose, then, consists of being called to a task: to realize God's reign as we implement the mission of the college.

A Just Community

This purposeful community, moreover, will be a *just* community. The community recognizes the worth of each member, because each person is made in the image of God. The college has affirmed that "we must try to make the student aware both of the Christian tradition and of contemporary Christian thought and activity. But also we shall seek to develop that which is unique in each student. We shall not seek to turn out every student from a common mold" (CLAE 35). This commitment to the unique individuality and giftedness in persons unified by a common purpose remains foundational to our sense of community.

This model, moreover, shows each image-bearer as one who has specific responsibilities to employ God-given gifts and talents in the larger community and to fulfill the purposes of that community. Such a task-oriented vision of community insists that these gifted members employ their gifts in responsible service. Guided by God's grace, community arises from the individual's engagement with tasks and responsibilities essential to the life of the larger college community.

A Compassionate Community

Purposeful in its commitment to mission, and just in its recognition of the worth of each person required in fulfilling that mission, the kingdom community will also be *compassionate*. Community depends on each individual being in concerted sympathy with the tasks and gifts of others, mutually supporting and encouraging one another, and recognizing the worth, dignity, and needs of others engaged in communal tasks.

189

Properly understood, compassion is a liberating force, for it consists of how we see ourselves in relation to others. Compassion enables one to admit to individual limitations; to confess the need for support, and to acknowledge that, no matter how stellar the contributions of one individual, such achievement could not occur without the labor and caring support of others. Moreover, compassion allows us to recognize that we are, finally, fallen and fragile creatures, and that even in our inability to achieve desired tasks or goals we are nonetheless worthy as image-bearers of God.

A Disciplined Community

Finally, compassion is tempered by *discipline*. The Christian community will be an orderly community. Genuine compassion requires discipline, including the orderly pursuit of the college's mission. A sense of disciplined order bears profound implications for the very governance of the college and the manner in which we conduct our daily affairs. At no time may the community permit a tyrannical exercise of will in lieu of leadership, nor may it tolerate imposition in lieu of the informed discussion and decision of all members of that community.

Having described these elements of community, we must identify what keeps a community centered on its purpose and vitally committed to its principles of justice, compassion, and discipline. Clearly, working and learning together keep us focused. But it is more than that. Maintaining community requires rituals, celebrations, worship, traditions, and experiences in which the members of the community remember the past, honor the present, and give promise to the future. They will be a people both of memory and hope, learning and living in community.

The college's mission to community must be true to its Reformed tradition and mindful of its rich heritage, but must also embrace the diverse challenges of new partnerships that the college has set for itself. Therefore, community must be understood both internally — that is, who we are and what we are about as a body of people upon this one campus — and also externally — that is, how we apply that sense of who and what we are to forge relationships with other communities.

The Qualities of Internal Community

Our common calling at Calvin College is to do our Lord's work. Our roles vary widely, but each person fills an important and necessary role in the mosaic of people that form Calvin's community. Despite the complexity and multiplicity of tasks in the college, despite what seems at times to be fragmentation into departments for teachers, majors for students, specialties for staff, the intrinsic and irreducible unity of the Calvin College community inheres in the fact that all these diverse tasks are directed to one fundamental mission of the college.

The tasks of our daily life together are guided by faithfulness to the Word. We aim to be conformed more and more to the likeness of God incarnate, willing to receive the mind and heart of Jesus. We also aim to be agents of reclamation, reconciliation, and renewal. We believe that we are individually gifted by God to be such agents of a common aim.

Most in our community readily affirm these givens about ourselves and our community. Yet, because we are also a community of broken, not-yet-completely-whole human beings, we are vulnerable to forces that erode our community's strength and stability.

Threats to community are manifold; none of us escapes them. In a college community, moreover, certain unique pressures appear, from the secular values that permeate higher education generally to the pressures of the academic calendar with its swings between teaching, advising, and grading demands.

Nonetheless, there appears much to encourage one in the college's commitment to community, even as that communal life is being redefined. First of all, the communal effects of scholarship and teaching have been in evidence through seminars and colloquia, as well as such student groups as the Writers and Dance Guilds. Communal life is also promoted, for example, through such organizations as Student Volunteer Services and Habitat for Humanity, which have increased dramatically in participation and range of activities. Here the different members of the Calvin community join to address the needs of those in a larger community. Furthermore, informal Bible studies and prayer support groups, and such organized groups as Intervarsity Christian Fellowship and Fellowship of Christian Athletes, have grown in numbers and presence on the campus. Cultural, religious, and athletic events extend our

191

campus community into the surrounding community, and provide opportunity for members within the college community to cooperate with and support one another in common projects. Increasingly, then, members of the college have seized opportunities to serve, learn, and worship together in varying forms.

Mission to Community Beyond the College

Particularly important to our internal community is the way college members work together to serve communities beyond the college. The Reformed vision of the Christian faith ever moves outward to engage, to learn, to transform, and to redeem. Community at Calvin College is not an end in itself, but a threshold for enacting in the world the *purpose, justice, sympathy,* and *discipline* that serve as the basis for our community. *Christian Liberal Arts Education* forthrightly asserts this fundamental conviction of Christian community: "Christian education . . . must not be based on those withdrawal tendencies which have so often invaded the church. Equally, it must not be based on accommodation tendencies. Rather, it must be of service to the community of believers as it seeks to implement its Christian vision in the midst of society. It must aim at preparing the student to live a life of faith in contemporary society" (p. 37). The college, then, does not see the world as a malevolent structure to be avoided; rather, it sees the world as God's creation and as a community of which we are a part even as we work to reclaim it for Christ. By so doing, the college has both benefitted its geographical community and benefitted from its involvement with other, external organizations.

The college has established significant academic relationships with both geographical and professional communities. A commitment to offering evening courses and a Continuing Education program brings the primary *purpose* in the mission of our college — shaping the hearts and minds of people for Christian living — to bear upon the greater Grand Rapids community. The work of educating, however, extends far beyond course work available in a limited geographical area. In recent decades the college has, through education and scholarship, forged partnerships whose scope is international.

The outreach to an external community, moreover, will be marked by an insistence upon *justice,* identifying clearly the injustice in this world, refusing to tolerate it, and working to eradicate it. The college has engaged remarkable efforts to effect this transformation, to let justice roll down like a river upon a needy world. In the face of spiritual relativism or the rejection of the spiritual, we proclaim the authority of scripture as the foundation for justice itself.

The college's involvement in society will not be motivated by solipsistic concerns, but out of a genuine *compassion* toward a needy world, even toward those who profess to have no need. Here, perhaps, lies one of the greatest challenges to the college's mission in the future, to shape in all its members hearts of servanthood. Concerted efforts must be made to inform this community of need and to work to redress that need.

Finally, the college's mission to the communities beyond the campus will be marked by *discipline.* On the one hand, that discipline will be an internal one as we discipline our hearts to move away from personal satisfactions and to the needs of others. Such discipline requires a spiritual reordering, an evaluation of who we are as God's people and what we do as Christ's disciples. On the other hand, that discipline will require the commitment to go out into the world to engage and to rectify the errors marring it.

CONCLUSION

To approve a statement of mission, to envision new directions and commitments, is to affirm the rich spiritual, cultural, and educational tradition of the college. Calvin College was born of a noble vision: to shape hearts and minds for Christian living and to send out agents of redemptive transformation in God's kingdom. The enacting of that vision has, moreover, ennobled those who have participated in it. This new mission statement recognizes the value of our past, affirms the moorings of our college, and applauds our forebears who have selflessly and often sacrificially dedicated their talents and gifts to the enactment of that vision.

Even when dissension has entered, the people of this college have not lost sight of that vision. In times of disappointment or retrenchment, they have dedicated themselves anew to kingdom service. In times of development and growth, they have given joyful thanks to the

God who rules all our ways and works, and to whom we dedicate our service. Throughout all such transitions, the people of this college have been blessed by an understanding that all our work is secondary to, but redeemed by, the eternal love of Christ, in whose community we are but servants, and by whose headship we are willingly guided.

On the basis of this heartfelt affirmation, this mission statement nonetheless presents an uncompromising challenge. We cannot rest upon the legacy of the past. We find there, instead, a place to stand from which we initiate new ventures and new partnerships. The spirit of this mission statement, then, is to employ such new partnerships and ventures in avenues of continued kingdom service.

We commit ourselves to doing even better those things that we are doing well. We seek a more vital educational program, one that meets in our studies the challenges of understanding and addressing the pressing needs of our time. We seek truly outstanding art and scholarship, in which Calvin College becomes a directing leader in forming and engaging the Christian mind. We seek partnerships in community that are more than mere relationships, but become means to transform society itself, to let justice roll down like rivers, to redress sin and wrongdoing, to further, in all instances, the kingdom of God until Christ returns.

SELECTED BIBLIOGRAPHY

Adult and Continuing Education at Calvin College. A faculty report prepared by the Continuing Education Committee, 1983 [cited as ACE].

Belenky, Mary Field, et al. *Women's Ways of Knowing: The Development of Self, Voice, and Mind*. New York: Basic Books, 1986.

Boyer, Ernest L. *College: The Undergraduate Experience in America*. The Carnegie Foundation for the Advancement of Teaching. New York: Harper & Row, 1987.

Cheney, Lynne V. *50 Hours: A Core Curriculum for College Students*. Washington, D.C.: National Endowment for the Humanities, 1989.

Christian Excellence: A Call to Leadership; A Five-Year Plan for Calvin College, 1988-1993. The report of the President to the Board of Trustees, February, 1988.

Christian Liberal Arts Education. A faculty report prepared by the Curriculum Study Committee, Calvin College and Wm. B. Eerdmans Publishing Co., 1970 [cited as CLAE].

The Comprehensive Plan for Integrating North American Ethnic Minority Persons and Their Interests into Every Facet of Calvin's Institutional Life. A faculty report prepared by the Minority Concerns Task Force, Calvin College, 1985.

Core Curriculum Study Committee: Final Report. A report of the committee, Calvin College, 1990 [cited as CORE].

Cross, Patricia. *Accent on Learning: Improving Instruction and Reshaping the Curriculum.* San Francisco: Jossey-Bass, 1976.

Dressel, Paul L., and Dora Marcus. *On Teaching and Learning in College: Reemphasizing the Roles of Learners and the Disciplines.* San Francisco: Jossey-Bass, 1982.

Gender Concerns Task Force Report. A faculty report prepared by the Gender Concerns Task Force, Calvin College, 1991.

Graduate Education: A Report on Advanced Degrees and Scholarship. A faculty report prepared by the Graduate Studies Committee, Calvin College, 1990 [cited as GRADS].

Holmes, Arthur F. *The Idea of a Christian College.* Grand Rapids, Mich.: Wm. B. Eerdmans Publishing Co., 1975.

Katz, Joseph. *"Does Teaching Help Students Learn?" Teaching Undergraduates: Essays from the Lilly Endowment Workshop on Liberal Arts.* Ed. Bruce A. Kimball. Buffalo, N.Y.: Prometheus Books, 1988.

Kuh, George D. and Elizabeth J. Whitt. *The Invisible Tapestry: Culture in American Colleges and Universities.* Washington, D.C.: Eric/ASHE, 1988.

Marsden, George. "Christian Liberal Arts Education." *The Reformed Journal* (September 1988): 2-4.

Perry, William G., Jr. *Forms of Intellectual and Ethical Development in the College Years: A Scheme.* New York: Holt, Rinehart, and Winston, 1970.

Professional Education in the Christian Liberal Arts College. A faculty report prepared by the Professional Programs Committee, Calvin College, 1973 [cited as PECLAC].

"Report of a Visit to Calvin College." The NCA evaluation conducted March 4-6, 1985. Appendix A in the President's Report to the February 1986 meeting of the Board of Trustees.

Servant Partnerships: To Multiply the Talents. The report of the President to the Board of Trustees, Calvin College, 1990.

Timmerman, John J. *Promises to Keep: A Centennial History of Calvin College.* Grand Rapids, Mich.: William B. Eerdmans Publishing Co., 1976.

Wilson, John D. *Student Learning in Higher Education.* New York: John Wiley, 1981.

Wolterstorff, Nicholas. *Keeping Faith: Talks for New Faculty at Calvin College.* Grand Rapids, Mich.: Calvin College Occasional Paper, 1989.

APPENDIX

————. "The Mission of the Christian College at the End of the Twentieth Century." *The Reformed Journal* (June 1983): 16-18.

Zylstra, Henry. *Testament of Vision*. Grand Rapids, Mich.: Wm. B. Eerdmans Publishing Co., 1958.

Bibliography and Selected Reading List

The titles in this list have been selected so that collectively they map out the ground of my inquiry into academic freedom. The list is not intended in any way to be exhaustive. Rather, it is intended to constitute a usable resource for those wishing to do work in the general area of academic freedom. It also includes most of the key works that I reviewed during my sabbatical dedicated to this project. Consequently, the list includes most of the primary sources for this book. Materials included concern academic freedom issues in the United States, the United Kingdom, and New Zealand.

A comprehensive review of the literature on any topic inevitably encounters redundancy of substance and argument. Such is the case on the topic of academic freedom. Consequently, some citations were excluded from this bibliography and reading list simply because they were repetitive of others which do appear. Where this has occurred, it was not a judgment of the quality of those works but, rather, one of simple efficiency in keeping this bibliography as usable and helpful as possible.

*　　　*　　　*

Academic Freedom 1990: A Human Rights Report. Edited by L. Fernando, N. Hartley, M. Nowak and T. Swinehart for World University Service. Zed Books, Atlantic Highlands, N.J. 07716 (1990)

"Academic Freedom and Tenure." AAUP documents, 1940, 1969, 1970, 1984, etc. (from AAUP), including (but not limited to) the following references:

AAUP Policy Documents and Reports, 1990 and 1995

AAUP 1915 Declaration of Principles

AAUP 1940 Statement of Principles on Academic Freedom and Tenure

AAUP 1970 Interpretive Comments

AAUP "Limitations" Clause in the 1940 Statement of Principles

AAUP Statement of Professional Ethics

AAUP Observations on Ideology, Competence, and Faculty Selection (in *Academe*, January-February 1986)

AAUP "Limitations" Clause in the 1940 Statement of Principles: Some Operating Guidelines (in *Academe*, January-February 1997)

AAUP Religion and Academic Freedom: Issues in Faith and Reason (in *Academe*, January-February 1988)

AAUP Statement on the Relationship of Faculty Governance to Academic Freedom (1994)

AAUP "Defending Tenure: A Guide for Friends of Academic Freedom" (1997)

Academe (a wide variety of issues and case reviews, but only those cited in the text or a footnote are listed here). Washington, D.C.: AAUP.

Allen, Charlotte. "Crossroads." *The New Republic* (February 15, 1999).

Anderson, Martin. *Imposters in the Temple*. New York: Simon and Schuster, 1992.

Arblaster, Anthony. *Academic Freedom*. Harmondsworth, U.K.: Penguin, 1974.

Baade, Hans, ed. *Academic Freedom*. Dobbs Ferry, N.Y.: Oceana Publications, 1964.

Barnett, Ronald. *The Idea of Higher Education*. Suffolk, U.K.: SRHE/Open University Press, 1990.

Bellah, Robert N. "Class Wars and Culture Wars in the University Today: Why We Can't Defend Ourselves." *Academe* (July-August 1997).

Bernstein, Richard. *The Dictatorship of Virtue: Multiculturalism and the Battle for America's Future*. New York: Alfred A. Knopf, 1994.

Bertilson, Hal S. "The Special Responsibilities of Academic Freedom." *Platte Valley Review* (Spring 1991).

Bligh, Donald, ed. *Accountability or Freedom of Teachers?* Guildford, U.K.: University of Surrey, 1982.

Bok, D. *Beyond the Ivory Tower: Social Responsibilities of the Modern University*. Cambridge: Harvard University Press, 1982.

———. *Higher Learning*. Cambridge: Harvard University Press, 1986.

Bouma, Hessel, III, ed. *Christian Faith, Health, and Medical Practice*. With Douglas Diekema, Edward Langerak, Theodore Rottman, and Allen Verhey. Grand Rapids: William B. Eerdmans Publishing Co., 1989.

Brandt, David H. "Talking with the Churches: Possibilities for Mutual Support." In Conversations for Christian Higher Education, a symposium essay. Grand Rapids: Calvin College Provost's Office, 1996.

Brennan, William. *United States v. Associated Press*. 1993.

Brigham Young University. "Statement on Academic Freedom at Brigham Young University." *BYU General Bulletin* (1992).

Brown, Ralph, and Jordan Kurland. "Academic Tenure and Academic Freedom." In *Freedom and Tenure in the Academy*, edited by William W. Van Alstyne, pp. 325ff. Durham, N.C.: Duke University Press, 1993.

Burtchaell, J. T. "The Decline and Fall of the Christian College." *First Things* (April 1991).

———. "The Decline and Fall of the Christian College II." *First Things* (May 1991).

———. *The Dying of the Light: The Disengagement of Colleges and Universities from Their Christian Churches*. Grand Rapids: William B. Eerdmans Publishing Co., 1998.

Calvin College. *An Expanded Statement of the Mission of Calvin College: Vision, Purpose, Commitment*. Grand Rapids: Calvin College Provost's Office, 1992.

Carter, Stephen. *The Culture of Disbelief*. New York: Basic Books, 1993.

———. "Evolution, Creationism, and Treating Religion as a Hobby." *Duke Law Journal* (December 1987): 977-96.

The Condition of the Professoriate: Attitudes and Trends. New York: The Carnegie Foundation for the Advancement of Teaching, 1989.

Chapman, J. *The Western University on Trial*. Berkeley: University of California Press, 1983.

Cheney, Lynne V. *Telling the Truth (Why our culture and our country have stopped making sense, and what we can do about it)*. New York: Simon and Schuster, 1995.

Coleman, James S. "On the Self-Suppression of Academic Freedom." *Academic Questions* 4, no. 1 (Winter 1990-91).

Connerton, P. *The Tragedy of Enlightenment: An Essay on the Frankfurt School*. Cambridge: Cambridge University Press, 1980.

Curran, Charles. *Catholic Higher Education, Theology, and Academic Freedom*. Notre Dame: Notre Dame University Press, 1990.

———. "Church, Academy, Law: Personal Reflections." Chapter 6 in Worgul's *Issues in Academic Freedom* (1992).

De George, Richard. *Academic Freedom and Tenure: Ethical Issues*. Lanham, Md.: Rowman and Littlefield, 1997.

Diekema, Anthony. Confidential Memorandum to the Executive Committee of the Board of Trustees. Calvin College, September 1990.

———. "Servant Partnerships: To Multiply the Talents." A report of the President to the Board of Trustees, Calvin College, 1990.

———. *Committed to Christian Excellence: Leadership, Scholarship, Partnership*. Grand Rapids, Mich.: Calvin College, 1995.

D'Souza, Dinesh. *Illiberal Education: The Politics of Race and Sex on Campus.* New York: Free Press, 1991.

Durkheim, Emile. *The Division of Labor in Society.* Translated by George Simpson. New York: The Free Press, 1933.

———. *The Rules of Sociological Method.* Translated by W. D. Halls. New York: The Free Press, 1982.

———. *On Morality and Society.* Edited and with an introduction by Robert N. Bellah. Chicago: University of Chicago Press, 1973.

———. *Moral Education.* Translated by E. K. Wilson and H. Schnurer. New York: The Free Press, 1961.

Ellul, Jacques. *The Ethics of Freedom.* Translated by G. W. Bromiley. Grand Rapids: William B. Eerdmans Publishing Co., 1976.

Ericson, Edward, Jr. "What the Radicals Did for Academic Freedom." *The Journal of General Education* (Winter 1978).

———. " 'Academic Freedom: Keeping It Complex': A Response to Samuel Logan." *Christian Scholar's Review* (December 1991).

———. "What If There Really Is a War between Christian Scholars and the Academy?" A critical review of *The Outrageous Idea of Christian Scholarship* by George M. Marsden. *Perspectives* (May 1997).

———. "A Place at the Table: Christians in the Postmodern Academy." *Perspectives* (October 1998).

Erikson, Kai. "On the Sociology of Deviance." In *Wayward Puritans*, pp. 3-29. New York: John Wiley and Sons, 1966.

Finkin, Matthew W. "The Assault on Faculty Independence." *Academe* (September-October 1997).

Fish, Stanley. *There Is No Such Thing as Free Speech, and It's a Good Thing, Too.* New York: Oxford University Press, 1994.

———. "Why We Can't All Just Get Along." *First Things* (February 1996): 18-26.

———. "Academic Freedom: When Sauce for the Goose Isn't Sauce for the Gander." *The Chronicle of Higher Education* (November 26, 1999).

Gaede, S. D. *When Tolerance Is No Virtue.* Downers Grove, Ill.: InterVarsity Press, 1993.

Gillespie, T. W. "The Opening of the Christian Mind." *Reformed Journal* (1988).

Glazer, Nathan. "Academic Freedom in the 1990s." *William Mitchell Law Review* 22, no. 2 (1996): 479ff.

Gordon, James, III. "Academic Freedom at Religious Universities." Unpublished paper at Brigham Young University (1994).

Gorovitz, Samuel. *Freedom and Order in the University.* Cleveland: The Press of Western Reserve University, 1967.

Habecker, Eugene. "Academic Freedom in the Context of Mission." *Christian Scholar's Review* (December 1991).

Hamilton, Neil. *Zealotry and Academic Freedom.* New Brunswick, N.J.: Transaction Publishers, 1995.

———. "Buttressing the Neglected Tradition of Academic Freedom." *William Mitchell Law Review* 22, no. 2 (1996): 549ff.

Hamilton, Neil, et al. Academic Freedom Symposium. *William Mitchell Law Review* 22, no. 2 (1996).

Hardy, Lee. "Between Inculcation and Inquiry: The Virtue of Tolerance in the Liberal Arts Tradition." Paper presented at RUNA Conference at Calvin College, March 1995.

Hatch, Nathan. "Evangelical Colleges and the Challenge of Christian Thinking." *Reformed Journal* (1985).

———. "Christian Colleges and Christian Scholarship: Finding Our Identity." Unpublished paper available from Notre Dame University (February 1989).

———. *The Democratization of American Christianity.* New Haven: Yale University Press, 1989.

Hawkesworth, Mary. "The Politics of Knowledge." In *Academic Freedom and Responsibility,* edited by M. Tight. Suffolk, U.K.: SRHE/Open University Press, 1988.

Heie, Harold. "Talking with Each Other: Christian Colleges as Models of Civil Community." In Conversations for Christian Higher Education, a symposium essay. Calvin College Provost's Office, 1996.

Herberg, Will. *On Academic Freedom.* Washington, D.C.: American Enterprise Institute, 1971.

Herrnstein, Richard J., and Charles Murray. *The Bell Curve: Intelligence and Class Structure in American Life.* New York: The Free Press, 1994.

Hesburgh, Theodore, ed. *The Challenge and Promise of a Catholic University.* Notre Dame: University of Notre Dame Press, 1994.

Himmelfarb, Gertrude. "Academic Advocates: Academic Freedom and Classroom Political Advocacy." *Commentary* (September 1996): 46ff.

———. "The Christian University: A Call to Counterrevolution." *First Things* (January 1996): 16-19.

Hoekema, David. "Politics, Religion, and Other Crimes Against Civility." Unpublished paper presented at the Conference on Advocacy in the Classroom. Pittsburgh, June 1995. Later revision published in *Academe* (November-December 1996).

Hofstadter, Richard. *Academic Freedom in the Age of the College.* New York: Columbia University Press, 1955.

Hofstadter, Richard, and W. P. Metzger. *The Development of Academic Freedom in the United States*. New York: Columbia University Press, 1965.

Holmes, Arthur. "Is a Christian University Possible?" *Faculty Dialogue* (Spring-Summer 1994).

———. *The Idea of a Christian College*. Grand Rapids: William B. Eerdmans Publishing Co., 1975.

———. *All Truth Is God's Truth*. Downers Grove, Ill.: InterVarsity Press, 1983.

———. *Contours of a Worldview*. Grand Rapids: William B. Eerdmans Publishing Co., 1983.

Hook, Sidney. *Academic Freedom and Academic Anarchy*. New York: Cowles Book Co., 1970.

———, ed. *In Defense of Academic Freedom*. New York: Pegasus, 1971.

Horn, Michiel. "The Mildew of Discretion: Academic Freedom and Self-Censorship." *Dalhousie Review* (Winter 1992-93).

———. *Academic Freedom in Canada: A History*. Toronto: University of Toronto Press, 1999.

Horner, David. "Academic Freedom." *Faculty Dialogue* (Winter 1992).

Hoye, William J. "The Religious Roots of Academic Freedom." *Theological Studies* (September 1997).

Huer, Jon. *Tenure for Socrates: A Study in the Betrayal of the American Professor*. New York: Bergin and Garvey, 1991.

Hughes, Richard T., and William B. Adrian. *Models for Christian Higher Education: Strategies for Survival and Success in the Twenty-First Century*. Grand Rapids: William B. Eerdmans Publishing Co., 1997.

Hunt, J. F., and T. R. Connelly. *The Responsibility of Dissent: The Church and Academic Freedom*. New York: Sheed and Ward, 1970.

Hunter, James Davison. *Evangelicalism: The Coming Generation*. Chicago: University of Chicago Press, 1987.

Kaplan, C., and E. Schrecker, eds. *Regulating the Intellectuals: Perspectives on Academic Freedom in the 1980s*. New York: Praeger, 1983.

Kerr, C. *The Uses of the University*. Cambridge: Harvard University Press, 1972.

Kirk, Russell. *Academic Freedom: An Essay in Definition*. Chicago: Regnery, 1955.

———. "Bargaining Away Academic Freedom." *Government Union Review* (Spring 1980).

Koestler, Arthur. *The Sleepwalkers: A History of Man's Changing Vision of the Universe*. London: Hutchinson, 1964.

Kohr, Leopold. *The Academic Inn*. Telybont, Wales: Y Lolfa Cyf, 1993.

Kurland, Jordan K. "Commentary on Buttressing the Defense of Academic Freedom." *William Mitchell Law Review* 2, no. 2 (1996): 545ff.

Kuyper, Abraham. "Bound to the Word: The Answer to the Question, How Is a University Bound by the Word of God?" Unpublished manuscript of speech delivered on June 28, 1899. Available in The Hekman Library, Calvin College.

Lattimore, Owen. "Ordeal by Slander." Unpublished paper, 1951.

Laycock, Douglas. "The Rights of Religious Academic Communities." *The Journal of College and University Law* 20, no. 1 (1993).

Lewis, Lionel. *The Cold War and Academic Governance: The Lattimore Case at Johns Hopkins*. Albany: State University of New York Press, 1993.

Lipset, Seymour. "Political Correctness, Historically Speaking." *Educational Record* (Winter 1992).

Logan, Samuel, Jr. "Academic Freedom at Christian Institutions." *Christian Scholar's Review* (December 1991).

London, Herbert. "When Civil Rights Protagonists Demand a Dictatorial Regime." *Measure* (April-May 1995).

Lundin, Roger. *The Culture of Interpretation: Christian Faith and the Postmodern World*. Grand Rapids: William B. Eerdmans Publishing Co., 1993.

Lutz, D. W. "Can Notre Dame Be Saved?" *First Things* (November 1992).

MacIntyre, Alasdair. *After Virtue*. Notre Dame: University of Notre Dame Press, 1984.

Magrath, C. Peter. "Eliminating Tenure Without Destroying Academic Freedom." *The Chronicle of Higher Education* (February 28, 1997).

Manier, Edward, and John Houck, eds. *Academic Freedom and the Catholic University*. Notre Dame: Fides Publishers, 1967.

Marsden, George. *The Soul of the American University*. Oxford: Oxford University Press, 1994.

———. "Theology and the University: Newman's Idea and Current Realities." In *The Idea of the University*, edited by Frank M. Turner. New Haven: Yale University Press, 1996.

———. *The Outrageous Idea of Christian Scholarship*. Oxford: Oxford University Press, 1997.

———. "Liberating Academic Freedom." *First Things* (December 1998): 11ff.

Marsden, George, and B. J. Longfield. *The Secularization of the Academy*. Oxford: Oxford University Press, 1992.

Marsden, George, et al. Symposium: God in the Academy. In *Academic Questions* (Spring 1996): 10-36.

Marty, Martin E. "Relatively Absolute and Absolutely Relative." Paper presented at the AAUP Conference on Academic Freedom at Religiously Affiliated Institutions. Chicago, October 24-26, 1997.

May, William W. "Academic Freedom in Church-Related Institutions." *Academe* (July-August 1988).

McConnell, Michael. "Academic Freedom in Religious Colleges and Universities." In *Freedom and Tenure in the Academy,* edited by William W. Van Alstyne, pp. 303ff. Durham, N.C.: Duke University Press, 1993.

McCormick, R. A., and R. P. McBrien. "L'Affaire Curran II." *America* (September 1990).

McIver, Robert. *Academic Freedom in Our Time.* New York: Columbia University Press, 1955.

McKim, Donald, ed. *Encyclopedia of the Reformed Faith.* Louisville: John Knox Press, 1992.

Menand, Louis, ed. *The Future of Academic Freedom.* Chicago: University of Chicago Press, 1996.

Menninga, C., H. Van Till, and D. Young, eds. *Science Held Hostage: What's Wrong with Creation Science and Evolutionism.* Downers Grove, Ill.: InterVarsity Press, 1988.

Metzger, Walter. "The 1940 Statement of Principles on Academic Freedom and Tenure." In *Freedom and Tenure in the Academy,* edited by William W. Van Alstyne. Durham, N.C.: Duke University Press, 1993.

————, ed. *Dimensions of Academic Freedom.* Urbana: University of Illinois Press, 1969.

Mill, John Stuart. *On Liberty.* Indianapolis: Hackett, 1978.

Minsky, Leonard. "The Politics of Political Correctness." *Educational Record* (Winter 1992).

Monahan, Edward. "Tenure and Academic Freedom in Canadian Universities." *Interchange-on-Education* (1983-84): 94-106.

Monan, J., and Edward A. Malloy. " 'Ex Corde Ecclesiae' Creates an Impasse." *America* 180, no. 3 (January 30, 1999): 6-12. (See also an editorial, "New Norms for Catholic Higher Education: Unworkable and Dangerous," in 179, no. 15 [November 14, 1998].)

Monsma, Stephen. "Christian Worldview in Academia." *Faculty Dialogue* (Spring-Summer 1994).

————. "The Supreme Court, Societal Elites, and Calvin College: Christian Higher Education in a Secular Age." In *Keeping Faith: Embracing the Tensions in Christian Higher Education,* edited by R. A. Wells. Grand Rapids: William B. Eerdmans Publishing Co., 1996.

Moots, Phillip, and Edward Gaffney, Jr. *Church and Campus: Legal Issues in Religiously Affiliated Higher Education.* Notre Dame: University of Notre Dame Press, 1979.

Moynihan, Daniel P. "Defining Deviancy Down." *The American Scholar* (1993): 17ff.

Neuhaus, Richard John. "Transgressions Against a Harsh Faith." *Measure* (April-May 1995).

————. "The Christian University: Eleven Theses." *First Things* (January 1996): 20-22.

————. "Why We Can Get Along." *First Things* (February 1996): 27-34.

Neumayr, John W. "Death of the Mind: The Anti-Intellectualism of 'Cultural Diversity' in Education." *Measure* (January-February 1994).

Neusner, Jacob. "An Infusion of the Whole." In Marsden et al., "Symposium: God in the Academy." *Academic Questions* (Spring 1996): 17-21.

Newman, John Henry Cardinal. *The Idea of a University*. 1931. See the 1996 edition with commentary by Garland, Castro-Klarin, Landow, Marsden, and Frank M. Turner, ed. New Haven: Yale University Press, 1996.

Noll, Mark. *The Scandal of the Evangelical Mind*. Grand Rapids: William B. Eerdmans Publishing Co., 1994.

Nuechterlein, James. "The Death of Religious Higher Education." *First Things* (January 1991).

————. "The Idol of Academic Freedom." *First Things* (December 1993).

O'Hear, A. "Academic Freedom and the University." In *Academic Freedom and Responsibility*, edited by M. Tight. Suffolk, U.K.: SRHE/Open University Press, 1988.

O'Neil, Robert. *Free Speech in the College Community*. Bloomington: Indiana University Press, 1997.

Oakley, Francis. *Community of Learning: The American College and the Liberal Arts Tradition*. Oxford: Oxford University Press, 1992.

Oldaker, Lawrence. "Threats to Academic Freedom in Higher Education." Unpublished paper given at NOLP conference in Scottsdale, Arizona, November 21, 1992.

Paulin, Roger. *Goethe, the Brothers Grimm, and Academic Freedom*. Cambridge: Cambridge University Press, 1991.

Pincoffs, Edmund, ed. *The Concept of Academic Freedom*. University of Texas Press, 1975.

Plante, P. R., and R. M. Atwell. "The Opening of the American Mind." *Educational Record* (Winter 1992).

Plantinga, Alvin. "The Twin Pillars of Christian Scholarship." 1990 Stob Lectures, Calvin College.

Poch, Robert. "Academic Freedom in American Higher Education: Rights, Responsibilities and Limitations." ASHE-ERIC Higher Education Report no. 4, 1993.

Polanyi, Michael. *The Tacit Dimension*. New York: Doubleday, 1966.

Pope John Paul. "On Catholic Universities." Apostolic Constitution, 1990.

Price, Christopher. "Academics and Society: Freedom's Seamless Robe." In *Higher Education into the 1990s*, edited by Sir Christopher Ball and Heather Eggins. Suffolk, U.K.: SRHE/Open University Press, 1989.

Rabban, David. "A Functional Analysis of 'Individual' and 'Institutional' Academic Freedom Under the First Amendment." In *Freedom and Tenure in the Academy*, edited by William W. Van Alstyne. Durham, N.C.: Duke University Press, 1993.

Reese, A. C. "Dimensions of Academic Freedom in Research." Proceedings of the Society for Experimental Biology and Medicine, 1994.

Rice, A. K. *The Modern University*. London: Tavistock, 1970.

Richardson, Peter. *Paul's Ethic of Freedom*. Philadelphia: Westminster Press, 1979.

Riesman, David. *On Higher Education*. San Francisco: Jossey-Bass, 1980.

Ringenberg, W. C. *The Christian College: A History of Protestant Higher Education in America*. Grand Rapids: William B. Eerdmans Publishing Co., 1984.

Rorty, Richard. *Achieving Our Country: Leftist Thought in Twentieth-Century America*. Cambridge: Harvard University Press, 1998.

Rosovsky, Henry. *The University: An Owner's Manual*. New York: W. W. Norton, 1990.

Roworth, Wendy W. "Why Is Tenure Being Targeted for Attack?" *AAUP Footnotes* (Fall 1997).

Russell, Conrad. *Academic Freedom*. London: Routledge, 1993.

Satorius, Rolf. "Tenure and Academic Freedom." In *The Concept of Academic Freedom*, edited by Edmund Pincoffs. University of Texas Press, 1975.

Schauer, Frederick. "The First Amendment as Ideology." *William and Mary Law Review* 33 (1992): 856ff.

Schlesinger, P. *Free Speech for All?* London: Council for Academic Freedom and Democracy, 1979.

Schmidt, Benno. "The University and Freedom." *Educational Record* (Winter 1992).

Schrecker, Ellen. *No Ivory Tower: McCarthyism and the Universities*. Oxford: Oxford University Press, 1986.

Schultz, James. "Stick to the Facts: Educational Politics, Academic Freedom, and the MLA." *Profession* (1988).

Schwehn, Mark. *Exiles from Eden: Religion and the Academic Vocation in America*. New York: Oxford University Press, 1993.

Scott, Joan Wallach. "Academic Freedom as an Ethical Practice." *Academe* (July-August 1995).

Scott, Robert. "Better Than Thou." *Change* (July/August 1995).

Sheinin, Rose. "Academic Freedom and Integrity and Ethics in Publishing." *Journal of Scholarly Publishing* (July 1993).

Shils, Edward. *The Academic Ethic*. Chicago: University of Chicago Press, 1984.

———. "Do We Still Need Academic Freedom?" *The American Scholar* (Spring 1993).

Silber, John. "Tenure in Context." In *The Tenure Debate,* edited by Bardwell Smith et al. San Francisco: Jossey-Bass, 1973.

————. "Resentment: The Academic Vice." In Symposium: Academic Freedom at Century's End, in *Academic Questions* 10, no. 4 (Fall 1997).

Simmel, Georg. *The Sociology of Georg Simmel.* Translated and edited by Kurt H. Wolff. Glencoe, Ill.: Free Press, 1950.

Simmons, Ernest, Jr. "Soli Deo Gloria: The Doxological Tasks of the Church College." *Cresset* (Valparaiso University) (June-July 1995).

Simon, Rita. "What Should Professors Do?" *William Mitchell Law Review* 22, no. 2 (1996): 573ff.

Sire, James W. *Discipleship of the Mind: Learning to Love God in the Ways We Think.* Downers Grove, Ill.: InterVarsity Press, 1990.

Sittler, Joseph. *Faith, Learning and the Church College: Addresses by Joseph Sittler.* Northfield, Minn.: St. Olaf College, 1989.

Sloan, Douglas. *Faith and Knowledge: Mainline Protestantism and American Higher Education.* Louisville, Ky.: Westminster/John Knox Press, 1994.

Smith, H. "Church-related Higher Education: Distinguishing Characteristics." In *Church and College: A Vital Partnership.* Austin, Tex.: The National Congress on Church-Related Colleges and Universities, 1980.

Smolla, Rodney. "Academic Freedom, Hate Speech, and the Idea of a University." In *Freedom and Tenure in the Academy,* edited by William W. Van Alstyne. Durham, N.C.: Duke University Press, 1993.

Sokal, Alan. "Transgressing the Boundaries: Toward a Transformative Hermeneutic of Quantum Gravity," *Social Text* (Spring-Summer 1996).

Stoltzfus, Victor. *Church-Affiliated Higher Education.* Goshen, Ind.: Pinchpenny Press, 1992.

Symposium: Academic Freedom at Century's End. In *Academic Questions* 10, no. 4 (Fall 1997). Published for the National Association of Scholars. New Brunswick, N.J.: Rutgers University, Transaction Periodical Consortium, 1997.

Synod: Acts of Synod 1991, Christian Reformed Church in North America, Article 86, June 19, 1991. See also Agenda for Synod 1991, Report of Committee on Creation and Science (pp. 367ff., Report 28).

Thomas, Cal, and Edward Dobson. *Blinded by Might: Can the Religious Right Save America?* Grand Rapids: Zondervan/Harper Collins, 1999.

Thomson, Judith. "Ideology and Faculty Selection." In *Freedom and Tenure in the Academy,* edited by William W. Van Alstyne. Durham, N.C.: Duke University Press, 1993.

Thomson, Judith, and Matthew Finkin. "Academic Freedom and Church-Related Higher Education: A Reply to Professor McConnell." In *Freedom and Tenure in the Academy,* edited by William W. Van Alstyne, pp. 419ff. Durham, N.C.: Duke University Press, 1993.

Tight, Malcolm, ed.. *Academic Freedom and Responsibility.* Suffolk, U.K.: SRHE/ Open University Press, 1988.

Trachtenberg, Stanley. "Profligacy and the Pursuit of Truth." *Academic Questions* (Fall 1997): 65ff.

Turner, James. "The Catholic University in Modern Academe: Challenge and Dilemma." Unpublished paper, 1992.

Van Alstyne, William W., ed. *Freedom and Tenure in the Academy.* Durham, N.C.: Duke University Press, 1993.

Van Harn, G. "Keeping Faith with One Another." Unpublished paper, Provost's Office, Calvin College, 1992.

———. "Academic Freedom, A Case Study." A paper on Howard Van Till delivered to the Association for a Reformed University, June 1994. Available from Calvin College.

Van Till, Howard. *The Fourth Day.* Grand Rapids: William B. Eerdmans Publishing Co., 1986.

Veith, Gene E. *Postmodern Times.* Wheaton, Ill.: Crossway Books, 1994.

Wacome, Donald. "Faithful Nonbelief." *Perspectives* (October 1998): 13ff.

Walhout, Mark D. "Christian Academic Freedom." An unpublished paper delivered as the 1999 Winifred E. Weter Faculty Award Lecture, Seattle Pacific University, Seattle, April 22, 1999.

Walsh, Brian J., and J. Richard Middleton. *The Transforming Vision: Shaping a Christian World View.* Downers Grove, Ill.: InterVarsity Press, 1984.

Watkins, Beverly. "Nine Groups Back International Statement on Academic Freedom." *Chronicle of Higher Education* (October 3, 1984).

Westphal, Merold. "The Ostrich and the Boogeyman: Placing Postmodernism." *Christian Scholar's Review* 20 (1990).

Whitehead, John. *Politically Correct: Censorship in American Culture.* Chicago: Moody Press, 1995.

Wilke, Arthur S., ed. *The Hidden Professoriate.* Westport, Conn.: Greenwood Press, 1979.

Wilson, Edward O. *Consilience: The Unity of Knowledge.* New York: Alfred A. Knopf, 1998.

Wilson, John K. *The Myth of Political Correctness: The Conservative Attack on Higher Education.* Durham, N.C.: Duke University Press, 1995.

———. "Myths and Facts: How Real Is Political Correctness?" *William Mitchell Law Review* 22, no. 2 (1996): 517ff.

Withham, Larry. *Curran vs. Catholic University: A Study of Authority and Freedom in Conflict.* Riverdale, Md.: Edington-Rand, 1991.

Witvliet, John, et al. "Report of the Special Committee to the Board of Trustees." Calvin College, February 1991.

Wolterstorff, Nicholas. "Keeping Faith: Talks for New Faculty at Calvin College." An Occasional Paper, Calvin College, 1989.

———. *Reason Within the Bounds of Religion*. Grand Rapids: William B. Eerdmans Publishing Co., 1976.

Worgul, George, Jr., ed. *Issues in Academic Freedom*. Pittsburgh: Duquesne University Press, 1993.

Zylstra, Henry. *Testament of Vision*. Grand Rapids: William B. Eerdmans Publishing Co., 1958.

Tenure

The literature on the topic of academic tenure is enormous. Consequently, the titles in this list have been selected for their value in assessing the relationship of tenure to the topic of academic freedom in the academy. It is a limited focus within the much broader topic of tenure. It will be most helpful, then, to the reader whose interests in tenure are directly related to academic freedom. Where a volume or article addresses both topics, for purposes of this bibliography it will be found above under the rubric of academic freedom.

Academe. A wide variety of issues and case reviews, but only those cited in the text or a footnote are listed here. Washington, D.C.: AAUP.

Andrews, Hans. "How to Dismiss a Tenured Faculty Member." *Administrative Action* 4, no. 6 (1994).

Bowen, Howard, and Jack Schuster. *American Professors: A National Resource Imperiled*. New York: Oxford University Press, 1986.

Byse, Clark, and Louis Joughin. *Tenure in American Higher Education*. Ithaca, N.Y.: Cornell University Press, 1959.

Cantor, Paul A. "It's Not the Tenure, It's the Radicalism." *Academic Questions* 11, no. 1 (Winter 1997-98).

Chait, Richard. "Thawing the Cold War Over Tenure: Why Academe Needs More Employment Options." *The Chronicle of Higher Education* (February 1997).

Chait, Richard, and Andrew Ford. *Beyond Traditional Tenure*. San Francisco: Jossey-Bass, 1982.

Davidson, James. "Tenure, Governance, and Standards in the Academic Community." *Liberal Education* (Spring 1982).

Dickson, David. "Law Weakens Tenure, University Autonomy." *Science* (August 5, 1988).

Finkin, Matthew. "A Higher Order of Liberty in the Workplace: Academic Freedom and Tenure in the Vortex of Employment Practices and Law." *Law and Contemporary Problems* 53 (Summer 1990).

———, ed. *The Case for Tenure*. Ithaca, N.Y.: Cornell University Press, 1996.

Flanigan, Jackson, et al. "Tenure and Promotion Procedures: An Analysis of University Policies." Unpublished paper presented at Society of Professors of Education, 1994.

Horn, Joseph M. "On the Ineffectiveness and Irrelevance of Tenure." *Academic Questions* 11, no. 1 (Winter 1997-98).

Kimball, Roger. *Tenured Radicals: How Politics Has Corrupted Our Higher Education*. New York: Harper & Row, 1990.

Levine, Martin. *Age Discrimination and the Mandatory Retirement Controversy*. Baltimore: Johns Hopkins University Press, 1988.

Licata, Christine M. *Post-Tenure Faculty Evaluation*. New York: Association for the Study of Higher Education, 1986.

Marchant, G. J., and Isadore Newman. "Faculty Activities and Rewards: Views from Educational Administrators in the USA." *Assessment and Evaluation in Higher Education* (1994).

Parini, Jay. "Tenure and the Loss of Faculty Talent." *The Chronicle of Higher Education* (July 14, 1995): A40.

Peters, John, and David Brinkerhoff. "Balancing the Reward Structures of Promotion, Tenure, and Merit." An unpublished paper presented at the American Educational Research Association, 1992.

Smith, Bardwell, ed. *The Tenure Debate*. San Francisco: Jossey-Bass, 1973.

Smith, Page. *Killing the Spirit: Higher Education in America*. New York: Viking Press, 1990.

Sykes, Charles J. *ProfScam*. Washington, D.C.: Regnery Gateway, 1988.

"Tenure and Teaching in the University of North Carolina." A report to the Board of Governors at Chapel Hill (1993), 39 pages.

Index

AAUP (American Association of University Professors), 22-23, 46, 48, 66-69, 71, 73, 76-78, 83, 85-88, 96, 98, 104-5

Academic freedom, in college and church, 115-22, common belief systems, 117, 120; mutual benefits, 118-20; different roles, 115-16, 120; essential relationships, 115-17

Academic freedom, definitions of, 6-10, 84-86; descriptions of, 4-5, 14-15, 76-81; corporate, 86; personal, 85

Academic freedom, threats to, 11-43; censorship, 27-33, 66; chilling effect, 33-35; 93, 106; dogmatism, 13, 22-23; faculty indifference, 38-39; governmental, 37; ideological imperialism, 12-13, 90, 94-95; institutional, 37-38; intolerance of religion, 22-23, 38, 67; faculty nostalgia, 26; political correctness, 15-22, 24-26; postmodernism, 13, 15, 20, 53-54, 66, 123-26, 128; prior restraint, 27-33; self-censorship, 34, 36, 66, 106; passim

Academic freedom, protection and promotion of, 132-43; specific advice to boards of trustees, 138-39; church officials, 141-42; faculty, 133-35; presidents and provosts, 135-37; students, 139-41

Academic freedom, in the context of worldview, 44-81; as Christian freedom, 74-75; and Christian worldview, 53-71; and Enlightenment objectivity, 45-53; as means rather than end, 71-73

American Philosophical Association, 61

Barnett, Ronald, 6
Bell Curve, The, 20, 95, 129
Bill of Rights, 8
Bligh, Donald, 6
Bouma, Hessel, 21, 94, 121, 129
Brennan, Justice William, 126
British Education Reform Bill (1987), 6
Brown, Ralph, 96
Burtchaell, James T., 118
Byse, Clark, 98

Calvin Alumni Association, 32
Calvin College, 17, 29, 94-95, 119-20
Catholic University of America, 23, 34

211

INDEX